WHAT WOULD SOCRATES SAY?

PETER KREEFT

What Would Socrates Say?

An Introduction to Philosophy
by the Socratic Method

IGNATIUS PRESS   SAN FRANCISCO

Art and cover design by John Herreid

© 2024 by Ignatius Press, San Francisco
All rights reserved
ISBN 978-1-62164-720-1 (HB)
ISBN 978-1-64229-316-6 (eBook)
Library of Congress Control Number 2024935672
Printed in the United States of America ∞

Dedicated to William Harry Jellema, Brand Blanshard,
Balduin Schwarz, and Father W. Norris Clarke, S.J.,
all of whom taught me to teach and philosophize
Socratically by their unforgettable example.

CONTENTS

PREFACE

I believe that a writer's first obligation to readers is to interest them. If this book does not interest you, it's a failure. Use it as firewood. Fire is at least interesting.

This book is based on what sixty years of teaching philosophy to students of all intellectual levels has taught me students identify with. Thus, one of my two interlocutors is a typical contemporary student, and the other is Socrates, the archetypal philosopher.

Since it is for beginners, this book has many beginners' arguments, which are usually oversimplified ones, but the ones that actual beginners in philosophy will use and understand more than the more sophisticated, advanced, long, and difficult arguments in the writings of most philosophers. This is not a book for geniuses *or* for dummies but for ordinary people.

Who Can Use This Book?

Anybody can use this book—either alone or in a discussion group or even in a classroom. It's appropriate for a one-semester upper-level high school course or as the beginning of an introductory college course, where it should be supplemented by some readings from the great philosophers, beginning with Plato. I suggest adding significant bits of Aristotle, Thomas Aquinas, René Descartes, David Hume, and Immanuel Kant as a minimum. Blaise Pascal, Jean-Paul Sartre, William James, Søren Kierkegaard, and Friedrich Nietzsche, though they are not as basic, write more charmingly and winningly.

Both teachers who prefer classical philosophy and those who prefer analytic philosophy should like this book because it is based on the Socratic method and is in the form of Socratic dialogues, which are both analytical and classical.

Why Is It So Long?

This book is long because most of it is dialogue, and it takes two or three times as much space to make a point in that form than in monologue. But the point of this book is not to make points or "takeaways" but to explore important and profound questions. Dialogue does that much better than monologue. Arguing is more interesting than preaching, and dialogue is much more interesting than monologue because it is drama, narrative, and contests—like sports (hurrah!) or war (boo!). Even solitaire is a contest, though only with yourself.

So what makes this book unusually long actually makes it easier, not harder, to read.

The length of the dialogues varies a lot. The first nine are longer because they are more basic and important. Quantity ought to be determined by quality.

INTRODUCTION TO PHILOSOPHY

I warn you that this introductory chapter and the two that follow are by far the most boring chapters in the book.

Why? Because they are not yet philosophy (which is definitely *not* boring) but are talking about philosophy (which is). Talking about something interesting is never as interesting as doing it, whether that something is birth, death, pain, pleasure, sex, sunsets, math, music, hamburgers, Heaven, surfing, space travel, or philosophy.

Philosophy is necessary. It makes a very big difference to your life. The difference between living and being killed is a pretty big difference, and a hundred million people is a rather large number, and well over a hundred million people were deliberately killed in World War II because the two sides had radically different philosophies. One side believed that might made right, so they believed in starting wars and killing people whom they thought had no right to live. They believed in the superiority of the strong to the weak, and of some races to others. The other side believed that all men are created equal and had inherent rights such as the right to life and liberty and the pursuit of happiness.

Not all wars are about philosophy, but many are. The Thirty Years' War, which decimated almost one-third of even the *civilian* population of Central Europe, was about two religious philosophies, Protestantism versus Catholicism. The American Civil War was about two ethical philosophies, slavery and the abolition of slavery. Lincoln said that the Union, America as a single *nation*, could not survive "half slave and half free". The Spanish Civil War was between two political philosophies, Communism and Fascism. The French Revolution was also about two philosophies, essentially tyranny and freedom, and the revolutionaries changed their philosophy from freedom to tyranny during their Reign of Terror. In each case the two *philosophies* were so at war with each other that the people who believed them went to war.

The same principle works on an individual level. Philosophy can join or separate individuals. If one of two married people believes in a philosophy of lifelong fidelity and respect while the other does not, the marriage will probably die. Today it is rare for a strong Democrat and a strong Republican to be even friends, much less spouses.

Wait a moment. Don't just agree with everything I say just because I'm writing this book. I might be wrong. In fact, I was, just now, when I used the examples of wars that made a life-or-death difference to millions of lives to prove that philosophy was necessary. That was a bad argument because it didn't really prove its point. (In the next introductory chapter, we will learn the basic rules of logic, which is the science and art that tells you when an argument really has proven its point, its conclusion, to be true and when it hasn't.)

My argument didn't prove its point because its point was that philosophy was *necessary*. And the premise, or reason, for that conclusion was that it makes a very big difference to your life, a life-or-death difference in war. The premise was obviously true, but what it proves is that philosophy is *important*, that it makes a big difference to your life when you believe it and live it, but not that it is *necessary*. The two concepts are not the same. It's *important* to be honest, to make a will, and to avoid addictive drugs, but all three of those important things are not necessary but are freely chosen and can quite easily *not* be chosen. They may be necessary means to some other end, but they are not necessary in themselves. Honesty is necessary only if you want to be morally good, or trustable; and making a will is necessary only if you don't want the state to determine who gets your money when you die; and avoiding drugs is necessary only if you don't want to scramble your brains and your life. What is in itself and always *necessary* to a human being is having a body and a mind and being in various relationships with other human beings, as well as growing and dying. What is necessary is unavoidable; what is only important can be avoided. All you have to do is to be stupid, lazy, or irresponsible, all of which are remarkably easy.

A much better argument to prove that philosophy is necessary is the argument the old Roman philosopher and senator Cicero gave: If you say you do not believe philosophy is necessary, that, too, is a philosophy. It's your philosophy, and it's a bad philosophy, but it is a philosophy. It's not science, or religion, or common sense. It's your claim to wisdom. ("Philosophy" means "the love of wisdom".) And it's unwise because it contradicts itself (it refutes itself).

That argument is similar to the one about total skepticism (which is one of the arguments we will explore in the first chapter): that it refutes itself because it contradicts itself. Total skepticism means skepticism (or uncertainty or doubt or disbelief) about every idea; but total skepticism is one of those ideas. Therefore, total skepticism means skepticism also about total skepticism. It does not even believe in itself, in its own philosophy of total disbelief.

So, What Is Philosophy?

Instead of immediately *answering* the question of what philosophy is, I'm going to examine the *question* first.

This question assumes two things.

First, it assumes that the writer or speaker wants to know something that he does not yet know, or fully know, namely, what philosophy is. "Philosophy" is not a word like "two" or "apple", that is, a word whose essential meaning is clearly known by everybody. In fact, one of the issues that divides philosophers is what philosophy is! The answer is not obvious and universally known.

There is also a second, and less obvious, assumption in asking the question, What is philosophy? It is the assumption that the speaker or writer already knows the meaning of the two other words in the question, the word "what" and the word "is".

"What is it?" means "What is the *essential nature* of it?" And that assumes things have essential natures. The question asks for a definition or a description of it so that we can understand it and identify it. To want to "identify" it assumes that it has an essential "identity", that all examples of it (here, "it" = philosophy) have something in common, some essential nature that is the same in all the different kinds of it (e.g., philosophies can be smart or stupid, optimistic or pessimistic, easy or difficult, scientific or nonscientific, religious or nonreligious), and that this essential nature remains underneath all the different changes it may undergo (e.g., old or new, popular or unpopular, embryonic or developed).

And the word "is" in the question, What is philosophy? assumes there is some objective reality to philosophy and asks what philosophy *really* is, not just what some people subjectively feel or think about it.

So you see that even in this innocent-sounding question there are already some deep and difficult philosophical issues. The question, What is philosophy? raises the prior questions, What is a "what"? and What is an "is"?

That's how philosophy usually works: backward, so to speak, first using ordinary words and then demanding definitions of them, and first giving an argument and then uncovering and evaluating the assumptions or presuppositions or premises of the argument, the reasons for its conclusion—uncovering and exploring hidden assumptions or presuppositions or reasons (reasons for an argument's point, or conclusion) and then evaluating them.

Philosophizing is more like detective work than engineering. The detective begins with the crime and wants to detect the criminal. The crime has already been constructed; he wants to "deconstruct" it. The engineer, on the other hand, constructs. He begins with materials (e.g., metals, chemicals, and computers) and constructs a machine (e.g., a rocket ship) out of them.

The philosopher wants to know why a thing is or why you believe a certain idea. He sees a logical structure of ideas, which includes that idea and other ideas it is logically related to. Some of these other ideas are the reasons or premises or assumptions behind that first idea, and others are the consequences that logically follow from it. A philosophy is like a mental building, and a second philosopher *evaluates* its foundations. Philosophy can also *build* mental buildings or systems beginning with premises or foundations.

Philosophy is in this way like science rather than technology: it wants to *explain* something that is already there rather than *make* new things. We need both, of course. For instance, a depressed person comes to a psychiatrist hoping to find both of these two things: first, an explanation of *why* he is depressed (i.e., the cause), and, second, the power to cure it, to change it. In medicine the first of those two things is called the diagnosis and the second is called the treatment or prescription.

Karl Marx famously said, "The philosophers have only interpreted the world differently; but what matters is to change it."[1] But that

---

[1] Karl Marx, *Theses on Feuerbach* (Stuttgart, Germany: Livraria Press, 2023), 6.

second thing is not philosophy's job. Thinking alone without acting can't change the world; that is the job of human actors, both in politics and elsewhere. But acting in a deliberate way always depends on some philosophy, at least implicitly, as a prescription always depends on a diagnosis. For instance, Marx's prescription, namely, a worldwide Communist revolution that eliminates capitalism and capitalists, depends on the diagnosis that all the world's ills come from the class conflict that capitalism has created between the "haves" (the bourgeoisie) and the "have nots" (the proletariat).

And if you did not fully and clearly understand that last paragraph, you are totally hopeless and should read no more of this book. I'm kidding, of course! It's just the opposite: please *expect* confusion and welcome it as a doctor welcomes patients.

That's my first answer to the question, What is philosophy? And here is answer number 2. It's a much easier answer. Both the thing itself (philosophy itself) and the word for it (the word "philosophy") were invented by the ancient Greeks, most especially Socrates; and the inventor has the right to define the invention. So since "philosophy" literally means "the love (*philia*) of wisdom (*sophia*)", that is simply the correct answer to the question; that is what the word "philosophy" means. "Philosophy" means "the love of wisdom".

There are two important words in that definition: "love" and "wisdom".

We all know what love is, and we all know that it comes in many kinds. One of those kinds is the love of wisdom, which is quite different from the love of pleasure, or of a spouse, or of a friend, or of ice cream. But it is probably surprising for you to learn that philosophy, according to those who invented it, is a form of love. Where there is no love (of wisdom), there is no philosophy. If you are not in love with wisdom, you are not a philosopher, no matter how much philosophy you read and no matter how many philosophy tests you pass. The heart (which loves) moves the mind (which understands) as well as vice versa. The heart pumps blood into the brain, and the brain directs the heart (through the autonomic or unconscious nervous system). The physical interdependence between the physical heart or blood pump and the physical computer or brain symbolizes the mental and psychological interdependence between the power to love and the power to think.

Of course that raises the further question what *wisdom* is.

Wisdom is not identical with knowledge. Knowing all the numbers in the phone book is not wisdom. Yet wisdom is a kind of knowledge. Knowledge of what?

For one thing, wisdom is knowledge not just of facts but of reasons and causes. Animals know facts by their senses (e.g., my cat knows that when I click such a switch, the light goes on or off) but not why, not the causes. They do not have rational minds. Animals cannot be scientists or electricians.

For another thing, wisdom knows *first* causes or *ultimate* causes. The bullet, the gun, the hand, and the muscles are all part of the chain of causes that explain a murder, but the murderer's choice and the motives that motivate that choice are the first cause. They are at least *closer* to the first cause, if that first cause is something further like fate or karma or predestination. So if there is a God, an intelligent Being who designed and created the universe, then the science that explains how the universe works is not as close to wisdom as the theology that explains (insofar as it can) the Creator of the universe. (Both of these examples are controversial "ifs" among philosophers.)

For a third thing, wisdom is not merely the knowledge of facts but of values, of what is good or beautiful or lovable—not merely of what is but of what ought to be.

And therefore wisdom is also practical; that is, it is able to be practiced, to be lived. And we expect those who have lived well to be wiser than those who have not. We learn wisdom by past experience, and then we apply that wisdom to future experience.

But suppose you think this goal is too high, that wisdom is unattainable and therefore that the love of wisdom (philosophy) is a wild goose chase. Well, then, that does not mean that you are not doing philosophy, but that you are. That is your philosophy: that philosophy's goal, wisdom, is unattainable. And that is a bad philosophy, not only because it is not true but also because it does not know itself; it does not acknowledge that it, too, is a philosophy.

We all judge others as more or less wise (e.g., we judge Lincoln as wiser than Hitler), so even if there is no infallibility in our judgments about others' wisdom, and no infallibility even in the most wise people's judgments about life (and, of course, there is not), there are at least degrees of fallibility and thus degrees of wisdom, and therefore there must be such a thing as wisdom.

Wisdom is like diamonds. When you discover how rare and how hard to find diamonds are, you do not for that reason deny their existence or their value.

Philosophy, Science, Religion, Common Sense, and Ideology

Philosophy is not one of the sciences in the modern sense of "science" as distinct from the broader ancient meaning. The ancients classified philosophy as a science because they did not limit science to the empirical and the mathematical. Philosophy is not limited to the scientific method of quantifying its data and testing hypotheses by empirical observation and controlled experiments. The scientific method is like a laser light: concentrating human thought into a narrow and therefore more powerful form. Philosophy is like ordinary light, or like a floodlight as distinct from a spotlight: its objective is the "big picture" rather than exact knowledge of the details. Or, to use another analogy, philosophy attempts to x-ray the data to find the things like the skeletal structure that do not appear on the surface.

Although some of the questions philosophy asks are the questions that religion claims to answer (like what is the greatest good and what is the origin of the intelligibility of the universe), philosophy is not religion because it does not appeal to religious faith, divine revelation, miracles, or mystical experience, only to natural reason. It is like science in that way, and its appeal is universal, since all of us have reason, though not all have faith.

Philosophy is not the same as common sense, though common sense may be a useful check on it. (At least, we instinctively seek stronger reasons to justify a philosophy that contradicts common sense than when the philosophy agrees with and reinforces common sense.) We all begin with at least some "fuzzy" universal and innate common sense and then try to improve it or refine it, by such enterprises as philosophy, religion, and science.

Philosophy is not an ideology, a system of ideas willed into existence for practical and political purposes of change in a predetermined
direction. Philosophy is a product of reason, not will; and its ultimate
purpose is simply truth and understanding, not political change, even
though radical political changes may be called for by a philosophy,
as in the ideological wars in our history, especially in modern times.
But the philosophy cannot be rationally justified by the ideology; the
ideology must be justified by the philosophy. An ideology always
goes beyond the work of reason and involves the work of the will. It
is made, not discovered.

Inductive and Deductive Thinking

There is another way of answering the question, *What* is it? All the
above answers are abstract and general rather than concrete and particular. They appeal to our deductive thinking. Deductive thinking
begins with a truth that is abstract and general (or universal) and
then applies it to concrete particular examples. In contrast, inductive
thinking begins with concrete particular examples and from them it
derives an abstract, general, common, or universal truth.

For a good inductive answer to the question, What is philosophy?
you could simply look at some of the philosophical questions listed
in the table of contents and ask yourself the question, What do all
these questions have in common, and how are they all different from
scientific, religious, commonsensical, or ideological questions? That
would not give you an *essential* definition of philosophy, but it would
give you some of the features or *properties* that philosophical questions
typically have.

That is how we learn most things: inductively, from the bottom
up, so to speak, rather than from the top down. When we want to
learn what a human being is, we usually begin by meeting a number
of actual, concrete human individuals and then we make generaliza-
tions about what is common to all of them. We do not usually work
the other way around, beginning with an abstract universal definition
and then proceeding to concrete examples. That's deductive thinking, and that's the way we usually *judge* things. We judge that X
is or is not a human being by whether it conforms to the essential

definition of a human being—for example, does it have both a body and a rational mind? Inductive thinking is the way we usually *learn* things. We need both inductive and deductive thinking.

How to Begin the Study of Philosophy

There are four ways to begin the study of philosophy, and thus four kinds of "introduction to philosophy" books.

One way, which is useful, instructive, interesting, and even dramatic, is the study of the history of philosophy as an intellectual narrative or journey or ongoing intellectual warfare. I have written such a book, *Socrates' Children*, a four-volume work about the one hundred greatest philosophers and how each reacted to the others in "the great conversation".

A second is apprenticeship: to begin with an in-depth study of a single philosopher or a single great philosophical classic. This has the advantage of depth and concreteness. I have also written such a book, *A Socratic Introduction to Plato's "Republic"*, about Plato's philosophy, especially in his *Republic*, and another, *Philosophy 101 by Socrates*, about Plato's *Apology of Socrates*. I have found assigning Plato the very best way to inveigle students into the love of wisdom.

A third way, which is the most common one today among textbook writers, is an anthology of short excerpts from classical philosophers and many short contemporary articles from professional philosophy journals. This is a scattershot approach and lacks depth, "big picture" context, and continuity. I also cowrote such a book, but its excerpts were from the classics only. It is currently out of print.

This book is a fourth, and unique, way. It imagines Socrates teaching you and presenting arguments for both sides of at least one centrally important and controversial issue in each of the divisions of philosophy. Someone once defined the ideal university as "Socrates on one end of a log and the student on the other end". I call that "Socrates University".

I think this works well mainly because dialogue (which is the heart of the Socratic method) is much more interesting than monologue. That's why the question and answer session at the end of a lecture is almost always more interesting than the lecture. It is dialogue and thus dramatic. It is not just a still picture but a movie. For Socrates, there is little or no lecture, only Q and A. For Socrates, philosophy is like a boxing match, an intellectual battle. But it is a friendly one; it is like psychoanalysis, not like war.

So I have put myself and you, dear reader, into this book, in dialogue. There has never been another Socrates, and if there were, I would not be one; but I am at least his admirer and disciple and imitator, so I put myself at one end of the log of "Socrates University" and you at the other end.

I do not know your name, so I have called you "Nat Whilk", which is Old English for "I know not who". Nat could be short for either Natalie or Nathan, so you can identify with Nat whatever your gender. I have put into your mouth the most common opinions, questions, answers, reactions, and responses that I find among beginners in philosophy who are intelligent and alive. (I assume only two things: that you are neither a robot nor a zombie.)

A Totally Unnecessary Point

The following is a totally unnecessary paragraph and should not be taken too seriously. Are you certain you are not a robot or a zombie? If so, how? How would you prove this to yourself? If you cannot, why not? That is an example of the kind of philosophical question contemporary philosophers love to ask. The more usual version is, How do you know you are not really a brain in a vat in the laboratory of some mad scientist who is programming your brain to think it perceives all the things that you seem to yourself to think or perceive?

If you think this is a ridiculous question and not a serious one, I personally sympathize with you, for I do too, deep down and in the long run. (That is one of the very few times you will learn anything about my own personal philosophical opinions in this book.) On the other hand, if you think it *is* a serious question, I also sympathize with you, for that is a philosophical question. It is similar to the question of whether we can ever be certain we know the truth, addressed in chapter 1 of this book.

How Is This Book Different from Other Introductions to Philosophy?

This book is different from other introductions to philosophy. For one thing, it tries to draw you inside philosophy. Its logic is not just deductive and inductive but seductive, since the love of wisdom is a kind of love. To understand everything in a book from the outside well enough to get an A on a test is not necessarily wisdom. The arguments in this book are meant to be not only like windows that you see through but also like doors that you walk through. I'm trying to seduce you into *doing* philosophy, not just looking at it. That's the strategy behind all of Socrates' arguments with Nat in this book. He values the process as much as the result, the reasoning as much as the conclusions.

For another thing, it focuses on existential questions, questions that make a difference to the lives of ordinary people, not just philosophers and scholars.

For another thing, it has no philosophical or ideological agenda, either overt or hidden. It tries to be open-minded and evenhanded and to do justice to both sides of every controversy. And it tries to inculcate that habit in you too, for if you do not fairly explore and evaluate both of two rival products, how can you know which one to buy?

Still another, and the most obvious, difference between this book and other introductions to philosophy is that it has a concrete historical model and master, namely, Socrates. This is not limiting, as it would be if Socrates were replaced with any other philosopher, because while Socrates taught a lot about the process of philosophizing, he came to only a very few conclusions himself, nearly all of which were paradoxical (e.g., that learning is really remembering, that virtue is really knowledge, and that the answer to the question why bad things happen to good people is that they never do). But none of these few distinctively Socratic opinions or conclusions are what is argued about in this book.

Finally, the Socratic method encourages us to see and learn from both sides of an issue, even the side that we may eventually reject. Every error has a grain of truth in it, and even a little grain of truth, like a seed buried deep in darkness, is valuable and can come alive and grow and become an edible plant.

A Word about Skepticism

One of the features of the Socratic method used in this book is that both sides of an issue or controversy are argued for and taken seriously. There are usually surprisingly good arguments for both sides of an either-or issue. Students naturally tend to feel that this method of presenting both sides of a controversial issue either presupposes skepticism or results in skepticism, which is the ism that claims that truth, or at least certain truth, cannot be found. "Who's to say, anyway?" is a very common response to an argument. It is found especially when great philosophical minds, far wiser than ours, are to be found on both sides of almost every question.

And the only possible answer to that question, the question of who's to say what's true, is neither "This philosopher as distinct from that one" nor "Nobody", but "You". You, Nat Whilk. You have the responsibility to make up your mind, just as you have the responsibility to make up your bed. You cannot let your mind be like an unmade, dirty bed with crumbs and stains and perhaps even bedbugs in it. Make your bed! Make your mind!

But not too quickly, please. Because your mind is yours, and "a mind is a terrible thing to waste."

Like Socrates, I will not *tell* you *what* to think, by preaching, but I will try to *show* you *how* to think, by example. I am not a skeptic (a skeptic is one who believes that certain knowledge of the truth is impossible), but I admire serious and unhappy skeptics who are in love with wisdom but have not yet found her and married her. She is indeed seductive and elusive. But I do *not* admire happy and satisfied skeptics, because they are not serious seekers after wisdom but just lazy minds that have thrown down their weapons (reason) and given up the battle.

Socrates begins his arguments with something that looks like skepticism—a skeptical *attitude* at least—and he often ends with the same attitude rather than with satisfaction or a claim to certainty. But he is not a skeptic. Some of his dialogues end with a form of thought that is somewhere between skepticism and rational proof, namely, with a symbolic "big picture", a myth or sacred story. These are usually narratives, or stories, that deeply move us because our life is itself a story, and they help us *understand* deep truths, but they do not either *define* them or *prove* them. They do not define because they are symbolic rather than literal, and they do not prove because they show rather than logically demonstrate. Great sages always use stories, such as Jesus' parables, the story of Job, and the teachings of Buddha, Confucius, and Lao Tzu.

I will describe the strategies of the Socratic method in the third introduction. I use some of them in this book, but I do not confine myself to them because I try to imagine how an actual conversation might proceed today between an intelligent beginner in philosophy and Socrates, if he were still here.

In writing this book, I did not first logically outline the issues and the steps that most efficiently address and try to resolve the issues, and then add the two speakers in order to make the logical progress of the argument a bit more interesting. That is a procedure that inevitably would have reduced the two speakers to puppets who speak in a more logical, clear, and ordered way than any real speaker, even a philosopher, ever really does. Instead of inventing these two stick figures to carry the arguments, I have tried to invent two real characters and imagine how a good conversation would actually take place between them. So the conversations include some meanderings, tangents, mistakes, changes of mind, and confusions. If this more literary and psychologically realistic technique does not make the arguments themselves clearer (and I think sometimes it actually does), it at least makes them more interesting, more human, and something with which we can identify. And that is the purpose of this whole book: to seduce the reader into actually philosophizing, into jumping into the great conversation.

INTRODUCTION TO LOGIC

I said the introductory chapters are the most boring parts of this book. Well, this second introduction is the most boring of the boring introductions. But it is also probably the most useful and necessary.

Logic is the science and art of reasoning well. There are two different kinds of logic today. The Socratic method, which we are going to use in this book, uses the old logic, ordinary language logic or commonsense logic, whose rules were first formulated by Aristotle. The new logic, which is called symbolic logic or mathematical logic, is only about a century old (although it has its roots in the eighteenth century). It is more useful for the hard sciences, especially computer science, but the old logic is the way real live philosophical conversations actually go. Never in my life have I heard anyone arguing in symbolic logic other than professional philosophers talking to one another.

For a rather technical but very short discussion of the difference between the two logics, see the last section of this introduction.

The ancient philosophers defined man as "the rational animal". Logic is the art and science of reasoning well. Reasoning, in modern parlance, usually means giving reasons for believing some things; in other words, it is trying to prove conclusions from premises—for instance, "If all men are mortal and I am a man, then I am mortal", or "No sane person voted for that candidate, but you voted for that candidate; therefore, you are not a sane person." (We are considering only the structure of reasoning here, not the content, and not how persuasive it is.)

But this reasoning to a conclusion from premises is only one of three powers of reason. It is the third of the "three acts of the mind" that distinguishes us from all other animals. The other two are (1) understanding, or simple apprehension, or conceiving an abstract concept, like "man" or "mortal", and (2) judging that a proposition or declarative sentence or truth claim is true or false, like "I am mortal."

Let's look at these three acts of the mind one by one.

Let's suppose you understand the meaning of "apple" but not "quasar". You have a *concept* of an apple in your mind, but you have no concept of a quasar. It's just a word to you. Even if you know that the word literally means "quasi-stellar object", you do not under-stand that it does not mean a UFO or a firecracker but something outside the solar system that acts in some ways like a star and in other ways not like a star. But you do know what an apple is, and on the basis of that knowledge, you can distinguish it from another fruit even though that other fruit may look like an apple. That act of the mind is conception (conceiving a concept), or simple apprehension, or understanding the meaning of a term.

Concepts are neither true nor false. The statement that "apples are fruits" is true and "apples are animals" is false, but "apples" in itself is neither true nor false. It is simply an understood meaning. It is expressed not by a statement or proposition or declarative sentence, which could be either true or false, but merely a word or phrase that could be either the subject or the predicate of a declarative sentence. (The subject is what you're talking about, and the predicate is what you say about it.)

Most of the concepts we have in our minds are somewhat fuzzy or vague or even ambiguous and misleading. For instance, "good" could mean something moral (a moral virtue or a moral act) or something physical (health or strength) or something military (victory, or the means to victory). So to clarify and limit the meaning of a concept (in our minds) or a term (in a proposition) or a word (in a sentence), we use a *definition*.

The second act of the mind is judgment, asserting a statement or declarative sentence or proposition as true. (Even when we say that a judgment is false, we claim to know that it is true that that judgment is false.) A *judgment* of the mind connects two concepts in the mind, and this is expressed in logic as a *proposition* that connects two terms, the subject term and the predicate term, and this is expressed in lan-guage as a *declarative sentence*.

Judgment depends on conception because if we do not understand the meaning of the concepts or terms, we cannot know or judge whether the proposition is true or false.

Argument, or reasoning, is the third act of the mind. Just as judg-ment connects two terms, argument connects two or more judgments by a process of reasoning, moving from the premise or premises, as assumptions, to the conclusion, which is proved by those premises. For instance, "man" is a term, "All men are mortal" is a proposition, and "All men are mortal and I am a man; therefore, I am mortal" is an argument.

The goal sought in the first act of the mind is clarity and understanding. The goal sought in the second act of the mind is truth. The goal sought in the third act of the mind is proof that the conclusion is true.

There are two kinds of reasoning (the third act of the mind). Deductive reasoning moves from a general principle to a particular example or application of it. All the examples of reasoning above are deductive. Inductive reasoning moves from a number of concrete, particular, individual examples to an abstract, universal, general truth. For instance, philosophers A, B, C, and D are all above average in intelligence; therefore, probably all philosophers are above average in intelligence. Inductive proofs do not even claim to produce certainty, as good deductive proofs do, but only degrees of probability, depending on the quality and quantity of the examples. Most, but not all, philosophical reasoning is deductive.

All three acts of the mind can be done well or badly: (1) Concepts can be either clear or unclear. They can be unclear by being either vague or equivocal, that is, with two different meanings. (2) Judgments (truth claims) can be either true or false. (3) Arguments can be either logically valid or invalid. In a valid deductive argument, the conclusion necessarily follows from the premises so that if all the premises are true, the conclusion must be true. In an invalid, or fallacious, argument, this is not so.

Clarity is a matter of degree. Truth and logical validity are not. Every truth claim, or declarative sentence, is either true or false, and every deductive argument is either logically valid or invalid.

For instance, all four of the following arguments are invalid because the conclusion does not necessarily follow from the premises:

"I hate yogurt; therefore, yogurt is bad."
"Three people I know love yogurt; therefore, everyone must love yogurt."
"Yogurt is soft and ice cream is soft; therefore, ice cream is yogurt."
"Every movie star eats yogurt; therefore, everyone who eats yogurt is a movie star."

So an argument has three checkpoints: (1) its terms must be clear and unambiguous, (2) its premises must be true, and (3) its logic must be valid. If an argument fails any one of its checkpoints, it fails in its mission to prove the conclusion to be true.

For instance, the argument "All philosophers are gods, and all gods are blue; therefore, all philosophers are blue" is a logically valid argument because *if* its premises were true, its conclusion would be true too; but it is a failed argument because its premises are not true.

In contrast, the argument "All philosophers are humans, and some humans are women; therefore, all philosophers are women" has true premises but its logic is invalid: the conclusion does not logically follow from the premises. It, too, is a failed argument.

So is the following: "Pens contain ink, and pig pens are pens; therefore, pig pens contain ink." This is a failed argument because it uses a term ("pens") equivocally.

Thus, the rule to try to follow in constructing an argument is always to use clear concepts, true premises, and valid logic. And the rule to follow in evaluating an argument is to ask whether there are any ambiguous concepts, false premises, or logical fallacies.

So if someone argues for a position you think is false, you can respond to that person's argument in one of four ways: (1) that it fails because one of its concepts is used ambiguously, (2) that it fails because at least one of its premises or assumptions is false, (3) that it fails because its conclusion does not logically follow from its premises, or (4) that it succeeds because none of these mistakes is made, and therefore its conclusion is true and you must admit that you were wrong in denying it.

None of those four responses is what you usually hear people say when someone else argues against a position they hold. What you usually hear is simply nonsense: "Well, that may be true for you but it's not true for me." As if each of us is God creating our own universe out of our own mind. Excuse me for shocking you, but you did not create the universe.

In fantasy, truth is invented. In Tolkien's invented world in *The Lord of the Rings*, elves are tall, serious, wise, and formidable; in Shakespeare's invented world in *A Midsummer Night's Dream*, elves are tiny tricksters like Tinker Bell who live in flowers. But philosophical argument is about the real world.

The following chart is for reference. It summarizes all of traditional commonsense deductive logic, organized by the "three acts of the mind". It applies most clearly to deductive reasoning, but except for the notion of logical validity, it applies to inductive reasoning too. (Inductive arguments are never simply valid or invalid but more or less probable or likely.)

This is far from the whole of logic, or of the Socratic method, but it frames what Socrates is doing in his arguments. It is not sufficient for understanding that method, but it is necessary—a minimum.

A Summary of Traditional Aristotelian Logic by the Three Acts of the Mind

	1st	2nd	3rd
Act of the mind	Understanding	Judging	Reasoning
Logical expression	Term	Proposition	Argument
Linguistic expression	Word or phrase	Declarative sentence	Paragraph
Example	"Man"	"All men are mortal."	"All men are mortal and I am a man; therefore, I am mortal."
Structural parts	None	Subject term and predicate term	Premises and conclusion
Question answered	What it is	Whether it is	Why it is
Aspect of reality	Essence	Existence	Cause (reason)
Good when	Clear	True	Logically valid
How achieved	Definition	Many ways	Obeys the laws of logic
Bad when	Unclear: vague or ambiguous	False	Invalid, fallacious
Question to ask	What do you mean?	What's your point?	Why? (Prove it!)

A Very Short Discussion of the Two Logics

The practical difference between the old Aristotelian logic and the new symbolic logic is that the old logic is how human beings think, while the new logic is how computers think. (Actually, computers do not think at all; they merely record and transmit human thoughts, like books. Computers do not have minds. They don't know us; we know them.)

The structural difference is that the old logic begins with the first act of the mind and insists on defining the universal essence designated by a term, which presupposes that there are such universal essences or forms or "the natures of things".

This assumption, technically called "metaphysical realism", the belief in the objective reality of universals, is rejected by many modern philosophers, who prefer "nominalism", the belief that universals are not realities but only words ("nomina") or class concepts that we invent and impose on reality to classify it for our own purposes.

The new logic begins with the second act of the mind and with propositions, and it puts propositions on a "truth table", calculating which other propositions are true, false, or uncertain, given the assumption that a given proposition is known to be true or false.

Propositions are either true or false. "True or false" is a zero-sum game. It is digital. This is how computers "think". The old logic begins with terms. Terms are neither true nor false. Thinking with terms is not digital. It is usually analogical, since words, unlike numbers, have ranges of meaning. This is how human beings usually think, until they take courses in modern logic. Thus, the Socratic method works within the old logic rather than the new logic.

This is a vastly oversimplified account of the difference between the two logics, but it is enough to justify using the old logic for our Socratic method book.

INTRODUCTION TO THE SOCRATIC METHOD AND HOW TO USE IT WITH DIFFICULT PEOPLE

These dialogues are "Socratic". They are poor imitations of Plato's Socratic dialogues, and my Socrates is a poor imitation of the real Socrates. Like the real Socrates, my fictional Socrates uses the famous Socratic method of teaching, but not all the time. He is not merely a faceless stand-in for the method but a personal friend, mentor, and guru to his student, Nat Whilk. He is me.

The method as used by Plato and described in this introduction is much more elaborate than Socrates uses in these dialogues of mine. So this introduction describes the fuller thing of which these dialogues are partial imitations.

After each dialogue are questions for discussion and personal essays. They are not test questions about whether you understood the dialogues; they assume that you did and go on from there to ask you actually to *think* about them. You are invited but not required to use the Socratic method in your essays and discussions.

The best way to understand the Socratic method is inductively, by experiencing many instances of it (the earlier, shorter dialogues of Plato) and gradually coming to see the common principles, both theoretical (essentially the three acts of the mind and the rules of logical validity, both of which are commonsensical) and practical (how he uses these principles).

But here is a "cheat sheet", a quick way of summarizing these principles, both the practical strategic principles of the use of logical laws and the practical psychological principles of the Socratic personal relationship, both of which are dimensions of what Socrates is doing.

First, some logical principles.

1. Understand, presuppose, and use the three acts of the mind in the previous section as the fundamental structure of logical thinking.

2. Presuppose the law of non-contradiction not merely as an agreed-upon rule of procedure ("Don't tolerate contradictions") but as the law of reality. No one has ever experienced or even conceived of a lion that is not a lion or a love that is not a love, even though there may be ligers (lions that are also tigers) or loves that are also hatreds. Those are not contradictions, only paradoxes, apparent contradictions. One can love and hate the same person at the same time, but one cannot both love and not love the same person at the same time. Logical consistency is the basis for personal consistency. See point 3 in the list of personal principles that follows (p. 34).

3. Begin with the first act of the mind (understanding the meaning of a concept) by trying to understand what your interlocutor or dialogue partner means by his key terms. Come to terms with him. Undo ambiguities by defining terms. This is not just a word game; you need to define not just words but the real things the words are trying to communicate. And you may need to go a step further (or many steps further) and also define the terms in the definition if they are ambiguous. Ask your partner which of two or more meanings he means.

The basic rule of a good definition is that it must be neither broader nor narrower than the thing defined. "Man" is neither "a male rational animal" (too narrow) nor "a two-footed animal" (too broad). Justice is not "whatever the boss says it is" because that is both too broad and too narrow.

This step is like turning on the light; the next steps are actions (repairs, enterprises, journeys) that work only in the light, not in the foggy shadows.

4. The object of the second act of the mind (judgment) is truth. To be sure you and your partner are arguing on the same basis, find a judgment (a proposition, a truth claim) that you agree is true and argue from there, taking it as your common ground, your premise, your starting point. All disagreement presupposes some agreement, some common foundation, some premise. Find it. Even two armies have to fight on the same battlefield. This means that you need to find a belief of your partner's that you agree with, or one of yours

that he agrees with. In that way you are moving in the same world of thought, and the dialogue is not just a collision of wholly different worlds. Then, if you critique your partner's thoughts, it will be an internal critique rather than an outside, foreign one. It's like judo: the small can move the great if he uses the weight and movement of the other against him.

5. The third act of the mind, arguing, moves in many ways. One way is to move forward, to deduce consequences from principles. This may be positive (a true premise proving a true conclusion) or negative (a false conclusion showing up a false premise). This latter case is technically called a "reduction to absurdity": a premise that may seem reasonable at first can sometimes be shown to entail or necessitate logically a conclusion that is unreasonable, thus indirectly proving the premise to be untenable.

6. Another way is to move backward, so to speak, and try to find the implied principles or premises behind a belief, an answer to the question, *Why* is this true, do you think? This is very useful even if nothing comes from it because it enlightens the other person about his own mind.

Keep in mind that refuting one of these whys or reasons or premises of your opponent's argument does not refute the truth of his conclusion, only the persuasiveness of this particular argument for it. There may be better whys, better reasons, better premises, and better arguments for that conclusion.

7. Refutation of a judgment that claims to be universally true can be shown simply by a counterexample. For instance, justice is not always "giving a person what legally belongs to him", because if this person legally owns a gun and threatens to kill with it, justice does not demand giving him what is legally his. Examples can often be found from ordinary experience that refute high-sounding general principles.

8. Socrates likes to use analogies that compare difficult or abstract or unfamiliar problems with similar problems from concrete ordinary and familiar experience. Analogies prove nothing, but they make difficult concepts simpler and clearer. They show parallels rather than prove them.

9. Socrates often uses what is called an "elenchus": You make a claim. Socrates gets you to agree with some other proposition. Then he shows, sometimes surprisingly, that the new proposition to which you

have agreed is inconsistent with what you claimed before. So he gets you to contradict yourself. You must give up at least one of those two contradictory propositions.

10. Socrates also uses dilemmas, either-or situations that logically lead to the same unwelcome conclusion no matter which alternative (which "horn" of the dilemma) you choose. This often results in the frustration called "aporia", which means literally "roadlessness", or "no way out". This forces you to retrace your steps to find where you went off the road. It often convinces you of your "double ignorance", your ignorance of your own ignorance of the truth. When this works, it induces humility and the willingness to rethink things; when it does not work, it induces frustration and skepticism and a desire to give up.

Second, some personal psychological principles.

1. The first and most necessary principle is in the will rather than the intellect. It is the will to truth. The aim of arguing is not personal victory but truth. There are no winners or losers. If the truth is found, or understood more clearly, both parties win. A Socratic argument is not a debate or a game or a contest; it is more like a scientific experiment.

Nietzsche was the philosopher who made famous this label, "the will to truth", in the process of being the first to question it and criticize it. The will to truth is the first assumption behind all other assumptions, and if it is not there, nothing but personal power remains. Nietzsche thought, darkly, that "the will to power" was the force that moved everything without exception. He had a more complete and passionate criticism of Socrates than of anyone else except Jesus.

2. Because truth is the end and rational argument is the means, we have as our second principle the agreement to follow the argument wherever it may lead. We do not follow personal fear or vanity or popularity or anything else. Rational argument moves us and leads us somewhere, like a river, and the Socratic method assumes that both parties move their boats into the river and let it carry them downstream.

3. The Socratic demand for logical consistency and the refusal to accept logical contradictions (the fundamental law of logic, the law of non-contradiction) has deep personal psychological ramifications. If you believe two ideas that contradict each other, you contradict

yourself, you are not one, you are at war with yourself, you are split into two people, you live in two different worlds, at least mentally. You are an enemy to yourself. So it is an act of charity for Socrates to try to unify and reconcile and harmonize your beliefs. It is the care of the psyche. Logic is a human instrument and serves a human purpose. Perhaps that's why the titles of most of Plato's dialogues are the names of persons, not ideas. The dialogues are exercises not only in logic but also in therapy, the care of the soul.

4. Dialogue requires two minds, not just one. Socrates does not preach or lecture; he asks and answers questions. A dialogue is an ongoing and often dramatic interpersonal relationship, a story. Questioning is much livelier than lecturing because it means thought is actually happening now; lecturing or preaching means that thought has already happened and is now merely being transferred to another mind. Socrates' "dialectic" shows us the road as well as the destination. He shows us (and includes us as dramatic actors in) the *process* of thinking, and the process is as important, and certainly as interesting, as the product.

5. Since the second most basic law of ethics, after to do good and avoid evil, is to love your neighbor as yourself, Socrates loves himself too and uses his "dialectical" or conversational method on himself, ruthlessly challenging his assumptions and demanding total consistency and clarity and not being satisfied until he gets them—and this means very, very seldom being satisfied! It's much easier to spot the faults in another person's arguments (or in another person's character) than in your own. Questioning ideas makes demands and puts pressure on whoever receives the questioning, including yourself; and if this is good for others, it is good for yourself too. If you can't find a dialogue partner to act as Socrates, find the Socrates in yourself and use the Socratic "dialectic" on yourself. Question yourself ruthlessly (out of charity to yourself).

6. The reason that last point is true gives us another personal and psychological principle of the Socratic method: humility. Socrates admits his own ignorance, not only at the beginning of each dialogue but often also at the end. He is very careful to avoid what has been called "the double ignorance", ignorance not only of the truth but also of your own ignorance of the truth. The weakest minds are those that are too weak to see their own weakness. And Socrates really does have a low opinion of his own mind—and an even lower opinion of

most other people's minds because they do *not* have a low opinion of their own minds.

7. One necessary step in the ability to argue logically with another is to understand what the other means, and this requires a kind of intellectual empathy, putting yourself in the mind of the other by asking probing questions. You cannot refute another without first understanding him, looking at the issue the way he does. Also, if you do this to him, your partner is much more likely to do it to you. Stop throwing stones down from the mountain of your own thinking at the person you disagree with, and instead climb down from your mountain and climb up his to see what he sees. Learn from him. Learn first; teach later.

8. This also involves treating your partner differently depending on where he is psychologically or emotionally. When he is losing confidence, encourage him; when he is overconfident, deflate him. Jesus was always doing this to His disciples, though religiously rather than logically.

9. All this requires total honesty and candor and trust. Say what you really believe, not what you think anyone else wants to hear, no matter how outrageous he may think it is and how stupid he may think you are. This is part of "the will to truth".

10. And never give up. Never take refuge in easy, passive, defeatist skepticism. Partial knowledge, or probable knowledge, or a slight but significant progress in clarity are noble goals; the whole issue need not be resolved and both parties need not agree totally at the end for the dialogue to be successful. Socrates begins with skepticism of your certitudes in order to end not with more skepticism and less certitude but with at least *some* more certitude and less skepticism.

Combining the personal and impersonal aspects of this method takes experience and intuition; there is no mechanical way of doing it. You can't teach a computer to be Socrates.

How to Use the Socratic Method with Difficult People

The question of how to use the Socratic method with difficult people is not a stretch of the Socratic method. It was *designed* for arguing with difficult people because Socrates was surrounded by difficult people. So are we. So are our friends, for those difficult people include us.

The following joke is a better way to make that point. Three men—Huey, Louie, and Dewey—died and went to that intermediate state before Heaven called Purgatory. They noticed that there were thousands of ducks everywhere. Saint Peter welcomed them and warned them that one of the rules was "never step on a duck." There would be serious punishments for stepping on a duck and serious rewards for avoiding it. A few minutes after they arrived, Huey noticed that Louie had stepped on a duck, and Saint Peter immediately summoned two angels. One of them carried a large iron chain, and the other led an astonishingly ugly woman. They chained Louie to the woman and said, "She is your Purgatory for the next hundred years." That made both Huey and Dewey very, very careful not to step on a duck. But eventually Dewey did, and the same punishment was immediately administered to him. This made Huey even more careful not to step on a duck, and he succeeded for a long time. But eventually the angel with the chain appeared for him. The angel brought to Huey an astonishingly beautiful woman and chained her to Huey. "I don't understand the rules here", Huey said. "Neither do I", said the woman. "All I did was step on a duck."

We all know difficult people. We see one every time we look into a mirror. We avoid arguing with them because they are not only wrong; they are not only under an illusion; but they are under the illusion that they are *not* under an illusion, ignorant of their ignorance. They are in the "double bind". How can that knot be undone? There is a way to deal with this and with them—the Socratic way— and Søren Kierkegaard understood it well. He wrote in *The Point of View for My Work as an Author*:

> An illusion is not an easy thing to dispel....
>
> What then is he to do? First and foremost, no impatience.... A direct attack only strengthens a person in his illusion, and at the same time embitters him. There is nothing that requires such gentle handling as an illusion, if one wishes to dispel it. If anything prompts the prospective captive to set his will in opposition, all is lost. And this is what a direct attack achieves, and it implies moreover the presumption of requiring a man to make to another person, or in his presence, an admission which he can make most profitably to himself privately.

This is what is achieved by the indirect method, which, loving and serving the truth, arranges everything dialectically [logically] for the prospective captive, and then shyly withdraws (for love is always shy), so as not to witness the admission which he makes to himself alone before God—that he has lived hitherto in an illusion....

If real success is to attend the effort to bring a man to a definite position, one must first of all take pains to find him where he is and begin there.

This is the secret of the art of helping others. Any one who has not mastered this is himself deluded when he proposes to help others. In order to help another effectively I must understand more than he— yet first of all surely I must understand what he understands. If I do not know that, my greater understanding will be of no help to him.... All true effort to help begins with self-humiliation: the helper must first humble himself under him he would help, and therewith must understand that to help does not mean to be a sovereign but to be a servant, that to help does not mean to be ambitious but to be patient, that to help means to endure for the time being the imputation that one is in the wrong and does not understand what the other one understands.

Take the case of a man who is passionately angry, and let us assume that he is really in the wrong. Unless you can begin with him by making it seem as if it were he that had to instruct you, and unless you can do it in such a way that the angry man, who was too impatient to listen to a word of yours, is glad to discover in you a complaisant and attentive listener—if you cannot do that, you cannot help him at all....

Be the amazed listener who sits and hears what the other finds the more delight in telling you because you listen with amazement....

If you can do that, if you can find exactly the place where the other is and begin there, you may perhaps have the luck to lead him to the place where you are.

For to be a teacher does not mean simply to affirm that such a thing is so, or to deliver a lecture, etc. No, to be a teacher in the right sense is to be a learner.[1]

[1] Søren Kierkegaard, *The Point of View for My Work as an Author*, trans. Walter Lowrie (New York: Harper & Brothers, 1962), 25–29.

Critical Epistemology: Thinking about Thinking

Epistemology is the division of philosophy that thinks about thinking ("episteme" in Greek). We can begin to do philosophy with any division of it—philosophy's house has many doors—but most modern philosophers begin with epistemology. One reason for doing that is to examine our tools before we use them to build things (in the other divisions of philosophy). This seems like a more critical rather than uncritical approach.

On the other hand, there is a problem with this beginning: using our (rational) tools to examine and judge our (rational) tools sounds like having the prisoner who is on trial also be the judge, or having the player also be the umpire. More about this problem later.

Epistemology is sometimes divided into "critical epistemology" (which we will explore in this chapter) and "positive epistemology" or "substantive epistemology" (which we will explore in chapter 2). The question of the second chapter is how knowledge works, especially how the senses and the reason interrelate. The former question, addressed in this chapter, is whether knowledge is possible at all, or at least any certain knowledge. It is a critique, or evaluative judgment, of skepticism, which is the "no" answer to that question. For if skepticism is true, all the other questions are really only a wild goose chase.

Epistemology, to most people, is the least interesting division of philosophy, the most abstract and empty and airy one, since it's not thinking about the real objects of thinking but rather thinking about thinking itself. So please don't judge the rest of the book by these first two chapters. The book gets more concrete and specific and practical as it moves along. (See the table of contents.)

Socrates here is my imitation of the real thing. It is only a thin slice of him. Nat is simply a good beginning philosopher. I hope

39

you identify with Nat's curiosity, open-mindedness, intelligence, and love of arguments. It does not matter whether you identify with his opinions or not.

Nat wakes up one day, unsure whether he is in a dream, in the world, or in a book, to find himself seated on a log with an ugly little old man sitting on the other side, dressed in clothing that went out of fashion about twenty-four hundred years ago.

NAT: Who are you, old man? And what are we doing here sitting on this log?

SOCRATES: My name is Socrates. Perhaps you've heard of me.

NAT: You're a famous philosopher, right?

SOCRATES: Right.

NAT: What's that? What's a philosopher?

SOCRATES: One who philosophizes, of course.

NAT: And what is *that*?

SOCRATES: Good for you! You keep asking questions, as I do. So you have just answered your own question.

NAT: How?

SOCRATES: By doing what you have asked about. By philosophizing.

NAT: You mean philosophizing is asking questions? I thought it was answering them.

SOCRATES: It can be both. But asking has to come first. What good is the answer to a person who hasn't asked the question?

NAT: And this thing that you do, this philosophizing—why is it a great benefit to mankind? What do you make better for us?

SOCRATES: What do you think?

NAT: I guess it's thinking.

SOCRATES: Thinking is indeed my "schtick", you might say.

NAT: Do you make it easier?

SOCRATES: No, I make it harder. Questioning is harder than answering. Answers are as plentiful as germs. But questioning—really questioning, really wanting to know, the will to know, the effort to know, the passion to know—that's harder than you think.

NAT: So you make trouble for us. That's your gift.

SOCRATES: Yes. For me, being a philosopher is being an intellectual troublemaker. I ask permission to snoop around in other people's minds and evaluate their contents. And if the food is edible, we eat it, and if it isn't, we throw it out and look for real food.

NAT: You're talking about food for the mind, right?

SOCRATES: Yes.

NAT: And what is that food?

SOCRATES: I think the word for it is "truth".

NAT: Ah, but now comes the troublesome question: What is truth?

SOCRATES: Oh, I welcome troublesome questions, and I think there are very many of them, but I don't think that's one of them. I think we all know what we mean by truth.

NAT: I am very surprised to hear you say that. If we all know what truth is, then why are there so many disagreements about everything under the sun?

SOCRATES: Because we don't know which ideas *have* this quality that we call truth. But I think we all know and agree about what that word means. Old Aristotle, the most commonsensical of all philosophers, defined it in words of one syllable, something to the effect of, "If one says of what is that it is, or of what is not that it is not, he speaks the truth. But if one says of what is not that it is, or of what is that it is not, he does not speak the truth."

NAT: That's ... that's amazing! Forty-seven words, all of one syllable! Nothing hard to understand there. So truth means simply "telling it like it is"?

SOCRATES: Right. It's quite easy to define but very hard to find.

NAT: I can't believe it's that easy. Aren't there some philosophers who define it another way? Like mystical experience, or practicality, or logical coherence, or whatever you sincerely believe, or whatever those in power say it is?

SOCRATES: Indeed, there are philosophers who have other definitions of truth, alternatives to "telling it like it is", or "thoughts and words corresponding to reality". But I think all of them implicitly presuppose and use Aristotle's definition. Do you see how?

NAT: I think so. They all say that their definition of truth tells it like it is or corresponds to reality.

SOCRATES: Yes. So even if any of their definitions are right, they're right because they conform to Aristotle's definition. For any definition to be "right" means it's "true"; and for it to be "true" means that's the way things *really are*: that truth *really is* logical coherence, or mystical experience, or practicality, or whatever you believe, or power, or something else.

NAT: And if one of those other things is what truth really is, and if that means that Aristotle's definition is wrong, then these other philosophers with these other definitions of truth are saying that Aristotle's "telling it like it is" is *not* telling it like it is; that they rather than he are really telling it like it is by saying that it's *not* "telling it like it is", but something else instead.

SOCRATES: Yes. Well put, Nat. And what's wrong with saying that?

NAT: It contradicts itself.

SOCRATES: Yes, it does. And what is wrong with *that*?

NAT: That's illogical. That violates the first commandment of logic.

SOCRATES: Yes, it does. But what's wrong with *that*? Sometimes there are situations where we *ought* to break a commandment, aren't there?

NAT: But not this one.

SOCRATES: Why not?

NAT: Because it makes no sense. To say it is and it is not at the same time is to say nothing at all.

SOCRATES: Good! So that "law" is not like the man-made laws of a country or the rules of a game, but like the laws of mathematics: we didn't invent it and we can't change it.

NAT: But we can change the language systems we use to express it.

SOCRATES: Yes, but even then there is only one truth in all the different language systems.

NAT: How can you prove that?

SOCRATES: Because we can translate that one truth, that one meaning, from one language system to another. We can change the words, the pointers, but not the truth that the words point to. We can violate the law of non-contradiction in our thinking, as those philosophers do, but never in reality. When we try, we utter only meaningless words, like saying yes and no to the same question, or like saying something is and is not at the same time.

NAT: So logic is about reality? I thought logic was just a set of rules for us to play by. How can you prove that a logical law like non-contradiction is a law of objective reality and not just our invention?

SOCRATES: Well, if we invent something, we can uninvent it or reinvent it, can't we?

NAT: Yes.

SOCRATES: So if we invented the law of non-contradiction, we could reinvent it. But we can't. We can't make a real contradiction or even think a contradiction that's meaningful, any more than we can make 2 plus 2 into 5. And we can't ever discover any exceptions to the law of non-contradiction in reality. We can't even meaningfully *think* of one or imagine one. We can imagine a two-headed goat but we cannot even imagine one that has two heads and does not have two heads.

NAT: So what practical good does it do us to know that the law of non-contradiction is a law of objective reality, and not just our subjective invention? What difference does that make?

SOCRATES: Because it is only because we know that that law is true that we can know that when two ideas really contradict each other, they can't both be true. If that law were not true, we could never refute any argument at all. Every opinion would be equally irrefutable.

NAT: And how do we know that truth is not just opinion, "my truth" or "your truth"?

SOCRATES: In the same way we know that triangles have three angles. That's what the word "truth" *means*, just as "an enclosed figure with three angles" is what the word "triangle" means. And what "truth" means is different from what the word "opinion" means. Opinions are subjective. They are only in minds, and there are different opinions because there are different minds. And opinions have to be judged as true or false. There are false opinions, but there are no false truths. That's a meaningless self-contradiction.

NAT: OK, that's how we know there is objective truth. But how do we find it?

SOCRATES: Oh, that's a very different question, and that's not easy to answer, like the other one. I think we just answered the first question: it's self-contradictory to deny that truth is objective, to say it's true that there is no truth, that it's objectively true, and not just a matter of subjective opinion, that there is no objective truth but only subjective opinions.

NAT: But what about honestly and sincerely held opinions? Doesn't sincerity count? Isn't there a difference between a sincere opinion and an insincere one?

SOCRATES: Of course. And that changes the psychology and the morality, but not the logic. My personal sincerity or insincerity, my honesty or dishonesty, can't change objective reality. My sincere belief that you are not Nat but Aristotle cannot change the objective fact that you are not Aristotle but Nat. My subjective thoughts about reality can change me, but they can't change reality itself.

NAT: That seems awfully obvious. Why do so many people deny it?

SOCRATES: They are not here now to argue with us, so I don't know what arguments they would give. Let's confine ourselves to the two people who are here, all right?

NAT: All right.

SOCRATES: I said that truth is easy to define but hard to find. Are you willing to try to do some of that hard thing with me?

NAT: Yes. But I have a question I want to ask you first. It's not at all an abstract logical question, or a question of epistemology. I can't help being curious about *you*. Didn't you die over two thousand years ago? How come you're sitting on this log with me? Where are we? Are we in Heaven?

SOCRATES: If Heaven means everything delightful, then yes, this is a little bit of Heaven, at least for me, if you will consent to be my partner in the enterprise of searching for truth. I suspect it may seem like something more like Purgatory for you, if I do my job well. For this search may be a harder and longer journey than you expect. None of the questions we will discuss, if you consent to do it, will be as clear or certain or easy or quick as the one we agreed on, about truth and the law of non-contradiction. And often my job will be to block your way to easy answers and open ways to harder ones.

NAT: That's your "job"? Do you teach philosophy for some university? Who pays your salary?

SOCRATES: I am not an intellectual prostitute. I do not sell my mind for money. No university is my pimp. My only university is this log. And my student body is only one student at a time.

NAT: So why do you do this?

SOCRATES: I do it for love, not money. Philosophy is a form of love, you know. The word means literally "the love of wisdom".

NAT: Well, I think I know what love is, but what is wisdom?

SOCRATES: Perhaps some other day we will explore whether you really do know what love is or not. But today, since you asked about wisdom, let's talk about wisdom. That is, if you really want to know.

NAT: I do.

SOCRATES: Good. So you are not just patronizing me to be polite?

NAT: No. But I am still curious: How did we get here? And where is "here"?

SOCRATES: We're characters in a book. We're inventions of some second-rate philosopher named Kreeft, and so is this log, which is our university.

NAT: So we're not real?

SOCRATES: No, we are fictional.

NAT: Then how come we're asking each other questions?

SOCRATES: Because our inventor made us do it.

NAT: But I feel quite real.

SOCRATES: That's because he is a fairly good inventor. And because I have to qualify that word "real". In a sense you are real even though you are fictional because you are very much like many real people who are doing what you are doing: beginning to investigate philosophy. You're Everybody. There are millions of you in the world. Your author called you "Nat Whilk" because that's Old English for "I know not who".

NAT: But there's only one Socrates, right? You are unique.

SOCRATES: In my day, I was. But my "thing" caught on—or was caught and spread, like a virus. And if you hang around me long enough, you might catch that infection. That's my "thing", my job: not to give you answers but to clone myself, or to replicate myself like a virus, to spread the good infection of philosophizing.

NAT: And what is this "good infection" of philosophizing that you spread?

SOCRATES: Oh, there are many parts to the answer to that question. But I think the first and most important part is that philosophizing means loving wisdom and searching for it, which implies not claiming to possess it yet. That's why I see my task as a philosopher as not to give you answers to all your questions, even if I had them, which I don't, but to teach you, by example, the habit of asking them yourself, to inveigle you to do the thing I do, in the demandingly logical way I do it, which they have called the "Socratic method". Are you with me on that enterprise? Does that turn you on or does that turn you off?

NAT: To be completely honest, I think it's a bit of both. I feel both curiosity and hesitation. So it's not an either-or but a both-and.

SOCRATES: Thank you for being completely honest. That's one of the requirements of my method.

NAT: But isn't my double feeling a contradiction, both a yes and a no? I thought we agreed there are no real contradictions.

SOCRATES: Not in the world, but there are in the mind, and even more in the emotions.

NAT: So my "both-and" answer to your "either-or" question was not illogical?

SOCRATES: Not necessarily. Many questions do not admit of an either-or answer, but of a both-and. For instance, life is both pleasure and pain, and we seem to be both good and evil, and both fated and free, and both material body and immaterial mind. And we can both love and hate the same person at the same time. In fact, we often do that to ourselves. These are all paradoxes, or apparent contradictions. But they are not real contradictions. I can love and hate at the same time, but I cannot both love and not love at the same time unless I equivocate between two meanings of the word "love".

Practical questions like "Shall I practice this Socratic philosophizing now?" often force us into an either-or choice even when we feel the both-and of two opposite emotions about it, as you say you do now. And the practical question that is your either-or now is this: Will you stay on this log with me and converse for a while?

NAT: I will. I might even find some of that good stuff, that wisdom, whatever it is.

SOCRATES: Thank you! We are agreed, then, that we are going on a hunt together to find a quarry that is more elusive and more valuable than a lion or an elephant: its name is wisdom.

NAT: Where should we start?

SOCRATES: Well, when you want to start a search to find something, what is the first thing you must do?

NAT: I dunno. Tell me.

SOCRATES: No, I will not do your work for you. *You* tell *me*.

NAT: Won't you help me?

SOCRATES: Certainly. But not by telling you answers.

NAT: How, then?

SOCRATES: By asking you more questions. For instance, concerning this question of searching for something, let's use an analogy, a situation that looks similar. Suppose I was searching for something I lost, something I once had, like my watch, and I went to the Lost and Found Department, and I said, "Do you have any lost watches here?" And they might say, "Yes, we have quite a few. Here they are." And I would examine them, and if mine was there, I would recognize it. I would pick it out and say, "Aha! There it is." Isn't that how it would work?

NAT: Yes, of course.

SOCRATES: But just *how* would that work? Don't you think I'd have to go to the Lost and Found not with my watch on my wrist but with an idea of what my watch looked like in my mind? The idea has to be there already in my mind, for if I didn't have it, if I didn't remember what my watch looked like, how could I recognize it when I saw it?

NAT: You couldn't.

SOCRATES: So that "Aha!" experience of finding is really a kind of remembering: not just knowing but knowing again, not just cognizing but re-cognizing. I use the remembered appearance of my watch as the standard for judging which of the watches I see in front of me matches mine. Isn't that how it would work?

NAT: Yes.

SOCRATES: Now let's take a different example of searching for something. Let's say you are looking for a mate to marry, and you date many people, and none of them seems right for you, and then suddenly one of them stands out above all the others, and you suspect you have met your "soul mate". You would think, "That person comes up to my standard and resembles my idea of the kind of person I'm looking for", wouldn't you?

NAT: Yes.

SOCRATES: But this time there is no memory image in your mind because you never met such a person before and then lost this person, as you lost your watch. Yet you came to the dating scene with some idea in your mind of what kind of person you were looking for, right? For instance, both strong and gentle, and both tough and tender, or maybe both rich and generous, or good-looking and sexy, if you were thinking on a more materialistic level. Isn't that so?

NAT: Yes.

SOCRATES: But here, too, you have a kind of "Aha!" experience when you find that person, and you have it for the same reason you had the "Aha!" experience when you found your lost watch: the thing outside your mind matched the idea you had in your mind.

NAT: True. But there is a difference. Your idea of the watch, which you remembered having in the past, was very clear, while the idea of the ideal mate, which you did not remember ever having, was not clear.

SOCRATES: Yes, that is a great difference. But in both cases you use the idea in your mind to judge or to identify the physical object outside your mind, don't you?

NAT: Yes.

SOCRATES: Now let's take a third case of searching for something: our present search for wisdom. I think this is like the two previous examples in that we began by having in our mind an idea of what we were searching for (in the first case it was a clear idea, and in the second case it was a less clear one) and then we found the real thing that matched the idea, and that's why we had the "Aha!" experience of recognition. That "Aha!" experience might also occur in the search for a wise philosophy among philosophies, like the search for a watch among other lost watches or the search for a mate among other potential mates. For instance, you might be searching for the piece of wisdom that defines the nature of justice, and you read Machiavelli and Hobbes and Rousseau and Mussolini and Marx and you say "No, that's not it" to all of them, and then you read Plato or Aristotle or Jefferson or de Tocqueville and you say "Yes, that's it; that's what I was looking for." You have the "Aha!" experience.

NAT: I understand all three examples, I think. But how is the third one different?

SOCRATES: Because when we search for a philosophy that has wisdom, we first have to know what wisdom is, what its properties are, what it looks like to the mind, don't we?

NAT: Yes.

SOCRATES: But if we already know what wisdom is, there is no need to *search* for that knowledge. And if we do *not* know what it is, how will we recognize it if and when we find it? Let's suppose we think we found the wisdom we were looking for in Plato. (Of course we may be wrong; this is not infallibility we are dealing with.) When we do that, we are measuring and judging Plato by our idea of wisdom, which we had *before* we discovered Plato. So how can we *newly* discover that idea that we already had?

This problem shows up especially when we are looking for a definition, when we are asking the question, What is it? What is its essential nature? For if we do not know that "what", that nature, already, we cannot recognize it if we find it; and if we do know it already, we need not search for it as if it were lost.

NAT: I am confused.

SOCRATES: Then let's take it one question at a time. How do we judge whether we have found what we are looking for?

NAT: By whether it matches our idea of it.

SOCRATES: Yes. And now suppose what we are looking for is not a watch or a mate but an idea. How do we judge whether we have found the idea we are looking for?

NAT: By another idea, I suppose.

SOCRATES: And did we have that "other idea" in our mind already?

NAT: We must have had it, if we used it to judge.

SOCRATES: How did we get that other idea?

NAT: It must be in the same way we got the first idea we mentioned. It must have matched some previous idea that we used as our standard.

SOCRATES: And how did we get *that* idea?

NAT: We must have had it already.

SOCRATES: But if we already have the idea, why are we looking for it?

NAT: I don't know. So how would you solve that problem, Socrates?

SOCRATES: I won't tell you how *I* tried to solve it (although if you really want to know, you can read Plato's dialogue called the *Meno*); but right now, we're looking for *your* solution.

NAT: I don't know how I can possibly solve that problem. I guess I can't.

SOCRATES: Don't be satisfied with a guess. Think about it.

NAT: Thanks for the good advice.

SOCRATES: Then please take the advice. Think about it. Now. For a minute or two or three.

NAT: OK. (*Long silence.*) Hmm, I suppose we can have an idea of an idea before we have the idea. For instance, a definition. We can define ideas as well as things. So I guess what we need is a definition of wisdom so that we can recognize it when we find some of it, because it matches our definition.

SOCRATES: Good thinking, Nat. So what do you mean by a definition?

NAT: You want a definition of a definition?

SOCRATES: Why not? You just said you could have an idea of an idea.

NAT: OK, let's see. A definition is ... a definition defines a thing.

SOCRATES: But that just repeats the noun with the verb. What does "define" mean? How do you define?

NAT: I'm not sure how to define "define". We could look it up in a dictionary.

SOCRATES: If there were no dictionaries, could we still define it?

NAT: I guess so.

SOCRATES: Why?

NAT: Because we did it even before we had dictionaries. And also because we had to *have* a definition before we put it into the dictionary.

SOCRATES: Good reasoning!

NAT: But how do we do it?

SOCRATES: Look at your experience. How do we actually do it? How do we define things?

NAT: Well, when we did not yet have dictionaries, we just had the real world and our minds, so we checked the ideas in our minds by the real world. But that doesn't tell us how to check an idea by an idea.

SOCRATES: So let's look at how we do that, how we define an idea that is not a physical thing by another idea.

NAT: What field deals with nonphysical things?

SOCRATES: Well, we could look at theology, the study of God, or angelology, the study of angels, or psychology, the study of the psyche—but they are all not only mysterious and complex but also controversial. Let's find a field that is simple and clear and relatively easy that is not about physical things but which is non-controversial, that everyone in the world agrees about.

NAT: You mean logic?

SOCRATES: I was thinking of mathematics. For instance, geometry.

NAT: Isn't geometry about physical things?

SOCRATES: Is a triangle a physical thing? Can you put one into my hand?

NAT: Sure. Just give me a pen and paper.

SOCRATES: That would not be a triangle but a picture of a triangle.

NAT: OK, so geometry is not about physical things, made of atoms. So what is geometry about? It's not about gods or spirits or souls or angels.

SOCRATES: It's about the geometrical properties of physical things, like triangularity. The nature of triangles.

NAT: OK.

SOCRATES: Now, can we define a triangle?

NAT: Sure: it's a three-sided enclosed plane figure. I remember that from geometry.

SOCRATES: Good. Now let's take another idea that is not a physical thing: the idea of democracy, or the nature of democracy, or the essence of democracy. It can be defined, can't it?

NAT: Yes.

SOCRATES: So what is democracy?

NAT: It's government of the people, by the people, and for the people.

SOCRATES: All right. Now what is the common structure of both of those definitions, the definition of a triangle and the definition of democracy?

NAT: I learned this once. It's made up of two parts, the genus and the difference. First, you put the thing you want to define in a more general class—"enclosed plane figures" for triangles and "governments" for democracy. Then you say how it's different from the rest of that class: three sides instead of four or five for a triangle, and the authority vested in the people instead of a king or an aristocracy for a democracy.

SOCRATES: Good. So now let's do that with wisdom. What is its genus?

NAT: Knowledge, I think. Wisdom is a kind of knowledge. It's deep knowledge, or knowledge of values, or knowledge by experience, or something like that.

SOCRATES: All right, let's look at that genus, knowledge. That's what epistemology is: knowing what knowledge is, thinking about thinking. Then let's look at the difference that turns knowledge into wisdom. You mentioned three possible candidates.

NAT: But I have a question before we begin. Before we search for *what* it is, shouldn't we be sure *that* it is? Do we really know anything at all? Or do we just *think* we do? Aren't there some philosophers who think we can't really know anything at all?

SOCRATES: Yes, they're called skeptics.

NAT: Shouldn't we refute the skeptics first? Before we go looking for the definition of the beast we are hunting, shouldn't we be sure there is such a beast?

SOCRATES: I would prefer to define the beast first, for we can define both real and mythical beasts, both horses and unicorns. But perhaps we should postpone the other question, the knowledge of what knowledge is, until the next time, because it's going to be much more difficult than you think. Let's focus on whether we have any knowledge at all. Let's move to the examination of skepticism and see whether we can refute it, all right?

NAT: All right.

SOCRATES: What is the object of knowledge? What do we seek when we want to know something?

NAT: Truth.

SOCRATES: So if we have no truth, we have no real knowledge.

NAT: Yes. And that's skepticism, right? And if skepticism is true, we'd have to just give up. So how would you refute skepticism?

SOCRATES: How would *you*?

NAT: Oh, come on, Socrates, compromise a little for me, please. Don't expect me to be a great philosopher like you and refute a whole school of philosophers who are probably a lot smarter than I am. You've thought about this much more than I have.

SOCRATES: But I will not allow you to be passive, and I will not allow myself to be preachy. We both have to be active and critical for this to work.

NAT: OK, then, let's make a deal: we'll both be active but we'll exchange places. I'll play Socrates to you for a little while, and I'll question you and evaluate your answers, OK? But you have to at least give me something to work on, something to evaluate, something to refute.

SOCRATES: That's fine, and fair. I accept your proposal of role reversal at least for a little while.

NAT: So please tell me just this one thing: How would you refute skepticism?

SOCRATES: I would refute skepticism by being skeptical of it! If you want to be skeptical of all isms, be skeptical of skepticism too. The skeptic is not skeptical *enough*.

NAT: But then, if we are skeptical of even skepticism, we're left with nothing.

SOCRATES: No, we're just left with skepticism of skepticism, not skepticism of all other ideas. For not all other ideas contradict themselves, but universal skepticism does. If I say I have no knowledge, I am saying that I have *that* knowledge. If I say I have no knowledge of truth, I'm saying that I know *that* truth.

NAT: Suppose we say only that I do have some knowledge or truth but that it is only subjective truth, not objective truth.

SOCRATES: By subjective truth do you mean personal opinion?

NAT: Yes.

SOCRATES: Then when you say that what others claim is knowledge is really only personal opinion, you're saying that your skepticism, your personal opinion that we have only personal opinions, is more than just your personal opinion: that it's the true one, and that my contrary idea that we can know also some objective truths is false. My opinion and yours contradict each other.

NAT: No, I'm not judging your opinion, just airing mine.

SOCRATES: Then you're not arguing or doing philosophy. You're just "airing". You're not saying I'm wrong.

NAT: Well, then, suppose I say only that we know no *universal* truths, no truths without exceptions.

SOCRATES: Your use of the word "no" means that you are making a universal claim there. So you're saying that you know the universal truth that you can't know any universal truths.

NAT: Suppose I say I know some objective and universal truths but only with probability, not certainty?

SOCRATES: Are you certain of that?

NAT: No. That would also clearly be self-contradictory.

SOCRATES: Then if it's not certain, it's only probable that all knowledge is only probable. And if that's only probable, then maybe some is certain. So you're not disagreeing with me when I say that some knowledge is certain. So we're not arguing. We're not contradicting each other. One of us is saying he does know something, and the other is saying he doesn't. If I say "I feel sick" and you say "I don't", we're not arguing, just confessing.

NAT: So what does this all prove?

SOCRATES: That all forms of universal skepticism seem to be self-contradictory.

NAT: OK, I guess we've refuted universal skepticism. But didn't Descartes say we should begin with universal doubt?

SOCRATES: He did.

NAT: But wasn't he one of the most brilliant philosophers?

SOCRATES: Probably. Do you think that means he couldn't make a mistake?

NAT: No, any of us can make a mistake. That's why it seems to make sense to begin with doubting everything. Do you see any problem with that? I strongly suspect you do.

SOCRATES: Yes, in fact. Here is my problem. If doubt is to be universal, if we are to doubt every truth claim, then we should doubt that one too: that we are doubting.

NAT: Well, then, let's do that.

SOCRATES: I wonder whether we *can* honestly doubt that we are doubting when we are doubting. Isn't that like thinking you may not be thinking at all at a time when you are thinking about *that*?

NAT: But don't you agree that if we want to be rational about anything, we have to prove it?

SOCRATES: Do *you* think that?

NAT: Yes.

SOCRATES: Why? Prove it. Prove *that*. Prove that there is no rationality without proof.

NAT: I don't know what you mean by "rationality".

SOCRATES: You're right to question that word. Different philosophers have very different definitions of it. Let's substitute something much clearer. Let's talk about certainty. Do you think we all know what certainty is?

NAT: Yes.

SOCRATES: So do you think there is no certainty without proof?

NAT: Let's say I do.

SOCRATES: Can you prove that?

NAT: I don't think so. But I don't think you can prove the opposite either. Can you?

SOCRATES: I think I can. I think I can find an example of a certainty without a proof. Are you certain you exist? I think you are. Can you prove it? I think not.

NAT: Of course I can prove it: "Cogito ergo sum"—"I think, therefore I am." Descartes' first certainty.

SOCRATES: Doesn't that argument beg the question?

NAT: What's that?

SOCRATES: It's the fallacy of assuming the thing you claim to prove.

NAT: And how does that famous argument of Descartes commit that fallacy?

SOCRATES: It smuggles the "I" that it's supposed to prove in the conclusion back into the premise.

NAT: Oh. I think I misunderstood you, Socrates. I thought you, like Descartes, were the great defender of questioning everything.

SOCRATES: Oh, I am. And therefore one of the things I question is whether we should question absolutely everything.

NAT: I see. Like being skeptical of skepticism.

SOCRATES: And I also need to distinguish questioning from doubting. Doubting is only one kind of questioning. We can accept the existence of the sun without doubt and then go on to ask many questions about it, when we do astronomy. I have no objection to *questioning* everything, but one of the things I question is Descartes' method of beginning by *doubting* everything.

NAT: Well, we can doubt everything we see with our senses, at least, can't we? For sometimes we see illusions, and when we're under an illusion, we don't know it is an illusion. So how can we be sure that we're not under an illusion now? How do we know the whole world is not an illusion that some mad scientist is pouring into our brain, which is really not even in a body but in a vat in a laboratory?

SOCRATES: Ah, yes, the "brain in a vat" question. You have picked up a little philosophy somewhere, it seems.

NAT: And when we use our reason instead of our senses, we also often make mistakes, even in simple things like adding numbers in a checkbook. And at the time we're making the mistake, we can't at the same time be free from the mistake. So we can be under an illusion when we reason as well as when we sense. And that applies to *anything* our reason tells us, just as the possibility of sensory illusion applies to everything the senses tell us.

SOCRATES: I do not deny that our reason can make mistakes—many of them, in fact, and quite easily.

NAT: And here's a third thing we can doubt: How do we know we're not dreaming right now? We can dream we are dreaming, and then dream that we wake up, so there can be a dream within a dream, so how do we know our dreams at night aren't dreams within a dream instead of just dreams? Perhaps when we die we will wake up and see that our whole life was only a dream.

SOCRATES: Still another level of doubt, and even more universal.

NAT: And finally, how do we know that we're not being hypnotized right now by a vastly superior intellect, an evil spirit that wants to deceive us at every second and who succeeds at every second, so that every single idea we have ever thought is untrue, is just a lie forced into our mind by this powerful and intelligent and malevolent deceiver?

SOCRATES: I see you have read Descartes. Those were the four kinds of doubt he recommended we begin with, in his *Meditations*.

NAT: And isn't there also a fifth kind of doubt? Aren't there some Hindu and Buddhist mystics who say that the whole universe and the self are not really real at all? That there is really only one thing, and it's infinite and indefinable? That would be sort of the opposite of the fourth kind of doubt, that "all my thoughts are really the Devil's thoughts", because it's like thinking that all my thoughts are only God's thoughts. In Eastern religions, God didn't create a material universe out of nothing, so if there is a God, that's the only thing there is. There's a quotation in the Hindu Upanishads that says something like this: "The idea of 'one' is the only truth; the idea of 'two' is the beginning of all error."

SOCRATES: Parmenides had a philosophy similar to that: that only one Being was real, Being Itself, and that plurality and change were illusions. He even had logical arguments to support that.

NAT: So how would you escape from those five kinds of doubt?

SOCRATES: Well, I suppose we could examine each of the five separately, in its own terms. But we could also judge all five at once: by doubting whether the right way to begin is with any such form of universal doubt, as distinct from merely doubting some particular opinion. I think we ought to demand a good reason for such universal doubt, rather than assuming it, don't you?

NAT: Yes, I suppose so, if I want to be logically consistent.

SOCRATES: You sound reluctant and disappointed.

NAT: I'm surprised that you're not as skeptical as Descartes and some other philosophers.

SOCRATES: I think they are not really as skeptical as they claim to be. You see, they simply *assume* that we should begin with universal doubt and not with any beliefs or assumptions. I think that is a belief and an assumption. So I think my way, of simply questioning each opinion and trying to judge whether it is true or not, is actually doubting more, not less. It's more totally open-minded.

NAT: I think I still prefer to begin with doubt, like Descartes.

SOCRATES: Why? What reason do you have for beginning with doubt?

NAT: What else could we begin with, if we don't begin with doubt?

SOCRATES: There are a number of possible answers to that question, and we should try to explore some of them later. But your asking *your* question—"What else could we begin with?"—is not an answer to *my* question—"Why begin with doubt?" Please answer my question. Why do you think we should begin with doubt?

NAT: OK, here's my reason: because that's how science works. That's the secret of the success of modern science: the modern scientific method, which begins with universal doubt. Premodern, prescientific people were not stupid, of course, but their science never reached certainty because it always assumed something: that previous science was right, or that Aristotle was right, or that common sense was right, or that religion was right.

SOCRATES: I understand your reason. And I think you are right about science. But you are now assuming something else that I think is very questionable: that philosophy is a science, in the modern sense, or at least that it ought to use the scientific method in the same way as the other sciences. Isn't that a questionable assumption? Many philosophers question it. In fact, most.

NAT: Well, here's another reason: If you start by assuming nothing, and accept nothing except what you prove, you have a firm foundation. You are making higher demands. You are setting the bar high. You demand certainty, not just probability. If you begin in such doubt, you may end in certainty, but if you begin by claiming certainty, you will end in doubt, once you question your certainties and realize that there are no proofs for them or that the proofs for them are highly questionable.

SOCRATES: But there's another unproved assumption there: that we should demand certainty, not just probability or reasonability or something less than certainty. Not all of our knowledge is certain, is it?

NAT: No.

SOCRATES: In fact, there are five possibilities here, five different things that are frequently confused: reality, knowledge, certainty, proof, and science. Not everything real is known—for example, the number of stones on the moon. And not all knowledge is certain—for example, my awareness that Ireland, which I have never seen, is green. And not all certainties are proved—for example, that I exist, or that I am alive. And not all proof is scientific proof—for example, most philosophical arguments, even good ones. Knowledge has many levels. Isn't that right?

NAT: That's true. So what? What follows from that?

SOCRATES: So if there is knowledge that is not certain, why not begin with that, with something less than certainty, and then try to get as close to certainty as we can, and accept that we have made some progress even if we have not gotten to indubitable certainty, at least not yet and not for everything we want to know? That's how most of our knowledge works in life. Why shouldn't philosophy imitate life?

NAT: So you don't think we should begin with Descartes?

SOCRATES: I don't think philosophy begins in doubt; I think philosophy begins in wonder. But doubt and Descartes are not identical. If you want to begin with Descartes, I have no problem with that. In fact, that's what we've been doing here today. And there's a good reason for doing that: Descartes is the hinge, the turning point, in philosophy, the father of modern philosophy and the one who demanded we do philosophy as we do science, at least in this first step: universal methodic doubt. So I think the question we are exploring now is a good one and not a waste of time. In fact, I think it may be the best point to begin with if we are to begin to philosophize today, as distinct from premodern times like mine.

NAT: So do you agree with Descartes that we should begin by looking at our instruments before we use them to build our philosophy? That we should begin with a critique of reason itself?

SOCRATES: No, I think not.

NAT: Why not?

SOCRATES: Because I don't see with what we could possibly critique reason. Is there something superior to reason?

NAT: I don't know. Maybe so, something like mystical experience or faith in a divine revelation.

SOCRATES: But even if that existed, it could convince only the individual that had it, not everyone else. We have to appeal to reason because that's universal, in everyone. So we'd have to give reasons for accepting this mystical experience or faith in divine revelation, if we are doing philosophy.

NAT: OK, so we can't validate reason by anything like that.

SOCRATES: And could something *inferior* to reason have the authority to critique reason? Something like animal instinct or feelings or desires?

NAT: No, they all have to be evaluated by reason.

SOCRATES: That seems reasonable. And here is the only other alternative: reason validates itself.

NAT: And that's what Descartes wanted to do.

SOCRATES: But how could reason validate itself? How could one particular act of reason—the act by which reason itself is critiqued and validated—how could that have the authority to critique and validate all of reason, universally? Think of all our acts of reason as prisoners on trial. How could one of the prisoners on trial have the authority to climb out of the dock, jump up onto the judge's bench, and be the judge of himself and all the other prisoners?

NAT: I guess it has to be no to that alternative too.

SOCRATES: And are there any other options than what is superior to reason, what is inferior to it, and reason itself?

NAT: No.

SOCRATES: So a critique of reason seems impossible.

NAT: But what alternatives to universal doubt and the critique of reason itself do we have for our beginning? The question is important to me because I remember, from geometry, Archimedes' discovery of the power of the simplest of all tools, the lever. He said, "Give me a lever long enough and a fulcrum point to rest it on, and I can move the whole world." I think that that "Archimedean point" must be crucial because it will guide our whole subsequent quest. If I walk westward from New York to the Pacific Ocean in a straight line, if I choose to turn that line just a little bit to the left or to the right at the beginning of my journey, that would make the difference between ending up in San Diego or in Seattle.

SOCRATES: An apt analogy. It shows the importance of the first step in any journey, mental or physical. We Greeks had a saying: "Well begun is half done."

NAT: So what are our options? Where might we begin our quest for wisdom, our philosophy?

SOCRATES: There are numerous options. For one thing, we could begin with direct sense experience, which we do not in fact doubt until we do this kind of philosophy, and which we can only *pretend* to doubt universally in real life. It assumes a trust in the senses, which we correct only by further sensations, as when we realize that the stick that appears bent in the water is really straight when we correct sight with touch, or when we correct sight with measurement so as to discover that the sun and the moon are not the same size, as they appear in the sky, when we measure their different distances from us. We can live out that empirical beginning, and it works well; but we cannot live and work with universal doubt, as the universal skepticism calls us to do. We can use it only as an initial thought experiment to refute skepticism, as Descartes tried to do.

Or we could begin with the laws of logic, especially the law of non-contradiction, which it's literally impossible to doubt. We did, in fact, assume and use that beginning a few minutes ago in our refutation of skepticism. We can know that any idea that contradicts them must be false, and that will guide our journey. In fact, it seems necessary. But it is not sufficient because we cannot deduce any positive content from that logical law alone. "A horse is not not-a-horse" does not tell us what a horse is. Descartes began not with our sensory experience of real things like horses but with only universal doubt and the law of non-contradiction, and I suspect that may be the mistake of putting Descartes before the horse.

Or we could begin not with sensation or with reason but with our will, our love, our desires, and our demands. And if that seems irrational, how about the will or love or desire or demand for truth? Is that not also necessary though insufficient, like both sense experience and the laws of logic?

Or we could begin with the experience of interpersonal dialogue, which is what we are doing now. That seems to refute
skepticism well and answer questions like, How do you know you
are not really a brain in a vat, or, How do you know the Devil is
not hypnotizing you in all your ideas? How could the two of us be
inventing each other?

Or we could begin with asking the question, What difference
to our life and our experience would the answer to this question make? That's the question the pragmatist begins with. That
alone does not tell us truth, but it is at least a criterion and test of
the meaning and even the meaningfulness of a question, and also
seems necessary, for practical purposes, though not sufficient.

Or perhaps we could claim that we all do, in fact, begin with
the most primitive experience that we have as soon as we are born:
that there is something there, that something exists, whatever it
is. That would seem to be the beginning that is the most realistic
because we all do pass through it. Though it, too, is obviously not
sufficient.

NAT: Wow. That's a lot of possibilities. Too many of them to argue
about every one of them today. Which one do you think is the
best alternative to universal doubt?

SOCRATES: My lived answer, as distinct from my theoretical answer,
is the one I did begin with in fact, in practice, in conversing with
you. That was interpersonal dialogue, which we are doing now.
But I did not do that in order to refute Descartes' doubt, because
I did not begin with his universal doubt.

Perhaps there is no good answer to that question of how to
begin that is the same for everybody. Perhaps different people
should have different beginnings because we have different ends
and goals and interests, and also different powers and abilities. For
instance, Descartes demanded not only truth but certainty; I did
not. My conclusions are open to more doubts and questions. Perhaps it is only in math that we get the kind of certainty that is both
unquestionable and total and that therefore convinces everyone
in the world. So perhaps there is no one answer to this practical
question of how we should begin that is best for everyone.

NAT: Aren't all those other beginnings uncritical?

SOCRATES: I don't think so. Beginning with these other things does
not mean we are forbidden to question them. The question is not

whether we should question everything that we possibly can—I think we agree that we should—but merely where it's most helpful to begin. And that means "Helpful to what? Helpful for what end?"

NAT: But wherever we begin, aren't there rules we all need to follow?

SOCRATES: Of course. And some of them are rules of logic, and some are rules of conduct, practical rules like listening and honesty and not substituting personal insult or rhetoric or feeling for logical argument.

NAT: Perhaps we should review them first.

SOCRATES: I think that is an excellent suggestion. Perhaps, then, we should take some time with two of the introductions in the first part of this book that we are in, then: the one about the basic structure of logic and the one about the basic strategy of what has come to be called the Socratic method in dialogue.

NAT: I shall read them, and then come back and try to apply them to our dialogue. Will you still be here at the other end of this log?

SOCRATES: I will be here until and unless our common creator removes me from this log. Which I think he does not want to do.

NAT: See you in the next chapter then. Although I have to admit I am a little disappointed that we did not arrive at a clear and certain and adequate answer to our quest for wisdom, except for our refutation of that universal skepticism which would have doomed that quest from the outset.

SOCRATES: I, too, am disappointed, though not in you. But we have only just begun. We must be patient. And disappointment is a good motivator to keep going, don't you think?

NAT: I can't deny that. In fact, I can't deny most of what you say, Socrates.

SOCRATES: But I have really said very little, and of that little, most of it is interrogative. And you can't either affirm or deny a question, because it's not a truth claim.

NAT: But don't you think that our very first concern should be to find the truth?

SOCRATES: No, I do not think that.

NAT: What could be first even above that?

SOCRATES: How about looking for it first?

Questions for Discussion or Personal Essays

There are too many questions here to do justice to more than a few, but I offered this "too many" in order to give you more choice to focus on the ones you found interesting and not *totally* confusing.

1. Which of the logical techniques of the Socratic method (see the third introduction) did you find in the dialogue?
2. Which of the psychological techniques of the method did you find? Were any disobeyed?
3. How many analogies did you find? (Hint: the first one is at the very beginning.)
4. Why do analogies work so effectively?
5. Why do you think many people today are suspicious of analogies or find it hard to invent them or to understand them? Do you think it has any connection with the fact that digital computers cannot understand analogies? If, as Socrates says, computers cannot understand anything, how is it meaningful to say that they cannot understand analogies but only literal meanings and zero-sum mathematics?
6. Do you have any other definitions of truth than the one Socrates quotes from Aristotle? Compare yours to his.
7. Do you agree with Socrates about the unthinkability and meaninglessness of real contradictions? Why or why not? Do you think the law of non-contradiction is a descriptive law of everything real or only a prescriptive law for our proper use of logic? Give reasons for your answer. Can you come up with any real exceptions to the law of non-contradiction? Why are there apparent exceptions, paradoxes?
8. Why does Socrates call college professors intellectual prostitutes? Is he serious or joking?
9. Would you swap your present university for the log that is "Socrates University"? Why or why not?
10. What kind of "love" does Socrates think philosophy is? What are some other kinds? (The question is not about various *objects* of love but about various *kinds* of love.)
11. Evaluate Socrates' epistemology of the "Aha!" experience from your own experience.

12. If you want a longer assignment, read and critique Plato's explanation of learning in his *Meno*.

13. Do you think we have (a) innate wisdom? (b) innate information? (c) an innate, intuitive "truth detector"? (d) an innate knowledge of the laws of logic? (e) innate categories? Give examples for all your yes answers.

14. How would you explain how we can find and learn and identify not a *thing* but an *idea* like "justice" or "wisdom"?

15. How would you answer Socrates' dilemma that if we knew it before, then we did not *find* it or *learn* it, and if we did *not* know it before, we would not have been able to recognize it when we did find it. What other explanations are there than the one Socrates gave in the *Meno*?

16. A definition tells you "what" a thing is. What is a "what"? Does the question, What is it? assume that things have real natures or essences, as distinct from our inventing classes and imposing them on things to classify them and to invent groups of them for our many different personal and subjective purposes? If so, can we prove that assumption? If not, how can some answers to the "what is it?" question be objectively true or false if there are no objectively real "whats"?

17. Why is it so hard to obey the two simple logical rules for a definition, that it be not too broad and not too narrow? Give examples.

18. Do you think physical things are real? Why or why not? Do you think that nonphysical things are real? Why or why not? Do you think the mind is a real thing? If so, is it physical or nonphysical? Give reasons for your answers.

19. The dialogue did not define wisdom. How would you define it? Defend your definition.

20. The dialogue defined "truth" but not "knowledge". How would you do that? (Warning: it will probably be much more difficult than you think not to use the word "know" or a synonym for it in your definition. This is probably the most difficult question in this chapter.)

21. Imagine you are a skeptic. Can you answer Socrates' argument that skepticism is self-contradictory?

22. In what ways is Socrates skeptical and in what ways is he not?

23. How would you answer all five different kinds or levels of doubt that Nat proposes? How do you know you are not just a brain in a vat? How do you know you are not dreaming or being hypnotized?

24. Can you doubt you are doubting? If so, how? If not, why not?

25. Could one of the most brilliant philosophers in history (Descartes) have committed a basic logical fallacy in his most famous argument ("I think, therefore I am"), as Socrates claims? How would Descartes respond to Socrates?

26. Why do you think Parmenides and the Upanishads are wrong? Do you *know* they are wrong? If so, how? If you don't think they are wrong, why do you think they are right?

27. Do you think Descartes' method of universal doubt is useful in science? In common sense? In philosophy? In religion? Why?

28. Religion appeals to the infallible mind of God, "divine revelation". Science demands logical, mathematical, or empirical proof of everything. Which do you think is more certain? Why do many people think the opposite?

29. Do you think Nat, quoting Descartes, is right to say that if we begin in doubt we may end in certainty, while if we begin with certainty we will probably end in doubt? Why or why not?

30. In what sense is philosophy scientific? Hint: How is a scientific theory tested?

31. Which of the three gaps between the four following things do you think is the greatest and why? (a) ignorance, (b) knowing without having a reason, (c) knowing with a merely probable reason, and (d) knowing with a certain reason.

32. How useful did you find Descartes? How useful did you find Socrates? Why?

33. Evaluate Socrates' argument that a critique of reason is impossible. What consequences for philosophy and philosophizing flow from agreeing or disagreeing with that critique? If Socrates is right, why was this whole dialogue on "critical epistemology" not a waste of time?

2

Substantive Epistemology:
Rationalism versus Empiricism

NAT: Socrates, I wonder whether we did the right thing in beginning our conversation about philosophy and philosophizing with epistemology. It seems to be the trickiest division of philosophy because it tries to think about thinking or to know what knowing is. It twists itself into a pretzel.

But I have some hope that our conversations will become a little easier from now, even within epistemology. Because you said there were two basic questions in epistemology, not just one, and I think we're ready for the easier one now. We discussed the first one, whether we really have knowledge of truth at all, and how to avoid universal skepticism, and whether we should begin with methodological skepticism as Descartes said. But we didn't get to the second question, What *is* human knowledge? How does it work? I suspect you want to discuss that one now, right?

SOCRATES: If you do, yes. But if not, no. If you don't have the curiosity, the will to know, then I don't want to try to pretend that you do.

NAT: I do, even though the questions of philosophy seem awfully abstract and tricky and impractical.

SOCRATES: Many of them are indeed abstract and tricky, but I do not agree that philosophy is impractical.

NAT: Why not?

SOCRATES: Well, what do you mean by "practical"?

NAT: I'd say an idea is practical if it makes a big difference to us, to what we do or what we know or think.

SOCRATES: And we do many different things, don't we?

NAT: Yes, of course.

SOCRATES: And we like to think about all those different things that we do, don't we?

NAT: Yes.

SOCRATES: And what is the common factor in all our thinking about all those different things?

NAT: I don't know.

SOCRATES: Oh, I think you do. Let's analyze the act of thinking to find out in which aspect of it we can find the common factor. Would you agree that thinking is an act?

NAT: A mental act, yes.

SOCRATES: And an act comes from an actor?

NAT: Yes.

SOCRATES: So we could call the actor—in this case, the thinker—the subject of the act?

NAT: Yes.

SOCRATES: And an act is directed to something or other, isn't it?

NAT: Yes.

SOCRATES: So we could call that the object of the act, couldn't we?

NAT: Yes.

SOCRATES: So we have analyzed thinking into three aspects: the subject, or actor, the act itself, and its object.

NAT: Yes.

SOCRATES: So which of those three aspects is the most diverse? In which of them does it seem we will not find much in common?

NAT: The objects.

SOCRATES: Why?

NAT: Because the same person can think about many things. About almost anything at all.

SOCRATES: And which of the three aspects is always the same?

NAT: The thinker. The self.

SOCRATES: And does that self change with every act of thinking, as its objects do? Are there as many thinkers as there are objects of thought?

NAT: No. There is only one. Whatever I think about, it is I who think it.

SOCRATES: Then that is the common factor.

NAT: Yes.

SOCRATES: Then "know thyself" would be the most practical thing we could do, would it not? Since whatever we are, whatever is the right answer to "know thyself", that right answer would make a difference to every act of knowing, since that self is the common factor in all our knowing. For instance, if the knowing self was an angel, it would know what an angel can know and only in the way an angel can know it. And if it was a fish or a worm or a horse, it would know in the way that knowing subject can know it.

NAT: Yes. That logically follows.

SOCRATES: So if I do not know myself, if I do not know the knower, the common factor in all my knowing, then I do not know who or what it is that *has* all my knowledge, that has in its mind all those objects, right?

NAT: Right.

SOCRATES: It would be like having millions of dollars in a bank but not knowing which bank it was, or what a bank was.

NAT: I see. So epistemology is indeed practical.

SOCRATES: Yes. And if a study is practical, we ought to practice it, right?

NAT: Right.

SOCRATES: Therefore, we ought to do epistemology, even though it is abstract and difficult.

NAT: Yes.

SOCRATES: But epistemology is about the act of knowing, and that's the act of human knowing, not angel or animal knowing, so "know thyself" presupposes anthropology, doesn't it? So we need to do anthropology before we do epistemology, then, don't we?

NAT: But that would take a much longer time.

SOCRATES: Yes, but I think we could also work the other way round, so to speak: from epistemology to anthropology. Instead of deducing our epistemology from our anthropology (which we could also do, of course), we could deduce our anthropology from our epistemology, from our observation of how we do in fact know. That way, we could defer anthropology to another time and concentrate on epistemology today.

NAT: All right, so let's do that. Let's think about our thinking, how it works. Where do we begin?

SOCRATES: Let's do it inductively: let's begin with the different ways of thinking that we observe ourselves doing, instead of first trying to define thinking in general, which would be much more difficult, I think.

NAT: All right.

SOCRATES: Let's see. Can we think by a kind of direct intellectual intuition or understanding? For instance, when I say "apple" or "triangle", you immediately and intuitively know what I mean, don't you?

NAT: Yes.

SOCRATES: And can we think also by calculating, by moving from premise to conclusion? For instance, I deduce that apples are probably good for you by calculating that apples are fruits and most fruits are good for you.

NAT: Yes.

SOCRATES: And can we think also by analysis, by mentally taking things apart, as we just did a minute ago when we distinguished the three different aspects of the act of thinking?

NAT: Yes.

SOCRATES: And can we also think by synthesis, by mentally putting them together in a single "big picture"?

NAT: Yes.

SOCRATES: And can we think by using our senses as well as our minds, as in physics or chemistry?

NAT: Yes.

SOCRATES: And can we think by using our minds alone and not our senses, as in mathematics?

NAT: Yes.

SOCRATES: So there are a number of different kinds of thinking, or aspects of thinking, or dimensions of thinking, then.

NAT: Yes.

SOCRATES: But that is a much smaller number than the number of things we can think about.

NAT: Yes.

SOCRATES: So this would be a good question to begin with, since it is fairly specific and we can appeal to our experience. It's also a good question because one aspect of that question, namely, the relation between the sensory or empirical component in our knowing and the intellectual or rational component, was the main question of early modern philosophy, from Descartes onward for the next two centuries. It was the dispute between the rationalists and the empiricists, and between both and the solution offered by Kant and the idealists.

NAT: OK, you've given me two reasons for taking the time to think about this question now: the practical one and the historical one. So let's go. How do we begin?

SOCRATES: I think you know the answer to that question. Do you?

NAT: Well, I've already done the first and most necessary thing, I think. You famously said that "philosophy begins in wonder", so I'm now wondering about it. I want to know. The will to know, the will to truth—isn't that the first thing, for you?

SOCRATES: It is indeed. And I see that it is the first thing for you too. So what do you think comes next?

NAT: Well, I suppose we should do what you always did, demand to define our terms.

SOCRATES: Fine, but why? You can't be satisfied with just my example: do it because that's what Socrates did. *Why* did I do it?

NAT: Because if we don't know the "what", if we don't know what we're talking about, then we are not talking rationally.

SOCRATES: So "talking rationally" means something more than just talking consistently, following the rules of argument, arguing logically?

NAT: Yes. It means being clear, understanding our terms.

SOCRATES: And we do that by defining them.

NAT: Yes.

SOCRATES: So let's define rationalism and empiricism.

NAT: You know more about philosophy than I do, so could you define them, please?

SOCRATES: All right, I will depart from my usual method and do that preliminary work for you, since we are talking about historical facts that I know better than you do—how those who engaged in this great dispute defined their terms—but I will do this only so that you can do the rest of the work yourself, as my method demands.

NAT: Fair enough.

SOCRATES: Well, rationalism is the epistemology that claims that reason or intellect is prior to sensation both in time and in authority, and empiricism claims the opposite: that sensation is prior to reason both in time and in authority. Kantian idealism tries to combine these two, in a way that is not easy to state in one sentence.

NAT: I understand the first difference between rationalism and empiricism—do we in fact begin with abstract universal ideas, the objects of the intellect, or do we begin with the concrete particulars of sense experience? But what do you mean by the second difference—which of the two is prior in authority?

SOCRATES: Rationalism claims that reason has the authority—the right, not just the power—to judge sense experience since reason gives us certainty while mere sense experience does not. Empiricism claims that sense data have the authority to judge reason and its theories because the theory must be judged by the data, by how well it explains the data of experience, and not vice versa.

NAT: That's pretty clear. There seems to be a good argument for both sides.

SOCRATES: Rationalism claims that since sense experience does not give you certainty, but reason does, we should begin by doubting sense experience and relying on reason as a surer foundation. Empiricism, on the other hand, says that since abstract theories or principles should be judged by the data of sense experience, we both should and do, in fact, begin with sense experience. So the two questions, regarding time and regarding authority, are related to each other so that rationalists almost always say reason is prior in both time and authority, while empiricists almost always say that sense experience is prior in both.

NAT: Thank you for being un-Socratic, Socrates. Do you think we should continue this role reversal, with me asking you questions instead of vice versa?

SOCRATES: What I think is this: that we should be agreed about whatever answer we both give to that procedural question so that we are playing by the same rules. So what is your preference?

NAT: I would like to continue the role reversal that has me asking the questions and you answering them for a little while more, if you consent.

SOCRATES: All right. But I suspect that you may find, to your surprise, that asking the right questions may be more elusive than finding the right answers.

NAT: I don't understand that.

SOCRATES: I think you will, eventually, but only after you have more experience in philosophy.

NAT: Let's begin with history. You were sort of the Descartes of your day, weren't you? So you were a rationalist rather than an empiricist, right?

SOCRATES: What I was in Athens has little to do with what I am doing now. I am not trying to lead you into any particular philosophy, including mine. I will try to lead you into understanding and critiquing both of these philosophies, not just one of them. As to what I think now, I thought we established how different I was from Descartes in our last conversation, at least in method.

NAT: So will you first argue me into rationalism and then into empiricism?

SOCRATES: Yes and no. Yes, in the sense that I hope that at the end you will understand both by following reason's chain of argument. But no in the sense that I will not try to prove by argument that one is true and the other false.

NAT: So you will be both the defense attorney and the prosecuting attorney for both clients.

SOCRATES: I think that is a good analogy. So I think we should begin with the simpler question, the question of fact: Do we have nonsensory knowledge before we have sensory knowledge, or not? The technical term for nonsensory and presensory knowledge is "a priori knowledge", knowledge that is prior to sense experience. Another name for essentially the same thing is "innate ideas". The rationalist says we do have that, and the empiricist says we do not.

NAT: So what are some reasons for believing we do have a priori knowledge, as the rationalist says?

SOCRATES: Well, let's begin with a fact. Man and the other animals both have sensory knowledge, is that not true?

NAT: Yes.

SOCRATES: But no other animal writes philosophy books, or calculates the distance to the moon by trigonometry, or understands the principles of quantum physics or of Christian Trinitarian theology.

NAT: True.

SOCRATES: Why?

NAT: Perhaps the animals' reason is present but just more primitive than ours.

SOCRATES: Tell me, then, which animal understands the abstract general principle that 2 + 2 = 4, or criticizes an obviously invalid argument as violating the laws of logic, or invents languages?

NAT: None. But how do we know what goes on in the minds of animals?

SOCRATES: By their behavior.

NAT: What behavior?

SOCRATES: Primitive human tribes often dye their skin or their clothes with different colors, which they derive from different plants. Do animals do that?

NAT: No.

SOCRATES: Why?

NAT: I don't know.

SOCRATES: I think you do. Consult your own experience. Why can we do that? What mental power enables us to do that?

NAT: Imagination, I think.

SOCRATES: Yes. We can *imagine* things being different than they are in nature, and that's why we try to *make* them different.

NAT: So imagination is the origin of technology. I did not realize that.

SOCRATES: And what else do we have to do with our minds before we can imagine white skin becoming green when we dye it?

NAT: I don't understand what you are looking for.

SOCRATES: We cannot transfer the whole concrete thing, the green grass, to our skin to make it green, but we can transfer the color of it, the color green, to our skin to make it green, can't we? First in our imagination and then in the world?

NAT: Yes.

SOCRATES: So what are we doing, then, what do we have to do, before we can transfer greenness to our skin?

NAT: We have to take it from the grass.

SOCRATES: And how do we do that? Is it like stealing a ring from one person and putting it on our own hand?

NAT: No. The grass does not lose the greenness as the victim loses the ring.

SOCRATES: So what is our mind doing, then, between the time it sees the green grass and the time it imagines the green skin?

NAT: It is abstracting the greenness from the grass.

SOCRATES: Exactly! Animals cannot abstract the universal quality of greenness from the particular green thing, the concrete grass. That is why they cannot imagine transferring it to a white piece of cloth or white skin. And what they can't imagine, they can't do. They don't do it in the material world, as we do, because they can't do it in their minds, as we do. So ironically, that empirical fact seems to indicate that simple empiricism is not true; that we have a mental power that no animal has; that we are not just animals with bigger brains. Animals know the world only concretely; we can know it abstractly.

NAT: But that doesn't prove we have a priori knowledge. Because even when we do abstraction, we have to do sensation first. We have to see the green grass before we can abstract the greenness from the grass. And rationalism denies that temporal primacy of sensation, and empiricism affirms it, so our example counts for empiricism, not rationalism.

SOCRATES: Good argument, Nat! But this example can also seem to prove the opposite, the rationalist point, because we have to know the universal we want *before* we can abstract it from the sense experience. We have to seek a thing, and therefore know what we are seeking, before we can find it.

NAT: This is confusing! The priority seems to work both ways.

SOCRATES: Can you come up with an example where it does not seem to work both ways?

NAT: Let's see ... give me some time ...

SOCRATES: I admire your habit of taking time to think before you speak. I find it very rare.

NAT: Thanks. Other people think that makes me slow.

SOCRATES: They are wrong about you. But go ahead: keep on thinking of an example that has only one priority.

NAT: When I am surprised to see something I never saw before, and never thought of before, like some very strange animal, I did not begin with the idea but with the sensation. And there are many examples of that.

SOCRATES: What about examples of the other one-way priority, of a priori knowledge?

NAT: Well, we all know that everything must be what it is, and that nothing can be what it is not, at any one point in time, although it can change from what it was to what it was not.

SOCRATES: You have just pointed to two examples of a priori knowledge: the logical law of identity and the logical law of non-contradiction.

NAT: But is this really *knowledge*?

SOCRATES: Why not? It's true; in fact, it's always and everywhere true.

NAT: Yes, but is it what most people would call *knowledge*?

SOCRATES: Why not?

NAT: Because if you know something, that makes a definable difference. Something changes because of that knowledge. But nothing changes because of these two laws. You can never deduce anything else from them. They make no specific difference to anything else. They are not facts but laws. In fact, logicians call them tautologies.

SOCRATES: But they are not mere human conventions about words, because we can change our conventions, but we cannot change these two laws. They are objective truths about real beings, about all real beings.

NAT: Yes, but what difference do they make to real beings? What alternative do they eliminate? None. There is no thinkable alternative.

SOCRATES: What about the law of cause and effect? Isn't that a priori knowledge? We see things change, but we also know that if there is change, there must be a cause of it. And that makes a difference.

NAT: What difference?

SOCRATES: The difference is that nothing that appears ever just pops into existence for no cause or real reason at all. If it did, we would not be surprised to see a large elephant suddenly appear on our front lawn, and we would say, "Oh, yes, elephants just happen." We can *imagine* such a world. In fact, Ionesco did in his play *Rhinoceros*, and I think the scene with the thousands of frogs falling onto the car out of nowhere in the movie *Steel Magnolias* uses the same weird image. It does not happen in our world, but it is imaginable. So it makes an imaginable difference that that does not happen. And since that makes a difference to our thought, it's some kind of knowledge, although it's not knowledge of the fact that that actually happens in our world. But it is knowledge: knowledge that that does *not* really happen in our world. And since we know it *before* we ever experience elephants on our front lawns or anything else, it's a priori. So there is a priori knowledge.

NAT: It seems your argument is persuasive. But I am not persuaded.

SOCRATES: Well, here is another example of a priori knowledge, and this one is both positive and specific and even empirical. We can't be sure of many things in life, but we can be sure we can die.

All men are mortal. How do we know that? We could not be certain of that merely by sense observation, because we can never observe all men, especially men of the past and the future. So that knowledge must be a priori, before experience. And that knowledge is very specific, even empirical: an empirical prediction of our future.

NAT: But is it certain and universal? Is an immortal man unimaginable? Not at all. It's in some science fiction stories. In fact, aren't the so-called transhumanists working on the genetic engineering that would produce such a man?

SOCRATES: That's true.

NAT: So "All men are mortal" is not certain or universal. So it's not knowledge at all, only probability or prediction.

SOCRATES: So how do you think we know that all men are mortal?

NAT: I don't know. But if we had never seen human bodies, or if we had never seen them die, would we know that all men are mortal? I think not. I think a two-year-old does not know that. Therefore, that is not a priori knowledge.

SOCRATES: You are becoming a formidable philosopher, Nat! Well, what about the knowledge that we are obligated to do good and not evil? That seems to be a priori knowledge. We don't derive that from empirical observations. We use it to judge our observations of human behavior as good or evil, and on that basis we blame ourselves and others for doing evil.

NAT: Some say that when we do that, we are only confusing our negative subjective feelings with objective facts. As Hamlet says, "There is nothing either good or bad, but thinking [or feeling] makes it so."[1] In other words, ethical judgments are not knowledge at all, only feelings.

SOCRATES: That's essentially Hume's account of ethics. But I think that only someone who has never honestly listened to his conscience could say that. If Hamlet was right and "there is nothing either good or bad, but thinking makes it so", then we could change the whole world from bad to good just by thinking differently.

---

[1] William Shakespeare, *Hamlet*, ed. Joseph Pearce, Ignatius Critical Editions (San Francisco: Ignatius Press, 2008), act 2, scene 2, lines 248–50. All subsequent *Hamlet* quotations are from this edition.

NAT: Some say we can.

SOCRATES: Do you?

NAT: No. We can change deserts into farms or an atom into an atom bomb or maybe even water into wine, but we can't change evil into good—for instance, torturing children, or raping women, or a mass terrorist attack that kills many innocent people for no reason except to give vent to the terrorist's hate. If it were true that we made those things evil just by our thinking or our feeling, then we could make them good just by thinking or feeling the opposite way. But we can't.

SOCRATES: Yes. And you know that not from sensory experience but from moral experience, right?

NAT: Right. So that does seem to be a priori knowledge. We seem to "bump up against" the fact that such things are evil with our conscience just as we bump up against mathematical facts like "2 + 2 = 4" with our reason and just as we bump up against physical facts, like walls, with our bodies. It seems to be discovery, not invention—although I think Freud claims it's merely our subconscious internalization of society's desires about our behaviors. But it seems to be more than that because we can morally criticize society as well as individuals for things like slavery and racism. And when we experience that discovery of moral obligations in our conscience, not through our senses, it's a priori. And since it's a discovery of truth, truth about good and evil, it's knowledge. So that is a priori knowledge, whether or not the other examples are.

SOCRATES: You argue well, Nat. That's essentially Kant's argument. He saw ethics, or practical reason, as more certain than theoretical reason, which he thought could never know things in themselves, or objective reality as it existed outside of or independent of the mind.

But let's set aside the example of moral knowledge of good and evil for now in arguing about rationalism versus empiricism, because ethics is knowledge of what *ought to be* rather than knowledge of what *is*. Is there also any a priori knowledge of what is?

NAT: What do you think would be a good example?

SOCRATES: What about "all events have causes"?

NAT: Is that really a priori knowledge? If we did not first have sensory experience of events and changes, could we ever come to that knowledge?

SOCRATES: So what do you conclude from this discussion?

NAT: I conclude that I'm getting a bit bored with this whole question. It seems very airy. Does it really make a difference to anyone but a philosopher?

SOCRATES: Oh, I think it does. And I shall try to show you why.

NAT: Can you summarize it briefly instead of leading me to it gradually? I know you like your method better, but it takes such a long time. You want to motivate me to look carefully at this question, and I am reluctant to do that because it seems kind of unimportant to me right now, so please show me where your long roads lead to. What important difference does it make if I embrace rationalism? What difference does it make if I embrace empiricism? What difference does it make if I embrace Kant's third epistemology, idealism, whatever that is?

SOCRATES: I thank you for being honest with me, and I understand why the question itself seems "airy", as you put it. I will try to meet your demand. What difference does it make? A fair question, since I promised you I would do role reversal and answer rather than ask for a while.

Well, if rationalism is true, if we all have a priori knowledge, then we can be much more hopeful and optimistic about the ordinary person's ability to find certain truth because we already *have* it; it is just a question of getting it out, from the unconscious level to the conscious level, one might say. And that makes a difference because it is the stronger antidote to skepticism; and most people in your culture, I think, are much more tempted to skepticism, which underestimates our reason's powers, than to its opposite extreme, to overestimate it.

And if empiricism is true, it seems to lead to skepticism, unless it is modified and added to, since we can always doubt particular sensory impressions, but we can't doubt self-evident universal principles.

And if Kantian idealism is true, that means that all the apparently certain aspects of our knowledge do not make for a knowledge of objective reality, or "things in themselves", as Kant calls them, which he said were unknowable, but only a knowledge of the universal structures of the human mind. And that's even more skeptical than empiricism because empiricism at least admits that we have some probable knowledge of objective reality.

NAT: Thank you for being so short and sweet.

SOCRATES: I was also being radically inadequate. Please do not thank me for that.

NAT: Well, your compromise was at least adequate to motivate me to keep up this very abstract discussion. OK, let's continue. If rationalism, with its a priori knowledge, is questionable, let's try empiricism then. It seems more commonsensical. Doesn't everyone learn by experience? And don't most psychologists agree that that is where everyone always begins?

SOCRATES: You have given me two reasons for embracing empiricism: that it is "commonsensical", that everyone knows that we all do learn from experience, and that most psychologists agree with it. Let's examine those reasons, shall we?

NAT: Oh dear, here we go again into a long logical analysis by your Socratic method.

SOCRATES: No, I am in my compromise mode today, so I think we can do that pretty quickly. Your arguments are both versions of the same argument, the "argument from authority", either the authority of common sense, of "everybody", or of the "experts", of most psychologists.

Common sense is called that because it's "common" to the majority. But you know that you can't tell the truth by polls and numbers, that we are infallibly fallible, and that the majority can be wrong.

And the same is true of the second argument, from the consensus among psychologists. But psychologists are notoriously divided about many, many other things, and they can't all be right insofar as they contradict one another.

NAT: Is there a better argument for empiricism, then?

SOCRATES: Well, there is the argument used by Aristotle, Aquinas, and Locke against a priori knowledge: that the blind have no innate idea of colors, nor the deaf of sounds, and that only when we restore the sense do we restore the knowledge. But this does not prove that there is no a priori knowledge at all, only that there is no a priori knowledge of sensory things like colors and sounds.

NAT: So are there different versions of empiricism, then?

SOCRATES: Yes. Perhaps there are only innately known *laws*, like the basic laws of logic and ethics, but no innately known *content*. Aristotle is often called a "soft empiricist" because he says that, and also because he says that even though all our knowledge *begins* with sense experience, it's not *limited to* sense experience and does not *end* there. Aristotle said that we can also abstract universals by our intellect from our experience of particulars known by the senses. Hume is a "hard empiricist" because he says knowledge cannot transcend sense experience either in priority in time or in scope.

NAT: Aristotle sounds like a nice, moderate compromise. But how did he say we get from sense experience at the beginning to something more at the end, namely, abstract universals? That sounds like the effect being greater than the cause.

SOCRATES: He said that sensation was the *necessary* cause but not the *sufficient* cause of all our knowledge.

NAT: And that means that it had to be there but that there was also something more, right?

SOCRATES: Right.

NAT: And what was the "something more"?

SOCRATES: The power of the intellect and its act of abstracting.

NAT: What does that mean?

SOCRATES: Abstracting means distinguishing in our mind the universal, unvarying essential form or nature of a thing from its material embodiment in varied concrete particulars that we experience. For example, we know that all men are mortal. How do we know this? We cannot know "all men" by sense experience alone, so it is not by sense observation alone that we know this, but something more. After beginning with sense observation of others' deaths, we then may come to understand that death is necessary and essential to human nature, and we do this by abstracting that universal essence from its changing accidental examples that we see.

NAT: That sounds kind of vague. What did he say that "essence" was?

SOCRATES: The unity, in one single substance or entity, of an animal body and a rational soul. That essence is abstracted, or distinguished, from the accidental and changeable qualities like age, sex, gender, height, race, personality quirks, and so on.

NAT: And "hard empiricists" like Hume don't believe in abstraction, right?

SOCRATES: Right.

NAT: Why not?

SOCRATES: Because they don't believe in objectively real universals. They are nominalists. That means that they think universals are only names ("nomina"), either mere words or also vague concepts or mental categories that we impose on things and use to classify things for whatever purposes we want. Nominalists claim that only concrete particular things are real, not abstract universals like "human nature". That's an issue in metaphysics, which we may want to explore later.

NAT: I've been doing a little research on your epistemology, Socrates; and if Plato reported what you taught back in ancient Athens correctly, you did not speak of abstraction as Aristotle did, and you were pretty down on "hard empiricism" in the *Theaetetus*. So you were a rationalist rather than an empiricist, then?

SOCRATES: No one knows to what extent Plato reported my views correctly and to what extent he simply used my name for his own views; and I'm not going to enlighten you on that historical bit of trivia now.

NAT: OK, but whether or not you were a rationalist, Plato certainly was. Why didn't Plato use the concept of abstraction to explain how we could know universals?

SOCRATES: Because he believed these universal Forms were already abstract, or separate from concrete material instances. They were not in material things; those things were only images or shadows of the Forms. For instance, he believed that if all triangular things in the universe disappeared, the essence "triangle" would still exist, and the laws of trigonometry would still be true about it. And he believed that even if no men or states or laws were just, justice itself would still exist. Aristotle did not believe that universals existed separately from particulars, as Plato did, so he needed abstraction to get them.

NAT: So Plato believed we had a priori knowledge of his eternal Platonic Forms, or Platonic Ideas, while Aristotle did not.

SOCRATES: Right. Aristotle took a middle-of-the-road position between Plato's rationalism and Hume's hard empiricism.

NAT: Because he just sort of instinctively gravitated to the middle, right? "The golden mean"?

SOCRATES: It was not just a personal preference; it was based on reasoning. He took that middle-of-the-road position in epistemology because it logically followed from his middle-of-the-road position in metaphysics. He believed that universals were objectively real, as the nominalists didn't, but not that they were already separate from particular material things, as Plato did.

NAT: So when we do epistemology, as we are doing now, we are also implicitly doing metaphysics.

SOCRATES: Yes. But it's not clear yet whether the epistemology is the premise and the metaphysics is the conclusion or vice versa. Do you want to explore that interesting tangent now?

NAT: Frankly, no. I don't find it as interesting as you do. I care more about life than logic.

SOCRATES: That's fine. Thank you for being honest with me. One of the aspects of my method is always to appeal to my interlocutor's will to truth, which is wonder, and curiosity. If "philosophy begins in wonder", then if you do not have that beginning, you will not have its end either. If no cause, no effect.

NAT: Oh, I want to philosophize, all right, but not about that particular question now. There are far more important questions I want to explore.

SOCRATES: But what if the questions you don't want to explore are the logically most important questions of all?

NAT: I guess if they are not psychologically important to me, I will not be motivated to explore them, even though I ought to.

SOCRATES: So let's continue with what *is* important to you. Our previous discussion was about skepticism, and that was of interest to you. So I am guessing that the most important argument against empiricism, at least hard empiricism, is going to be that if it is true, skepticism logically follows. Is my guess correct?

NAT: It is, Socrates. It's like the argument about whether there is such a thing as free will or not. I'm more interested in practical ethics than in theoretical psychology, but the two are necessarily connected because if theoretical psychology proves that free will is an illusion and that all our choices are predetermined by causes in our heredity or our environment, then all ethical argument and all ethical language is meaningless. We don't praise or blame or command or forbid or even recommend the right choices to machines. So this question interests me in the same way as the question of free will versus determinism—not for its own sake but for its practical consequences, especially in ethics. If skepticism is true in epistemology, then it's true in ethics too, and then all of ethics is subjective and relative, not objective and absolute. And if hard empiricism is true, and if that premise leads to skepticism, then it also leads to ethical subjectivism and relativism—which obviously makes a big difference to my life.

But I'm not sure whether that practical consequence counts for or against either epistemology. I've heard arguments both ways, and I can't be sure whether rationalism makes us rigid, self-righteous, judgmental, intolerant, narrow-minded, and unfeeling, or whether it makes us serious, trustable, faithful, unselfish, principled, and responsible. And I'm not sure whether empiricism makes us warm, compassionate, tolerant, humane, and flexible, or whether it makes us unprincipled, hedonistic, compromising, indulgent, and untrustworthy. That's not obvious to me. What *is* obvious to me is that there are ethical consequences of these two epistemologies.

And since we're supposed to be discussing empiricism now, I'd like to see whether "hard empiricism" does logically lead to skepticism.

SOCRATES: Well, then, if you want a high-level argument to show that, I'd recommend you read David Hume's *Enquiry concerning Human Understanding*. That is exactly the progress of the argument there.

NAT: What is his argument in a nutshell?

SOCRATES: A nutshell is far too small to contain his argument, unless he is nuts. But if you insist on a radically inadequate summary, it is that ethical qualities like good and evil do not appear to the senses, which are the only ways we know objective reality.

NAT: I think there has to be a way to avoid both bad ethical consequences—both the too-hard and too-dogmatic absolutism and the too-soft and too-skeptical relativism. And if that demands avoiding both rationalism and empiricism, then let's look for that: an alternative to both.

I know we've only barely scratched the surface of the argument between rationalism and empiricism, and I know my opinions are kind of shallow, but it seems to me there are strong reasons for and against both rationalism and empiricism. And that makes me suspect that even though it seems they simply contradict each other, maybe both are making the same mistake. Maybe the senses and the mind are mutually dependent on each other. After all, the mind and the body seem to be related in that double way.

SOCRATES: Then let us explore the possibility of that desirable synthesis of reason and sensation, instead of simply declaring one of the two the master and the other the servant.

NAT: I think there is a good analogy here with men and women. They work best, and they are happiest, when they listen to each other and respect each other and each other's distinctive powers, and they work worst when they try to master and dominate each other.

SOCRATES: That seems to be a fruitful analogy. I am very willing to accompany you on your journey to find a happy marriage of reason and sensation, if that is your quest now.

NAT: You mentioned Kant as trying to do just that. What roles did he give to reason and sensation?

SOCRATES: He said that concepts without percepts (that is, sensations) were empty, and that percepts without concepts were blind.

NAT: Hmm, when I remember my own experiences of knowing something, I find that he is right there. A concept like the law of non-contradiction, or the law of causality, all by itself, does not tell me anything concrete or specific, and I can't deduce anything further from them alone. On the other hand, my sensations make sense to me only if they are *understood* in the very act of sensing them. For instance, if I see a fingerprint and I deduce that a finger made it, I'm using the principle of causality. I don't think that I started with the abstract principle rather than experience; but neither did I start with a bare, uninterpreted, unformed sensation without any rational structure. So I think perhaps both reason and sense experience come first, if that's possible. Because what comes first is the knower, before his act of knowing, and the knower is both reason and sensation, both body and soul, at once.

SOCRATES: I think you are thinking with admirable clarity and logic so far.

NAT: But when we *do* know some rational principle like "Everything that happens has a cause" or "All men are mortal", where do we get that from? Do we get to that principle by already having it innately and imposing it on our experience, like a cookie cutter imposing its form on the cookie dough? Or do we get it out of our experience instead of imposing it on experience, like an X-ray getting the skeletal structure of the body out of the body? Is the universal form or law or principle like a lion that lives in the jungle, and we go out and hunt it and abstract it from the jungle and put it in a cage in the zoo, which is the concept in our minds? Or do we have the lion in the cage to begin with and put it in the jungle?

SOCRATES: I think you have just used an excellent analogy to formulate the difference between the two ways Aristotle and Kant see reason and sensation combining.

NAT: And I think I see a reason for preferring Kant's ordering of these two powers over Aristotle's. Aristotle begins with sense experience and then moves to universals, while Kant says we begin with these universal categories and then use them to structure our sense experience, right?

SOCRATES: Yes.

NAT: But it's a logical fallacy to conclude to a universal conclusion from particular premises, isn't it? "All men are mortal" does not logically follow from "This man is mortal" or "These men are mortal."

SOCRATES: That's true, but that can still be an inductive argument and give us probability. The more men we find who are mortal, as long as we don't find any that are not mortal, the more probable it is that all men are mortal. And probable knowledge is a kind of knowledge, though it's not certain. It can still be useful.

NAT: Did Aristotle say we had only probable knowledge?

SOCRATES: No, he said we had some knowledge that was certain.

NAT: Did he think it was certain that all men are mortal?

SOCRATES: Yes.

NAT: How did he think we knew that, then? What road led there, according to him? What let us move from the particular, concrete men we see die to the universal principle that all men are mortal?

SOCRATES: As we saw before, his answer was "abstraction".

NAT: But it seems that abstraction is fallacious. If it's deductive, it commits the fallacy of concluding "all" from "some". And if it's inductive, it confuses probability, which is all that induction ever gives us, with certainty, which can't come by induction.

SOCRATES: If he was talking about the third act of the mind, reasoning, that would be true and he would be committing a logical fallacy. But abstraction is about the first act of the mind, not the third—about concepts, not arguments. According to Aristotle, what is abstracted from many particular men is the universal form, or the essence, or the nature of man. We abstract the essence from the accidents.

NAT: But how do we know what's essential and what's accidental?

SOCRATES: Not just by sense observation but by understanding.

NAT: That sounds kind of fuzzy.

SOCRATES: It is. Understanding, that first act of the mind, is not the same in everybody, as the laws of logic are. That's at least one of the reasons why some people are wiser than others, and that's also why philosophers will never agree: because they rely partly on that first act of the mind, and its logic can be a kind of fuzzy logic.

NAT: Isn't fuzzy logic a self-contradiction? A logical argument is either valid or invalid.

SOCRATES: If we mean by "logic" only the third act of the mind, reasoning, then there is indeed no such fuzzy logic; a deductive argument is either simply valid or simply invalid. But what I mean by fuzzy logic is the first act of the mind, understanding the meaning of a concept. That's a more-or-less thing rather than simply a yes-or-no thing, and that's part of the old logic but not part of the new logic, mathematical logic, or digital logic, or computer logic, which doesn't deal with essences or with any real distinction between essential and accidental properties. Digital logic is like laser light: it is powerful but narrow. It gets its power from its narrowness. It leaves out almost everything interesting, all qualities that can't be quantified.

NAT: I see.

SOCRATES: That's why Descartes, long before the invention of mathematical logic and computers, tried to erase all fuzziness by demanding that we confine ourselves to what he called "clear and distinct ideas", which are like numbers in that way.

NAT: What do you mean? In what way?

SOCRATES: Numbers are not fuzzy. They are clear, and they are distinct from one another. You can't confuse 2 with 3, but you might confuse an unintelligent man with an intelligent man or even with an intelligent ape.

NAT: That demand for total clarity and distinctness seems admirable in science, but how can we talk about things like human nature and moral goodness and wisdom in such quasi-mathematical terms?

SOCRATES: I don't think we can. All we can do is to try to quantify them, as we do in measuring IQs. But I don't think the intelligence of the first act of the mind can be quantified; only performances on examinations that are not in essay format but in quantitative format, such as true-false or multiple choice, can be quantified. But that presupposes that there is at least an analogy between the two formats, the qualitative and the quantitative, and the very use of analogies goes beyond the scientific method and quantification. Analogies require an intuitive "seeing" of the point, and that's why they are at least one form of intelligence that computers are not competent to do.

NAT: But even if we can't quantify everything, we can still clarify the meaning of our terms a little more, if not perfectly, by defining them, can't we?

SOCRATES: Yes indeed. But we can't get as far as Descartes' "clear and distinct ideas" because we can't define qualities by quantities. So we can't reduce everything to numbers.

NAT: I think I am reluctantly but inevitably abandoning my demand for scientific certainty in philosophy. So perhaps we can't prove, with conclusive arguments, which of these four epistemologies is true—or perhaps anything else in philosophy insofar as it rests on the amount of understanding we have of the essential terms, which is always somewhat fuzzy, or a matter of degree, that is, the degree of light, of wisdom, of understanding.

SOCRATES: But we can at least be certain that if two truth claims or propositions or declarative sentences really do contradict themselves, they cannot both be true. So we can disprove some philosophical ideas with certainty even if we cannot prove any. We simply cannot doubt the law of non-contradiction, no matter how hard we try. Every time we try, we have to argue, and all arguing presupposes that law, at least.

NAT: I am convinced that is true.

SOCRATES: And I suspect we can also prove some philosophical points positively, not just disprove some negatively.

NAT: Why?

SOCRATES: Because positive and negative propositions always imply each other, don't they? So we can always translate or reformulate positive propositions into negative ones and vice versa.

NAT: But that's just the rules of formal logic. What about positive content? What about things like moral absolutes and God and free will and life after death?

SOCRATES: Well, we can at least measure our truth claims by experience if they claim to be "big pictures" or comprehensive hypotheses that explain that experience. As in science, if two theories or hypotheses both claim to explain the data, the one that explains more of the data is always the right one to choose, even if it is not yet proved with certainty.

NAT: Well, yes, but how does that help us to choose between philosophical theories as complex as the four epistemologies we have been discussing today?

SOCRATES: Well, for example, Plato's rationalism explains the "Aha!" experience of recognizing the truth when we discover it, as empiricism does not.

NAT: But empiricism also explains why those born blind have no innate understanding of color, as rationalism does not.

SOCRATES: But rationalism explains why both the arguments for rationalism and the arguments for empiricism depend on the law of non-contradiction, which is a law we learn from pure reason, not from experience.

NAT: Wouldn't a "soft empiricist" like Aristotle say that we do learn it from experience, by abstracting the universal from the individual examples of it that we know by experience?

SOCRATES: No, he said that it is "self-evident", not abstracted.

NAT: So that's why he is not simply an empiricist, even a "soft empiricist" who adds abstraction.

SOCRATES: You are becoming a formidable philosopher, Nat. I congratulate you.

NAT: Honestly, I'd rather be corrected than congratulated for not knowing.

SOCRATES: And that is what I congratulate you for the most. You have learned that principle of my Socratic method even if you have not been persuaded of my rationalism—or of Plato's.

NAT: What about common sense? Does your method give that a rightful role?

SOCRATES: If you mean taking a poll of the opinions of individuals in your culture, it does not. If you mean our common knowledge of the principles of logic, of all three acts of the mind, then I do take that as the common starting point in my dialogues.

NAT: I think I have learned much more about your Socratic method today than about epistemology. But I'd still like to find at least a probable argument for one of the four epistemologies. But this conversation is already too long and tiring for me. Is there a shorter and easier way to at least a probable conclusion and a revisable choice?

SOCRATES: There may be such an argument. I think we seek two things in a philosophy: it explains, and does not contradict, our experience; and it is not logically inconsistent or self-contradictory. Do you agree with that principle?

NAT: Yes.

SOCRATES: Well, then, by the first part of the principle, both rationalism and empiricism seem to explain only half of our experience but not the other half of it. So we come to the other two epistemologies, Aristotle's and Kant's, both of which seem to do greater justice to both the rational and active aspects and the empirical and receptive aspects of our thinking. How do we choose between them? Well, there may be a simple and quick way: if there is a single self-contradiction in either one, it must be rejected. If there is any argument that conclusively disproves either of these two epistemologies, we shall have to reject the epistemology it has disproved. Do you agree with that principle?

NAT: Certainly. So do you think there is such an argument against Kant?

SOCRATES: There seems to be. The most obvious argument against Kant's epistemology is that its fundamental idea is self-contradictory. That fundamental idea is what Kant called his "Copernican revolution in philosophy". The point of the analogy with Copernicus is that instead of making the sun relative to the earth, Copernicus made the earth relative to the sun, and instead of making the human mind relative to its object, Kant made the objects of our mind relative to the mind and its innate categories. Instead of thought

corresponding to things, things correspond to thought and its categories and structures.

NAT: What thought structures? What categories?

SOCRATES: Three kinds of structures. What he called "the forms of
perception" are the two categories of space and time for everything we could sense or imagine; and then the twelve basic categories of abstract logical thinking, like cause and effect, necessity
and contingency, for everything we can think logically about; and
then the so-called "ideas of pure reason", the ideas of world, self,
and God for metaphysical thinking.

NAT: He thought these were innate ideas? Like the rationalists?

SOCRATES: No, not ideas, just empty categories, structures. But
they were known a priori. But the problem is that he said that
the reason we think in these categories is not because objective
reality really *is* the way it is but because our minds are the way
they are. Kant said we could not know things-in-themselves, or
how things were independent of our minds, but that we could
only know "phenomena", or how things have to appear to us—
to all of us, always, and universally, in these three realms. The
problem is that he denied knowledge of things-in-themselves.
The major idea of his epistemology is the claim that it is our
knowledge that shapes the world rather than the world shaping
our knowledge. That was his so-called Copernican revolution
in philosophy.

NAT: In other words, we cannot know objective reality.

SOCRATES: Yes.

NAT: That sounds even more skeptical than Hume's "hard empiricism". On the other hand, when I think about it, I wonder—
perhaps it is right. For how could we possibly know how something
is outside our knowledge rather than inside it? That seems to be a
self-contradictory idea, because to know anything is to claim that
it is *in* our knowledge. What's not in our knowledge is, by definition, unknown! So the commonsense idea that can know how
things-in-themselves are, outside our knowledge, seems to be self-
contradictory! And a self-contradiction is necessarily false, and its
opposite is necessarily true. But Kant's alternative to this apparent
self-contradiction is the most skeptical of all four epistemologies.

How strange that greatest skepticism, that of Kant's Copernican revolution, seems self-evident, and the nonskepticism of common sense, which says that we *can* know things-in-themselves, seems self-contradictory! I thought we proved the opposite in our last dialogue!

SOCRATES: And do you see any apparent contradiction in Kant's idea that we *can't* know things-in-themselves, how they are outside our knowledge?

NAT: Hmm, let me think about that for a moment.... I think so. If we can't know any things-in-themselves, if we can't know how the world really is outside our consciousness, if we can't know objective reality, if we can't know facts, then how can we know *that* fact, that bit of objective reality, that truth, that reality, namely, that that's the way the relation between our mind and the world *really is*? How can we know as an objective truth that we cannot know objective truth?

SOCRATES: Yes, that's the problem. Wittgenstein put it this way: Kant is trying to draw a wall around all possible human thought, a wall that separates thought from things, a limit to all human thought. But to draw a limit to thought is impossible because to limit anything we have to think both sides of the limit, so we would have to think the unthinkable. You don't have to *live* on both sides of a wall or a border to *think* both sides of the wall or the border, like a border between countries; but when the border or the wall is thought itself, you can't think both sides of that border—you can't think what is unthinkable—so you can't make that distinction.

NAT: Well, there must be a mistake in one of those two arguments, because they both seem to prove that first anti-Kantianism and then Kantianism are not only false but self-contradictory!

And here's another problem with Kant's epistemology. You mentioned causality as one of the twelve categories of logical thinking that Kant said we unconsciously impose on phenomena. But "imposing on" is a kind of causality, like star-shaped cookie cutters causing cookies to come out shaped like stars. So Kant is saying there is real causality between the *idea* of causality, or the category of causality, and the things we apply the idea to. Whether we say that things shape thought, as Aristotle says, or that thought shapes things, as Kant says, we're claiming to know the real cause-and-effect relationship between things and thought. So Kant, too, is assuming that causality is objectively real—that the categories of the mind really cause what we know to conform to them. But he's also saying that causality is *not* objectively real but only our thought category. That looks like another self-contradiction.

So it looks like all four epistemologies have problems.

SOCRATES: And perhaps that's the best we can do. Perhaps the best we can do is like choosing the least bad candidate in an election.

NAT: If that's typical of the way philosophical arguments end up, that's a bummer.

SOCRATES: Judged by the standards of science, yes. But philosophy isn't like science.

NAT: Maybe it should be. Maybe all knowledge should be done by the scientific method.

SOCRATES: Can you prove that by the scientific method?

NAT: Oops again. No. So that won't work either. That would be another self-contradiction. What do we do?

SOCRATES: Well, we either give up or we keep trying. Which do you think would be better?

NAT: That's like asking whether I'd rather die or keep living.

SOCRATES: And now we come back to the first principle of my Socratic method, the will to truth. Never, never, never give up. I think that has to be our first and fundamental choice.

NAT: I'm still on this log, so you know what choice I've made.

Questions for Discussion or Personal Essays

1. Did you find the second dialogue harder or easier than the first? Why?
2. Which did you find more interesting? Why?
3. What is the relation between theory and practice that this dialogue teaches, at least implicitly, by practice, if not explicitly, by theory? Evaluate that implicit teaching.
4. How is epistemology a necessary part of "know thyself"?
5. How is this very theoretical subdivision of philosophy also practical, according to this dialogue? Evaluate.

6. The dialogue speaks of at least five different powers of the mind or the soul or the psyche: intuition, or understanding; deductive and inductive reasoning; the will; the imagination; and the senses. Do you see any others that are omitted? Where do you think conscience fits?

7. What important terms were left undefined? How would you define them? Do you see any relevant difference defining them would make to this dialogue?

8. What seems to you to be the strongest point and the weakest point of each of the four epistemologies (rationalism, empiricism, Kantian idealism, and Aristotelianism)?

9. The dialogue began by discussing Descartes' rationalism since Descartes was the focus of the previous dialogue. What difference do you think it would have made if it had begun with Aristotle instead and related each of the other three epistemologies to his?

10. What compromises to the principles of the Socratic method appear in this dialogue? Do you think they were justified? Why or why not?

11. There are two aspects of the issue between rationalism and empiricism: whether reason or sensation is prior in time and in authority. These two aspects are obviously related. How? Can you perhaps separate them so as to give a rationalist answer to one and an empiricist answer to the other?

12. Judge the four epistemologies by the standard of your own experience of coming to know something. Which explains the most aspects of your experience? How decisive do you think the standard of experience should be in evaluating philosophies?

13. Did you find Socrates' technique of giving arguments both pro and con for both sides of an issue helpful or confusing? Why or why not?

14. Metaphysics, anthropology, and epistemology are all logically related. Which do you think comes first logically? Why?

15. Explain in your own words and evaluate "abstraction".

16. Explain in your own words and evaluate Kant's "Copernican revolution in philosophy".

17. Do you think that there is at least one other self-evident principle that is known a priori, in addition to the law of

non-contradiction (or the law of identity) and the principle of causality, namely, the principle of intelligibility, that reality is knowable and that we can know reality?

18. The principle of causality says that everything happens by a cause that is adequate to produce the effect, and this means that more cannot come from less. People can make books, but books cannot make people. Things that lack intelligence cannot produce intelligence or intelligent thoughts or designs. So how do you explain the evolution of higher species from lower? How do you explain the evolution of mind from matter? (This question is not primarily about epistemology, but it is too fascinating just to let go.)

19. Do you think you know that all men are mortal with certainty? If so, how? If not, why not?

20. What is the difference between a priori *concepts* (like "cause") and a priori *judgments* or principles (like "everything that happens has a cause")? What difference does this difference make? (This is probably the most difficult of all these questions.)

21. How is moral knowledge different from factual knowledge? How does this difference make a difference to epistemology, and not just ethics?

22. Do you agree that "all men are mortal"? If so, what kind of knowledge do you think that is? (For example, is it mere opinion, certainty, or something in between? If so, what?) How do you think you acquired that knowledge? Which of the four epistemologies do you see as the most accurate answer to that question?

23. Do the same with the knowledge that "everything that happens (all changes, all events, everything that has a beginning in time) has a cause." Can you think of anything real that is not an event with a beginning?

24. Do you think that the difference between soft empiricism and hard empiricism is greater or less than the difference between soft empiricism and rationalism? Why?

25. Do you believe that essences or essential natures or universals are objectively real or not? Why?

26. Evaluate Aristotle's habit of seeking a "golden mean", or middle position, on almost every issue.

27. If you want an advanced assignment, read Plato's *Meno* or Hume's *Enquiry concerning Human Understanding* and evaluate their arguments.

28. Evaluate Socrates' arguments that criticize Kant's "Copernican revolution in philosophy" as self-contradictory. Evaluate the opposite idea that its denial is self-contradictory. Find the error in at least one of those two arguments. (This is not easy!)

29. Evaluate Socrates' assumption (which he does not take time to prove) that "we can't define qualities by quantities, so we can't reduce everything to numbers."

30. What do you think are the limits of the scientific method?

31. What do you think are the limits of the Socratic method?

3

Philosophical Anthropology:
The "Mind-Body Problem"

Socrates found his philosophical vocation in obeying the inscription over the entrance to the temple of the oracle at Delphi, "Know thyself." He interpreted that to mean to do philosophical anthropology, not individual psychology—not to explore his unique, individual personality but to understand his species, his essential nature, his and our common humanity. We alone among the animals ask, What are we? What is it to be a human being? Is human nature material, spiritual, or both? If both, then how are these two related?

This issue of anthropology involves epistemology and metaphysics as well. For what we are depends on whether mind and matter are both *real* (thus, it involves metaphysics), and if so, how they are related. And it also depends on epistemology because knowing this depends on how we *know* what is real: by thought or sensation or both, and if both, how *they* are related.

This "theoretical" philosophical issue is directly relevant to the more interesting and "existential" (personal and practical) question of whether there is life after death, an issue that comes up in this dialogue but is dealt with directly in the next one.

Most people believe we are both material and spiritual, some kind of unity of body and soul (or spirit or psyche or mind)—neither body alone (materialism) nor soul alone (immaterialism) nor two separate substances or entities (Cartesian two-substance dualism), but a psychosomatic unity, or a hylomorphic (form-and-matter) unity, as Aristotle thought. Most people also believe that the soul does not die when the body dies, though this seems easier to justify in two-substance dualism than in one-substance dualism, and, of course, impossible in materialism.

Since this dialogue covers a number of different arguments for and against different anthropologies, it illustrates only a little of the careful, long, step-by-step analysis of a single idea that is typical of a Socratic dialogue. But it does illustrate Socrates' two broader logical and methodical habits of (1) tracing ideas both backward, to their necessary logical assumptions or premises, and forward, to their logically entailed corollaries, and (2) the demand for truth—that is, correspondence to the data (the world as we experience it, both empirically and mentally)—and for logical consistency.

SOCRATES: Both of our two previous dialogues about epistemology have already touched on our topic for today, namely, anthropology, or a philosophy of human nature, especially by dealing with the issue of the nature of reason and its relation to the senses. And if the senses are powers of the body and the reason is a power of the mind, that raises the issue of the relation between the body and the mind. So I think it is natural to move to that issue next, the so-called mind-body problem.

NAT: Do you think that is the most important question in anthropology?

SOCRATES: It is at least an aspect of the most fundamental question of anthropology, which is, What is *anthropos*? What is man? What is human nature? We want to define ourselves; we want to "know thyself".

NAT: Why is that of such primary importance?

SOCRATES: Because if we do not know who or what we are, we do not know who or what it is that knows everything else. If bits of knowledge are like deposits of money in the bank, and if we are the bank, then to know a million other things but not to know who we are is like having a million dollars deposited in our bank but not knowing what or where the bank is.

NAT: And what do you think is the fundamental controversy about what we are, about human nature?

SOCRATES: There are many important and controversial questions, such as whether human nature is good or evil or both or neither; but the one we have been destined by our author to argue about today is the so-called mind-body problem. However, I think there is a controversy that is even more basic in your culture today: whether there even *is* such a thing as human nature.

NAT: How could that be controversial?

SOCRATES: Because to speak of natures, or essential natures or essences, seems to presuppose that such universals are objectively real and not just nominal, not just names or words, or vague or confused concepts. That is a position in metaphysics; and that position, like metaphysics itself, is much less popular today than in the past. Today the most popular position is nominalism, which claims that universals are only names.

NAT: But if one is a nominalist, it seems that one cannot even ask any question about human nature, much less answer it. We can't define essential natures if there are none. And we haven't discussed metaphysics yet, so we haven't dealt with nominalism. Maybe we should postpone our exploration of anthropology until we have explored metaphysics.

SOCRATES: That would be the most logical way to proceed. But we could also simply *assume*, as most people do by common sense, that questions about human nature are meaningful, and therefore implicitly assume that there is such a thing as human nature. We always have to assume *something* if we're ever going to start. A journey has to begin somewhere, not nowhere. So let's just put that metaphysical question of nominalism into brackets, for another day, in order to focus on the argument about human nature today.

NAT: All right. Question one: bracketed. What is question two, then?

SOCRATES: I think it, too, is a metaphysical question, but easier to deal with than the more abstract question of nominalism versus realism about universal essences. It is the question of whether there is such a thing as an immaterial soul or spirit or mind or self or person or psyche that is not simply the body or a part of the body or an act of the body.

NAT: In other words, the question of whether metaphysical materialism is true or false—whether only matter is real or also something else, something that is not material. That's a nice either-or question that has only two possible answers.

SOCRATES: Actually, I think there are three. And we see each of these in the history of philosophy.

One possibility is materialism: that only matter exists, and that we are therefore 100 percent matter. Thomas Hobbes was a famous example of that philosophy, as was Karl Marx. That view is increasingly popular in your Western culture today, especially among scientists and philosophers.

A second possibility is the exact opposite: immaterialism, or spiritualism—that everything that exists is not matter but spirit, or mind. That is much more popular in the East than in the West. Many forms of Hinduism and Buddhism hold that, but so do a few Western philosophers like Berkeley and perhaps Hegel (though Hegel is very hard to pin down).

And the third possibility is dualism: that both matter and spirit, or both body and mind, are real. That is the position of Descartes and Plato and Aristotle, and of the few philosophers who explicitly defend common sense, like Thomas Reid and G. E. Moore. And it is still the most popular position.

And if this last position is the true one, the next question is how these two things, body and mind, or body and soul, or matter and spirit, are related to each other. Descartes says we are two separate "substances" or entities or beings, namely, matter and spirit, body and mind, while Aristotle says that these are not two separate substances but that the soul and body are the "form" and the "matter" of one substance, that is, two *dimensions* of one thing, like the meaning and the words of a text. In Aristotle this is called "hylomorphism", from *hylē* and *morphē*, which mean "matter" and "form".

NAT: By "form" did he mean simply the form *of the matter*? The shape?

SOCRATES: No, he used the word "form" (*morphē*) to mean not external shape but inner essence, the thing's essential nature. A sculptor thinks that way: he knows that the form of his statue is not the outside of the statue but the inside, so to speak. And an author would say that the form or essence of his writing is not its words but its meaning, since he could put the same meaning into different words, either in the same language or by translating it into another language.

NAT: Well, that example seems to be a fact that disproves materialism. The fact is that we can translate an abstract meaning, which is something we cannot see with our bodies as we can see the words on the page with our bodies, from one concrete and specific language to another. That seems to disprove materialism because the meaning that is common to the two material languages is not material. It does not have sensory qualities. Meanings are not red or triangular or have physical weights. It also seems to refute nominalism because the meaning is universal and common to both languages. So have I refuted both materialism and nominalism?

SOCRATES: Perhaps you have, but that is not clear and certain merely from a few sentences! We shall have to explore much deeper into both: into materialism today, because it immediately impacts anthropology, and into nominalism when we do metaphysics.

NAT: OK. So there are three anthropologies then: materialism, immaterialism, and dualism.

SOCRATES: Actually, there are four. Because there are two kinds of dualism, two-substance dualism and one-substance dualism. For Descartes, body and soul are two entities, two different "substances", as he called them, because they have nothing in common: matter has no mental properties, while the mind has no physical properties. But for Aristotle, we are only one substance with two dimensions, which he called "matter" and "form". Modern psychologists call that the "psycho-somatic unity", or the oneness of the psyche (or soul or mind or spirit) and the body. One-substance dualism says that even though the attributes of mind and matter are different, they are not two *things*, not even two things that are very close together and have intimately close interactions with each other, like a married couple.

NAT: Should we say "body and soul" or "body and mind"?

SOCRATES: Well, the broadest meaning of "soul" is simply "life", or "source of life". In that broader, ancient sense, as Aristotle used it, animals and even plants have souls because they are alive. But in a narrower, more modern sense, "soul" means "human soul" or "spiritual soul" or "rational soul". Mind, or intellect, or "reason" in the broad sense of the word, is one of the powers of the soul. Free will would be another. Perhaps some emotions or feelings, like guilt and gratitude and compassion, are a third. They are not just animal feelings like pleasure and pain.

NAT: Why do you say "reason *in the broad sense of the word*"?

SOCRATES: I mean by "reason" what traditional logic calls "the three acts of the mind", or the three powers of the mind: understanding the meaning of a concept, judging a proposition to be true or false, and reasoning from premises to a conclusion. The word "reason" is often used today more narrowly, to mean merely the third act of the mind, reason*ing*, or the second and third, as in modern mathematical logic, which begins with propositions, which are expressions of the second act of the mind, rather than terms, which are expressions of the first.

NAT: So computers can do the third act of the mind, and perhaps also the second, but not the first?

SOCRATES: Apparently so—although there is a lot of controversy about that, and about so-called artificial intelligence. Another topic for another day, perhaps.

NAT: So Descartes taught two-substance dualism and Aristotle taught one-substance dualism, or—what's the word?—hylomorphism. Did Plato agree with Aristotle or with Descartes about that?

SOCRATES: Technically, neither, though he was closer to Descartes. He did not use the Aristotelian terms of "form" and "matter", but he seemed to think we were one substance, a soul or spirit, but one that was trapped in a body, like a prisoner in a cell or a corpse in a coffin. The Greek word for body, *soma*, is almost the same as the Greek word for tomb, *sema*.

NAT: So if the soul and body are related as two substances, as Descartes says, then the soul can survive the death of the body, but if they are related as form and matter of a single substance, as Aristotle says, it can't, right?

SOCRATES: Well, it seems at first that it can't, if the soul is not a substance but only a form. And Aristotle apparently thought so. But Aquinas, who adopted Aristotle's hylomorphism, thought that the soul was substantial as well as formal—that it had its own act of existence, like a substance, and was *also* the form of the body, or the form or essence of the whole person. That's another issue.

NAT: You mean life after death.

SOCRATES: I mean whether the soul can be both a form and a substance. But life after death is certainly a more practical issue. What we are now and what we will be after death, if anything, are not the same issue, although they are obviously closely related. I think that second issue requires another whole conversation. So I think in this conversation we should concentrate on two questions of philosophical anthropology: first, whether dualism is true, whether both body and mind exist, as most people think, and second, if they do, then how they are related to each other—by one-substance dualism or two-substance dualism. That would seem to be the logical order.

NAT: Then let's first examine materialism, because that would seem to make the biggest difference if it's true. If only matter is real, then only material goods are real, so the whole apparatus of cultivating the spiritual life, any kind of religious life, and even the intellectual life, or the contemplative life, knowing the truth just for the sake of knowing, not for any material gain, would seem to be a waste of time, a fiction. And that would seem to be true of the moral life too, if only things with material qualities are real, since moral virtues and vices are not material qualities. And that radical moral consequence would seem to be the strongest argument against materialism.

SOCRATES: Logically, that's called a "reductio ad absurdum" argument, an argument that tries to prove that an assumption (here, materialism) is false by showing that the consequences that logically and necessarily follow from it are absurd or unlivable.

NAT: Like the argument against skepticism, right? If it's true that we have no reliable knowledge of truth, as skepticism says, then the absurd consequence follows that we can't even have any reliable knowledge that skepticism is true either.

SOCRATES: Yes, that kind of argument.

NAT: How would a materialist answer that argument?

SOCRATES: Well, if there are no ambiguous terms, there seem to be only two possible answers, logically, to any "reductio ad absurdum" argument. One would have to show either that these consequences are not absurd, not false, or that they do not necessarily follow from materialism as a premise.

NAT: And how would a materialist do that?

SOCRATES: In the same way an immaterialist would try to answer the similar "reductio ad absurdum" argument against immaterialism, the argument that immaterialism is false because absurd consequences logically follow from immaterialism, for instance, that we need not fear disease or physical pain or death because the so-called material body that they seem to harm is only an illusion.

NAT: Like the famous joke about the Hindu mystic who taught immaterialism and who was seen running away from a man-eating tiger. His students called out to him, "Teacher! Remember your teaching! That tiger is not real. Stop running." And he called back, "Running? Who's running?"

SOCRATES: Someone told me a similar story, which he said was true, and not just a joke. He had a friend who was an immaterialist, a follower of Mary Baker Eddy's "Christian Science" religion, which taught that matter was an illusion and everything was spirit. But this friend taught physical chemistry at a prestigious university. When he was asked to explain that apparent contradiction between his belief and his profession, he said that he told his students that although matter is an illusion, the illusion, like a significant dream, has very interesting properties that were worth investigating.

NAT: Well, I don't think many people in our culture believe immaterialism, so I don't think we should waste much of our time on that. Instead, I'd like to explore materialism, which seems very popular among scientists. And I'd like to use your Socratic method of logical dialogue, your question-and-answer critique. And since you know philosophy much better than I do, I'd like you to defend materialism, even if you don't believe it yourself, and see whether I can refute it, with just common sense and only a little knowledge of philosophy. Will you act the part of the materialist in this little thought experiment for me?

SOCRATES: Gladly.

NAT: So tell me what is the most attractive argument for materialism.

SOCRATES: In a word, science. It seems more scientific.

NAT: Why?

SOCRATES: Because one of the principles of science and the scientific method is "Ockham's Razor". It is a way of choosing between two or more alternative hypotheses or theories or explanations of the data. It says that if neither of two theories or hypotheses has any logical inconsistencies or self-contradictions, and if there is no empirical data that simply refutes either one of them, then the simplest hypothesis that explains the data is always the best one to choose.

NAT: So since materialism is the simplest, Ockham was a materialist, right?

SOCRATES: No. Ockham was not a materialist, but he was a nominalist, mainly because of his Razor. Nominalism is a simpler metaphysics because it gets rid of real universals and says there are only particular things, so that there are human individuals but no universal human nature. For universals are only words ("nomina"), or, at best, confused concepts that ignore differences.

NAT: But Aristotle explained that these concepts are not confused, just abstracted.

SOCRATES: Ockham criticized Aristotle's theory of abstraction of universal forms from particular matter because he said there existed no such forms to abstract, positively, only differences to ignore, negatively.

NAT: If all rivers are different, how can we truly call them all "rivers"?

SOCRATES: Obviously, Ockham could not reduce all language to particulars without absurdity, but he could reduce *realities* to particulars.

NAT: But if language is supposed to picture reality, why don't we have particular names, proper names, for everything in our language, if that's all there is in reality, viz., particular things? Why don't we call rivers or chairs or ants "Socrates" or "Xanthippe" or "Peter"?

SOCRATES: For two reasons. First of all, he denied that language pictures reality directly. He said that the object of our thought is not reality but ideas. And secondly, he said that we don't have proper names like "Socrates" or "Xanthippe" for chairs or ants as we do for people only because we don't care to be that exact about individual chairs or ants, but we do about people.

NAT: Well, I still can't accept nominalism as a metaphysics, but I like the Razor in science. It sounds like a good principle for making scientific progress. For instance, if you can explain a war by observable forces, like mutual hate and suspicion between the people of two nations, it's not scientific to add the invisible influences of divine providence or of good and evil spirits to explain the war. Old Ptolemy had explained the movements of the planets by a very complex astronomy of epicycles, assuming the earth was the center of the solar system; but Copernicus explained the observable data much more simply by assuming that the sun was the center. So that was the better hypothesis. But what about using the Razor outside science? Why should we do that too? That's not science but scientism.

SOCRATES: The materialist would reply, "Because the only certain knowledge, or the only reliable knowledge, is scientific knowledge."

NAT: But that's not a statement that comes from any science. It can't be proved by any science. It's a statement *about* science, from outside science, from philosophy or ideology. So it's self-contradictory. Imagine science as a large book. Scientism says "Believe nothing but what is written in this book", but that sentence itself is not written in that book, so we shouldn't believe it.

SOCRATES: Good argument! But I think we need to define what we mean by "science" so that both the nominalist and the anti-nominalist and both the materialist and the nonmaterialist can use the word with the same meaning.

NAT: Yes.

SOCRATES: Well? How would you define "science"?

NAT: I think the simplest answer would be the use of the scientific method, which is what distinguishes modern science from what premoderns called science.

SOCRATES: I think everyone can agree to that definition.

NAT: Then one who says that scientific knowledge is the only reliable knowledge is saying that knowledge by the scientific method is the only reliable knowledge. But that seems to contradict itself too because that can't be proved by the scientific method. So it saws off the branch it sits on.

SOCRATES: Suppose one could show that it is not self-contradictory. Wouldn't that make materialism the most scientific hypothesis because of its conformity to the other two criteria in Ockham's Razor, that it is the simplest hypothesis and that it explains all the data?

NAT: But it *doesn't* explain all the data. It doesn't explain the act of *knowing* the data.

SOCRATES: Another good argument! We should argue about that too, later, when we talk about that strange property knowing has, which philosophers call "intentionality", being not just a thing but "about" things. But materialism surely obeys at least one of the criteria of the Razor: it's very simple. So it accuses dualism of complexifying things needlessly, of believing in something like flying saucers. You can explain all the phenomena without them. Or, to use another analogy, the materialist claims that belief in immaterial souls or spirits is like belief in Harvey, the giant invisible rabbit in the old Jimmy Stewart movie that no one can see except Jimmy. There may be no proof against it, but there is no proof for it either.

NAT: That sounds like a weak argument to me.

SOCRATES: No, I think it is quite an impressive argument. Here, do this little thought experiment. If you list, in a column, all the things you think are immaterial, and which thus constitute evidence against materialism, like the three acts of the mind and mathematics and moral choices and religious faith and mystical experience—if you make such a list or column, you can add a second column and list in it all the physical and chemical acts and activities in the brain that correspond to each of those supposedly immaterial acts. Not only sensations like color but also abstract thinking like mathematics and religious faith and moral conscience and even mystical experience—all the items in the first column, the immaterial column, can be explained by something that happens in the material brain in the second column. So by using Ockham's Razor, you can simply cut out the immaterial column and explain everything by the material column alone. That also explains all the data; it explains why mere physical surgery alone can restore powers of thinking and feeling. The brain surgeon does not have to take account of souls or minds at all, only brains. In fact, if he does worry about souls and minds, his surgery is probably going to be impeded and compromised and distracted. The point is that the immaterialist cannot point to a single supposedly immaterial thing or activity that cannot be explained by some material activity in the brain.

NAT: I see. Ockham's Razor really cuts off a lot of unnecessary hair from the hairy bear.

SOCRATES: Yes. How would you critique that epistemological argument for metaphysical materialism?

NAT: Well, obviously *any* monism is simpler than dualism. So immaterialism is just as simple as materialism. You could just as well eliminate the material column as the immaterial column if there is a total one-to-one correspondence between the two.

SOCRATES: So that would put both materialism and immaterialism on an equal footing.

NAT: No, because I don't think materialism is the simplest hypothesis; I think immaterialism is.

SOCRATES: Why?

NAT: Because matter is not simple but very complex in its structure, and it is always divided into parts—in fact, perhaps a potentially infinite number of parts if matter is infinitely divisible—because it is spread out in space. But the structure of the mind is much simpler, and the mind is not divided into parts—you can't cut a mind in half, as you can cut a body in half—because the mind is not spread out into space. So if we went by Ockham's Razor, we would choose immaterialism, not materialism. You can explain everything in the universe by one thing: the mind, the mind that dreams this dream that we call the universe into existence.

SOCRATES: But without material brains there are no minds. If I remove your brain, you cannot think at all.

NAT: But matter is just as much surrounded by mind as mind is surrounded by matter, because you can't point to any matter at all without pointing to it, without it being a part of your thought, since pointing to something is an act of thinking. You challenge me to point to a single spiritual thing that can't be explained by matter, and I challenge you to point to a single material thing that can't be explained by spirit.

SOCRATES: Can you really imagine believing that this whole universe is only a thought, like a dream?

NAT: Yes, I can! I don't believe it, but I can imagine it, and I think I can understand how some mystics can believe it, even though I don't. But I can't even imagine the opposite: that thought is just blind atoms of matter bumping into each other. That's like saying that if you take a big rock and do enough material things to it, it will become a philosopher.

SOCRATES: Let's back up and review our principle. The Razor has three criteria for any hypothesis or theory or explanation: that it does not contradict itself, that it is the simplest theory, and that it explains all the data, or the most data. So you are arguing, first, that the theory does contradict itself because it justifies not science but scientism, which is not scientific; and, second, that it is not the simplest because immaterialism is simpler; and, third, that it does not explain more data than dualism does, and probably less. But you have not yet proved this third objection. What data is there that materialism can't explain?

NAT: A lot. Abstraction, and understanding, and moral choice, and self-consciousness, and our experience of our body obeying our thought and will, and out-of-the-body experiences, and the very idea of mind as distinct from matter.

SOCRATES: Whoa, there, racehorse! That's seven things, not just one.

NAT: So let's take them one by one. We can think abstractly. We can think of universals, qualities like blueness or justice or triangularity or twoness. Even if these universals are not realities, as the nominalist claims, they are certainly at least concepts. And concepts are not material things. You can't put twoness into my hand, only two concrete things. You can visit the pyramids, but you can't visit triangles. You can hold a bluebird, but you can't hold the color blue.

SOCRATES: But the atoms and electrons, and the photons of light, and what's measured in angstrom units on the spectrum, and the optic nerve, and the electrical vibrations it sends to the brain, and the brain itself, are all material. All of those things together make up the color blue. Take any one away and you don't have any perception of the color we call blue.

NAT: No, you are wrong—none of those things *is* the color blue. Nor are all of them together. They are all quantifiable. Blue is a quality, not a quantity.

SOCRATES: But if we can explain qualities by quantities, we obey Ockham's Razor.

NAT: But we can't. Measuring the quantitative material aspects of all the links in the chain of perceiving a color does not give the blind person any idea of the color itself.

SOCRATES: Then this thing you call "the color itself" does not exist. It is a universal. Materialists are nominalists. There are no universals, really.

NAT: But "matter" itself is a universal.

SOCRATES: And therefore not a reality. The universe, the sum total of all material things, is the only thing that is real.

NAT: But within the universe, whatever is material is limited to one particular place. It can't be in many places at the same time, as universals like qualities or essences can. And it can't come to exist in one place without leaving another place. But our thought is not limited like that. When we think of two cities and compare Boston and San Francisco and say one is more beautiful than the other, both cities and both places are present to our mind at the same time mentally, as they cannot be physically. Also, the very same thought can exist in many minds at the same time. Nothing material can do that.

SOCRATES: An interesting argument.

NAT: And here's another thing: What about the act of understanding, the first act of the mind in traditional logic? It's the one thing a computer cannot do. A computer does not understand anything at all because it's only matter, not mind. All it does is record and communicate and relate and order all the stuff that we understand.

SOCRATES: If what you say is true, then there is simply no such thing as AI, or artificial intelligence.

NAT: Right.

SOCRATES: But there is such a thing.

NAT: No, there is not! There is no such thing as AI. There is no more intelligence in a computer than in a book. A computer will say that pigs fly if you tell it to because it does not understand either pigs or flying. It's like a blank page in a book. It's passive, not active. It has no will. It obeys everything you command it. It asks no questions unless you command it to.

SOCRATES: So even the greatest supercomputer, that mimics everything human intelligence can do, is not really intelligent at all? The computer industry will not buy that.

NAT: Well, they should! Because the biggest supercomputer works by the same basic principles and causes as the simplest little handheld calculator. Do they say those little things actually think? If not, where is the dividing line between little computers that do not think and big computer that do? There is none. Computers are just big calculating machines with lots of storage and instructions to sort out the logical relationships between its bits of data. They don't understand any of their data at all.

SOCRATES: Well, not all materialists think that computers think in that sense.

NAT: Every materialist I ever met thought they did. And they think that human thinking is just doing what a very complex computer does, within an organic body. They say that the brain is just a computer made of meat.

Look, there are only two things a materialist can possibly say about the relationship between what we do and what computers do. If the materialist is going to explain mind by matter, he's going to have to either lower what we usually think of as human understanding to the level of the thing a computer does, reduce it to a merely physical process with no more "mental reality" than a rock, or else he will have to raise what we usually think of as what a computer does to the level of what we usually think of as human understanding.

And the ethical problem is enormous. Common sense thinks persons are ends in themselves, not just means to further ends, like machines. If that distinction is not clear, there's no reason not to treat persons as means and go back to slavery, and no reason not to treat computers as ends and risk our lives to save them. That's morally insane. If we are computers, we don't deserve the right to vote, and if computers are persons, they do.

SOCRATES: Well, since practice is based on theory, let's start with the basic theoretical question, or metaphysical question, or epistemological question. What do you see as the central theoretical problem, or philosophical problem, or logical problem, as distinct from the practical, moral problem, with the notion that computers are intelligent?

NAT: That that either lowers us to machines or raises up machines to the level of persons—unless the only thing that makes us persons is our animal body, or our sexuality, or our feelings. Because if it's not thinking that distinguishes us from computers, it's got to be one of those other things.

SOCRATES: That's a problem with the consequences of the idea. What is the problem with the idea itself?

NAT: Even if I grant that the brain is only a computer made of meat, who is using the computer?

SOCRATES: I think most materialists say we do not *use* our computer brains as we use computers, but that we *are* our computer brains. There is no "user", no additional self there, no "ghost in the machine".

NAT: So they say *there's nobody there* using the computer brain as an instrument?

SOCRATES: No spiritual self, no. It's a machine, not a driver outside the machine. It's like a self-driving car.

NAT: Then why do we have self-consciousness and computers don't?

SOCRATES: Some deny that we have self-consciousness. But most say that computers do too. They say the brain is just a supercomputer that has a self-scanning mechanism. That's how the idea of the self arises. What's real is just the mechanism, not the false idea of the self that the mechanism gives rise to.

NAT: But how can there be self-scanning if there is no self to scan or to be scanned?

SOCRATES: You think, then, like Descartes, that the existence of the self is immediately self-evident and indubitable?

NAT: Yes. "I think, therefore I am."

SOCRATES: That argument begs the question: it assumes what it claims to prove, namely, the reality of the "I".

NAT: It's not an argument. It's a direct insight. It's nonempirical data.

SOCRATES: Materialists say that all data is empirical, that the false concept of nonempirical data presupposes nonmaterialism.

NAT: But to say that all data is empirical is just as much an unproved assumption as commonsense dualism makes in saying that there is nonempirical data, as our immediate experience tells us there is. So why not accept that experience?

SOCRATES: Because Ockham's Razor tells us to prefer the simplest of those two hypotheses.

NAT: So by the Razor, reductionism is a virtue, not a vice. And Hamlet was wrong when he said to Horatio that "there are more things in heaven and earth than are dreamt of in your philosophy."[1]

SOCRATES: Yes.

NAT: I don't see how intelligent people can simply ignore the direct data, the direct experience, that we have of the first act of the mind, of understanding a meaning, and of self-consciousness, which opens up the whole area of free choice and responsibility and guilt and justice. Or how they can say that a machine can do all that too if only it's big enough and complex enough. Granted that the brain is like a computer, how can you say that there is no you using it? That there is no self making the mistake of thinking that there is a self? That sounds self-contradictory.

---

[1] Shakespeare, *Hamlet*, act 1, scene 5, lines 166–67.

SOCRATES: Both Buddha, who was probably an immaterialist, and Hume, who was probably a materialist, were very intelligent, yet both thought there was no such thing as a real ego or self.

NAT: But we do have self-consciousness, which is the direct and immediate experience of ourselves as knowers, as subjects, not just as known objects. That's why we know what the word "I" means. That's part of experience, part of the data. Scientific theories are supposed to explain the data, not explain them away.

SOCRATES: They would reply that we are mistaken. We usually believe that we have direct and immediate sense experience of the material world too, but the immaterialist explains that as a dream, and that's not impossible and unbelievable, as you yourself admitted, even though you don't believe it. So what we think is immediate experience can be deceptive.

NAT: But why do we speak of "our" thinking and acting if there is no self? How do they explain that universal illusion?

SOCRATES: The materialist says that the self is just our name for this series of thoughts and actions. Buddhists say that what we think is a single self is really only a collection of acts, like the strands of rope, many little threads bound together into a single big rope. They are bound together at birth and separated again at death. Hume says that all we find when we introspect is a series of sense impressions and the ideas that weakly and vaguely copy them.

NAT: But these thoughts and actions, whatever they are, are all *my* thoughts. *Something* unites them. I am aware of a material heap of many material things, but this does not result in a heap of awarenesses. It is not a heap or a group of strands on the subject side, as it is on the object side. It is one and the same "I" that is aware of many different things. How can materialism account for that unifying of these many thoughts and acts by a single thinker and actor?

SOCRATES: The thought of a self exists, of course, but that does not mean the reality exists. There are many thoughts that people take for realities that are not in fact realities. For instance, the illusion that a rope, which is really many strands, is one thing. For Buddhists, there are really no *things* at all, anywhere, either material or immaterial.

NAT: So there is no self? The word "I" is an illusion? There is no "inner life" at all?

SOCRATES: Exactly.

NAT: Then why does that illusion do such good work? It gives us personal continuity in memory, and personal sense of responsibility, and promise-keeping. And loving. When I love you, there is really no I to love you and no you to be loved? That's absurd! These so-called illusions do remarkable work! They hold life together. Can illusions have that power?

SOCRATES: Some illusions might. Dreams can be quite convincing. We can invent ideas that are more attractive than reality.

NAT: And here's another piece of data that materialism cannot account for. What about free will and free choice? How can materialism explain that?

SOCRATES: They say there simply is no free will. It's another illusion. Materialists are determinists.

NAT: So we can't help how our brain works or how our tongue happens to wag. There is no "I" that causes and controls these thoughts and actions.

SOCRATES: Right. We're just links in a chain. Or the two chains of heredity and environment. Or of the megachain that is the whole universe.

NAT: Then why should I believe anything you say, if everything you say and do is determined by mechanical necessity? If you didn't freely choose to believe in materialism because you thought it was rational, then I can have no *reason* to agree with you if you can have no reason to believe it.

SOCRATES: That's just the way it is. To quote that great logician Bill Belichick, "It is what it is."

NAT: And if determinism is true, there is no difference between what ought to be and what is, and so nothing is evil, and that makes morality impossible.

SOCRATES: If they are consistent, they say that there is really no such thing as "ought". It's just our subjective feeling. A good feeling, and a practical and necessary one, but just a feeing, not a fact. There are no moral facts, no real "oughts". There is just what is, and what is does not include what ought to be. "Ought" is just our subjective feelings and desires.

NAT: Then there is no such thing as morality. All moral language is meaningless—all moral arguing and counseling and commanding and rewarding and punishing and praising and blaming and preaching is meaningless, if there is no free will, and we are only very complex machines. We do not preach to machines, or call them immoral or unjust, or expect them to feel guilty and repent and go to confession. We just junk them when they don't work or send them to the repair shop. Is that how we must treat one another, if materialism is true?

SOCRATES: No, most materialists do not draw that conclusion. In fact, many materialists have a very high and sensitive morality.

NAT: Then they are illogical, because if their theory were true, morality would be impossible. Machines have no morality, no matter how complicated they are. So if this philosophy is true, then we can't really be morally good, so this philosophy makes our two greatest absolutes, truth and goodness, into enemies of each other. What a horrible philosophy!

And that brings up another piece of data that materialism cannot explain: truth. Materialists claim that we can know the truth, at least in science, for they argue that materialism is true; but materialism cannot explain what that word means. The common sense meaning is that *thoughts* are true when they match or conform to objective reality. But if thought is only matter, there is no *relation between* thought and matter. If A is only B, there is no relation between A and B any more than there is between A and A or between B and B. If all men were only women in disguise, there could be no *relation* between men and women.

SOCRATES: No, that consequence does not necessarily follow. There can be relations between one piece of matter and another, as between a computer and the data it faithfully transmits about the world outside it, like a faithful Xerox copy of a text or a picture. There does not have to be spirit, and a relation between matter and spirit, for there to be relations. There are still relations between one piece of matter and another.

NAT: But truth is not simply material relations between two different chunks of matter. One piston on my car is not the truth about the other pistons. Thinking about matter is not one part of matter.

Thought is *about* matter. I don't see how my thought *about* the pistons in my car can be one of the pistons. That's like saying that the science of geology is not *about* rocks but that it *is* only a rock.

SOCRATES: The relation you refer to when you say that thought is "about" things is what philosophers call "intentionality". Materialists say that the thing you think of as a real relation is not a real relation at all, but only your false assumption, and they do not make that assumption.

NAT: Then who is the "they" who are not making that assumption and who am I who am making it?

And here's another logical problem in materialism. A true thought about a thing as a whole cannot be simply one of the parts of that thing. The whole is more than its parts.

SOCRATES: If that were true, then this tiny part of the enormous material universe that is you, or your brain, could not know truths about the whole universe. But we can do that; that is what science does.

NAT: Then the fact that we can do science—science that knows principles that are true of the whole universe, like gravity—proves that we are *not* merely parts of the universe. The knower must be more than the known, and we know some truths about the whole universe; therefore, we are more than the universe.

SOCRATES: They would regard that argument as a "reductio ad absurdum" argument that proves their point.

NAT: Only because they regard the idea that the human mind is more than the whole material universe as absurd. In other words, only because they are materialists. They are begging the question; they are assuming the materialism that they need to prove.

SOCRATES: I think they would say that every one of your arguments assumes that these things exist—truth and intentionality and mind and self and consciousness, all in the commonsense sense of the words, as something transcending matter. So it is you who are begging the question.

NAT: But they are denying the very self that commits fallacies like begging the question. They are committing intellectual suicide, denying with their minds that there is such a thing as a mind. That's insane.

SOCRATES: But materialists are usually very intelligent. Are you saying that all these intelligent people are insane?

NAT: Perhaps intelligence is not a measure of sanity. Perhaps one kind of intelligence is the ability to deceive yourself by very clever arguments.

SOCRATES: We are supposed to be doing philosophy, not psychoanalysis. Let's confine ourselves to arguments. Here is a modified form of materialism that you might find more "sane". It's called epiphenomenalism. It does not claim that thought *is* nothing but matter but only that it is caused and determined by matter.

NAT: Why is that called epiphenomenalism?

SOCRATES: "Epi" means "on" and a "phenomenon" is a material sense impression, so epiphenomenalism says that thoughts are not simply material phenomena—that's why they don't have mass or gravity or color—but that they are additions to matter, as riders are additions to a horse or fleas to a dog. Or like the heat generated by electricity running along a wire from a plug to an appliance. It is the electricity, not the heat, that does the work. The heat just dissipates in the air, like the puff of smoke coming out of a car's tailpipe. It does not cause the car to move; the car causes it to move.

NAT: So thought is like a puff of smoke coming out of the back of the machine. Like a fart. So thought is a fart of the brain. The fart theory of thought.

SOCRATES: Insults and jokes do not count as arguments.

NAT: Epiphenomenalism says causality works only one way, from matter to mind, and not from mind to matter, right?

SOCRATES: Right.

NAT: But we have direct experience of data that contradict that. Causality works both ways, and the evidence is equally clear for both. It is true that material slaps cause mental anger and physical blows to the head cause mental unconsciousness, but it is also true that thoughts like "I should speak louder" cause me to speak louder, and thoughts like "That is a candy that I will enjoy eating" cause me to buy the candy. Once you admit that thought exists at all, it's hard to explain all the interaction as a one-way street moving from matter to mind and never vice versa. There seems to be a lot of traffic going the other way, from mind to matter. For instance, the epiphenomenalist philosopher is deliberately moving his mouth to create physical sounds to try to argue with me.

SOCRATES: Well, at least epiphenomenalism admits the immediate evidence in experience for thought. So it is halfway between simple materialism and dualism.

NAT: So it's a little closer to the fullness of experience, but not much. It still does not explain how the mind can move matter, how my thought and will to move my arm makes my arm move. And that means it's not a good scientific theory because it does not explain all the data. Ockham's Razor doesn't just say to accept the simplest theory, but to accept the simplest theory *that explains all the data.*

SOCRATES: And which theory of mind seems to you to explain all the data?

NAT: Hylomorphism, I think. Descartes' dualism doesn't explain mind-body interaction. But I'd like to believe in the mind's survival of the death of the body too, and I wonder if hylomorphism can do that.

SOCRATES: I think that question should be our next one. You have done a remarkable job in critiquing materialism, and I have probably not defended it very well, so you have won most of the arguments today, I think. You are becoming a formidable philosopher, Nat.

Questions for Discussion or Personal Essays

1. Evaluate Socrates' image or analogy of the self as a bank, at the beginning of the dialogue. What limitations do you see in this analogy?

2. How can a nominalist participate in the question about human nature if universal natures or essences are not objectively real, as nominalists claim?

3. There is a cynical saying that goes, "That idea is so absurd that you have to have two Ph.D.s to believe it." Both materialism and immaterialism, or spiritualism, are not as popular among ordinary people as among philosophers. Why do you think that is? Why do you think philosophers so often believe worldviews or life views that common sense regards as almost unthinkable?

4. Why do you think the notion of "form" has changed from what it meant to Aristotle (the essential nature) to what it means to us (the external visible shape)?

5. How do Aristotle (the one-substance dualist) and Descartes (the two-substance dualist) both use the word "substance"

differently than we do today? Compare this with the previous change in the word "form".

6. How has the word "soul" also changed its meaning in popular speech? Why is that significant?

7. How can Socrates claim that there is no such thing as artificial intelligence? What would a computer scientist say to that? Evaluate Aristotle's position in terms of the three acts of the mind. If computers cannot perform the first act of the mind (understanding), how can they perform the third act of the mind (reasoning) if reasoning means moving from a premise that is understood to a conclusion that is understood? What, exactly, is understood? Is "understood" ambiguous?

8. List and formulate logically the numerous arguments against materialism in this dialogue.

9. Evaluate each of the arguments in the above list.

10. Use the three acts of the mind to explain the three ways a "reductio ad absurdum argument" could be answered. Illustrate by an original example.

11. Which argument (refutation) do you think is the strongest: finding a logical self-contradiction in the opponent's position, a logical (theoretical) "reductio ad absurdum" argument, or a practical "reductio ad absurdum" argument (like the guru and the tiger)? Why?

12. Why is the role-playing thought experiment that Socrates agrees to—defending a philosophy (materialism) that he does not believe—so helpful? Or is it?

13. Evaluate Ockham's Razor.

14. Evaluate Nat's argument that scientism is not scientific because it's self-contradictory.

15. Is the above argument also true of materialism? Of immaterialism? Of *sola scriptura*?

16. Is there a better definition of "science" than "the use of the scientific method"?

17. Evaluate the argument that immaterialism obeys Ockham's Razor better than materialism because it is simpler.

18. How does Nat show that materialism violates all three principles of Ockham's Razor? How would the materialist answer these three objections?

19. Evaluate Nat's seven examples of data that the materialist cannot explain.
20. Evaluate Descartes' "I think, therefore I am."
21. Why do you suppose the opposite philosophies of materialism and immaterialism are so similar in denying the reality of a substantial self?
22. How can anyone think that there can be thinking without a thinker? Can you explain and defend Hume's and Buddha's denial of the self? Is this as ridiculous as Nat's common sense thinks it is? If so, how can great philosophers like these two be so stupid?
23. Can a materialist account for free will? Why or why not?
24. How can determinism account for the choice to believe in determinism?
25. Why don't determinists contend that no one should ever be punished for crimes because no one has the power of free will to avoid committing them?
26. Can "intentionality" or "aboutness" be denied? Why or why not? If not, does this refute materialism? Why or why not?
27. At one point Nat calls materialism "insane". Why? Evaluate this judgment.
28. Do you think intelligence is a measure of sanity?
29. Evaluate Descartes' argument that matter and mind are two clear and distinct ideas, therefore two clear and distinct realities. Can they be two clear and distinct realities without being two substances?
30. Does the fact that we are both visible and invisible, and, according to most people, also both mortal and immortal, refute the logical law of non-contradiction? Why or why not?
31. How would Descartes or any other two-substance dualist explain the causal interaction between the mind and body?
32. Does AI exist or not? What definition of "thinking" is assumed in the no answer? What definition of "thinking" is assumed in the yes answer?
33. Can you *conceive* of a totally immaterial entity that thinks? Why or why not? Can you *imagine* it? Why or why not?
34. Evaluate Nat's argument against materialism from the fact that we can translate a meaning into different languages. (Remember

that there are three criteria of an argument: the terms must be unambiguous, the premises must be true, and the conclusion must logically, necessarily, follow from the premises.)

35. Why is there a problem for an Aristotelian hylomorphic thinker in making room for life after death? Do you see any way of doing that without abandoning hylomorphism (or the psychosomatic unity)?

36. What do you see as the consequences of a consistent materialism? What do you see as the relationship between theoretical materialism (nothing immaterial is real) and practical materialism (only material goods or goals are real)? Is it a necessary relationship? Could the practical be repudiated without repudiating the theoretical? If so, how?

37. Is scientism (the reduction of all trustable knowledge to scientific knowledge) really self-contradictory? If so, why is it so popular? If not, why not?

38. Do you think the fact that we can know some truths about the whole universe proves that we are more than the universe? Why or why not? Analyze the logic of this argument.

39. Do you think that memory, responsibility, and promise-keeping prove that there is a substantial self? Why or why not?

40. Do you think Nat's moral argument ("All moral language is meaningless ... [if] we are only very complex machines") proves that we have free will? Why or why not? How would a determinist and materialist justify living morally?

41. Do you think materialism and determinism imply or entail each other? Why or why not? How could one be true without the other?

42. Do you think Nat's argument from the meaning of "truth" refutes materialism? Why or why not?

43. Do you think Nat's self-contradiction argument against materialism (that "the thought that thought does not exist is a thought") is valid or not? Why?

44. Is epiphenomenalism closer to dualism or to materialism? Why?

4

Philosophical Anthropology: What Happens at Death?

Hardly any question can be more important to us than what happens at death. It's literally "a matter of life or death". For the one thing we can be certain of about our life in this body is that it will end in death. Whether we will survive death is as momentous as whether we survive birth. Literally, everything is at stake.

Many of the questions that religion claims to answer are also important philosophical questions, like, What is the greatest good? Does God exist? Are moral good and evil absolute or relative? What is evil? What is death? These questions are the most important because they make the greatest difference to our lives as well as our thought. But philosophy has a narrower focus and method than religion, just as modern science has a narrower focus and method than philosophy. As philosophy uses and appeals to only natural reason and common human experience, not religious faith, modern science uses and appeals only to the data of empirical observation, experiment, and mathematical measurement, not the philosophical dimensions of reason.

The question in this dialogue is a single and simple one: Do we survive death? The answer depends partly on anthropology, on what we are before death. And that, in turn, depends on metaphysics (e.g., whether reality is confined to bodies) and on epistemology (e.g., whether we can know philosophical truths that are neither empirically observable, like "hurricanes happen", nor logically necessary, like "$2 + 2 = 4$", and if so, how).

SOCRATES: Well, Nat, I see you were not so discouraged by the inconclusive ending of our last conversation that you did not return.
Here you are on our log once again to discuss what we postponed
from that dialogue on philosophical anthropology, namely, the
question about what happens at death. Is it the final end of us or
not? And what reasons are there for the yes or the no answer?

NAT: That is why I'm back at "Socrates University": to explore that
question.

SOCRATES: Since the answer to what we are after death, if anything,
depends on what we are before death—that is, anthropology—I
think we should review the options we came up with to the question of anthropology first. Agreed?

NAT: Yes.

SOCRATES: We distinguished three anthropologies: materialism (that
we are nothing but matter), immaterialism (that we are nothing
but mind or spirit or soul), and dualism (that we are both). And
within dualism, we further distinguished three views: epiphenomenalism, which says that the mind is only a byproduct and effect
of matter, not vice versa; Aristotelian hylomorphism, which says
we are single substances with material and immaterial dimensions,
matter and form, body and soul; and Cartesian dualism, which says
we are two substances, matter and mind.

We found arguments both for and against each of these anthropologies. But if either simple materialism or epiphenomenalism is
true, that settles the question of life after death in the negative,
because we know that our bodies do not survive, and if spirits
either do not exist or are only the effects of bodies, they cannot
survive either. And if immaterialism is true, the question is also
settled, it seems, since if bodies are unreal, or are merely disguises
of minds or spirits, or their dreams or ideas, then bodily death is
also unreal, and what is unreal cannot die. So today's discussion
will assume some dualism of body and mind, or body and soul,
whether Cartesian or Aristotelian, and then ask whether the mental or spiritual or immaterial part of us is mortal or not, whether
the soul dies when the body dies. We have only one very specific
issue to focus on, and there are only two possible answers to it: yes
or no. That should make today's discussion much easier to follow
than the last one.

NAT: When you philosophized back in ancient Athens, Socrates, you clearly believed that the correct answer was yes. So if we are going to dialogue about that question today, I think you should try to defend the position you held then and I should try to oppose it. If you are the real Socrates, you probably have not changed your mind about that since you are still here, more than two thousand years after you were killed in Athens. I, on the other hand, am somewhat uncertain and, you might say, agnostic about it.

SOCRATES: Reducing the issue to two sides like that is perhaps too simple to do justice to the thoughts of either one of us, and to the personal doubts we may each have. But it would make things much clearer for our readers, and it is they whom we are here for. So let's do it.

NAT: Then please try to prove life after death to me.

SOCRATES: Not before I define some terms. Most importantly, the term "prove".

Not all proofs are scientific proofs, in the modern sense of "science", and that makes our search for philosophical proofs possible, for I doubt whether there are any *scientific* proofs of life after death.

And among philosophical proofs, there are many kinds, and they differ in both clarity and certainty.

Inductive arguments and arguments from analogy are never certain, only probable, yet they are common and they do count as clues, at least.

Proofs from cause to effect, as in geometry, are stronger than proofs from effect to cause, as in physics. But that seems impossible for us here, since we are not the ones who designed and caused our lives.

Finally, arguments from authority are weaker than arguments from reason, but they are still some kind of argument, with some kind of at least probable weight, if the authority is relevant and reasonable.

So I would like to start with that one, the weakest argument but probably the most popular: the argument from the authority of the majority. That the vast majority of all individuals and cultures that have ever lived have believed in some kind of life after death. That is simply an empirical fact.

NAT: Agreed. But how is that an argument? "You don't tell truth by counting noses."

SOCRATES: True. To make it at least a probable argument, we must add a principle of probability: everything else being equal, the more people of all kinds believe a given idea, the more likely it is that that idea is true. Not certain, but likely. If less than 1 percent of baseball experts believe that the worst team in baseball this year will suddenly become the best team next year, and over 99 percent believe that they won't, that makes this nearly miraculous event very unlikely or improbable. Would you accept that principle of probability?

NAT: Well, yes, but surely you do not call that a proof?

SOCRATES: No, but it is an argument. The conclusion logically follows from the premises, but one of the premises is weakened to a mere probability, and therefore so is the conclusion. So it is only a probable argument, but it is an argument, a process of reasoning that leads the mind reasonably toward a conclusion.

NAT: I suppose you could stretch the term "reason" that much. But it is far from satisfactory and not a *proof* at all. It sounds more medieval than modern.

SOCRATES: Actually, there was a medieval cliché that stated that "the argument from (merely human) authority is the weakest of all arguments." I think your modern ideologues, both of the Left and of the Right, are much more authoritarian than the medievals were, who always loved to argue philosophically about the things you moderns love to proclaim so dogmatically.

NAT: So we agree, then, that the argument from authority is the weakest argument.

SOCRATES: Yes. But it has at least *some* force, doesn't it?

NAT: Yes. But there are some falsehoods that everyone, or nearly everyone, believes at some time, or even most of the time, for instance, that "I'm right and you're wrong."

SOCRATES: Agreed.

NAT: So arguments from authority can never prove anything with certainty.

SOCRATES: Except in one case: if the authority was infallible.

NAT: But even then you would have to have a certain proof that that authority was infallible before you could be certain of the idea you want to prove. And that is something which you could never have.

SOCRATES: Are you infallibly certain of that?

NAT: Well, no ... I must admit that I have to be skeptical of my skepticism.

SOCRATES: And to make such an argument stronger, if the authority were qualitative as well as quantitative, that is, if those in the majority were in other respects wiser and more trustable than most people, that would raise the likelihood of the idea they believed, would it not?

NAT: Yes. But never to the point of certainty.

SOCRATES: Correct. That is probably all I can claim for this argument.

NAT: Are you being ironic with the word "probably"?

SOCRATES: Probably.

NAT: Are you joking?

SOCRATES: Yes, but I think the argument from authority persuades more people than any other if the authority is weighty. For instance, a Christian, who trusts the authority of Christ, or a Muslim, who trusts the authority of the Koran, would argue that if Christ, or the Koran, were simply wrong about life after death, the entire religious system would collapse.

NAT: Just because there is no life after death?

SOCRATES: No, because the supreme, divine, infallible authority is now shown to be either a liar or a fool, either a deceiver or deceived. And they would argue that there are stronger arguments for the religious system as a whole than for this one idea that is part of it.

NAT: But that does not make it a rational proof, only a likelihood whose degree of probability depends on faith in the authority that teaches it.

SOCRATES: That's quite right.

NAT: So what is it doing here in a *philosophy* book?

SOCRATES: It is here because it is the reason most people who believe in life after death believe it. The people who read this book are not only philosophers; they are people with religious or antireligious dimensions too, and I think this argument would be persuasive to them.

NAT: Even though it's not strictly rational proof?

SOCRATES: Yes. Do you think it's reasonable to confine yourself to only what is strictly rational? I don't. That's why I often ended my dialogues back in Athens with religious myths, clues, parables, allegories, sacred stories, or symbols, none of which claimed certainty or proof.

NAT: All right. So now let's move to the arguments based on reason alone.

SOCRATES: I think I should here also begin with the weakest argument.

NAT: And what is that?

SOCRATES: Would you not agree that the weakest argument is the one with the weakest or least relevant premise?

NAT: Yes, all other things being equal.

SOCRATES: So where would we get the weakest premise? We can think about things below us, that is, less than ourselves in perfection, or about things within us, or about things above us, things greater and more perfect than ourselves.

NAT: But the thing above us would be God, and that would make arguments from above into religious arguments based on faith rather than philosophical arguments based on reason alone.

SOCRATES: Yes, unless we also had reliable arguments for the existence of God or whatever else is above us. Which we do not have time to go into today. So there remain the other two sources of data, then. And the weakest would be things below us, for the observation of things below us cannot tell us much about ourselves. But perhaps they, too, can give us clues, especially in the form of analogies.

NAT: Clues are not arguments, much less proofs. I'm getting impatient for proofs, but I shall listen to your "clues" from the world below us. What are they?

SOCRATES: One of them is the physical law of the conservation of energy. Energy may be transformed but not either created or destroyed. The amount of energy in a closed system is always conserved. And if the universe is a closed system, then this clue works as a relevant clue, while if it is *not* a closed system, that means it is open to supernatural forces, which would make immortality even more likely.

NAT: I don't understand. How is that principle of physics a clue to the soul's immortality?

SOCRATES: If even matter and energy (which are convertible) cannot be simply destroyed, is it not more likely that spirit cannot be destroyed?

NAT: That assumes that spirit is more than matter, of course.

SOCRATES: Yes.

NAT: But even if it cannot be destroyed, it can be transformed.

SOCRATES: Yes.

NAT: And perhaps it can be transformed from its present state of being individuated in human persons into another state, where individuality and personality do not survive, but simply return to a kind of universal pool of spirit as our individual bodies return to the earth—*if* that notion of an impersonal pool of persons is thinkable rather than self-contradictory: personhood without individuality, without "I-ness". But even if it is thinkable, that's cold comfort, and not what most people mean by life after death.

SOCRATES: Perhaps. I warned you that this was the weakest of arguments. But it at least gives you a reason for believing that spirit as such cannot be annihilated, for even matter and material energy cannot. It is an "a fortiori" argument, an "all the more" or "all the stronger" argument.

NAT: I don't see that as a strong clue at all.

SOCRATES: I admit that "clue" arguments like this one depend on intuition and insight as much as on logical reasoning. Well, let me give you what I think is a better clue from the world below us. It is about the origin of the word "soul".

NAT: How can a word origin prove life after death?

SOCRATES: I did not say "prove". I said it was only a clue.

NAT: All right, what is it?

SOCRATES: Imagine a primitive, preliterate farmer plowing with two oxen. One suddenly drops dead. The farmer looks carefully at the two oxen, one alive and one dead. (Primitives usually observe nature more carefully than literate people do.) He sees the great difference between them: one moves and the other does not. He needs a name for the difference. He calls one "alive" and the other "dead". The basic meaning of "soul" is "source of life". So what is this "life" or "soul"? Can he see it? He examines all the body parts. They are identical. Dead Ox lacks no part, not a hair. Yet something is obviously lacking, something that makes the body move in Live Ox but not in Dead Ox. But that thing is not visible and tangible and material. So the "soul" must exist, for it distinguishes Live Ox from Dead Ox, but it is not a body part, because no body part is missing in Dead Ox. Therefore, the soul, or the source of life, is not a body.

NAT: But this says nothing about life after death, especially for man. Do you think primitive man believes that everything that lives on earth goes to Heaven and lives again? Even plants?

SOCRATES: No, not necessarily. And this observation does not even prove life after death for Dead Ox. But it shows that *something* exists that is not material, even in animals, and therefore there is a *possibility* that that something, which leaves the body when the body dies, does not itself die when the body dies, since this something is evidently not made of any visible, material stuff. The argument does not prove the actuality of life after death, only the possibility.

NAT: But even if the soul does not die when the body dies (which I do not grant, especially with animals), that soul may still die in other ways.

SOCRATES: Well, Plato had an argument in the *Republic* about that. The diseases that harm the soul do not kill it, before death; and we have no reason to think that there are forces after death that kill souls. Therefore, nothing can kill souls. But I will explore that argument later. This argument leaves room for doubt, but also room for belief.

NAT: Why bother with such imperfect arguments?

SOCRATES: Because their cumulative force adds to their probability, like strands to a rope. If there are a hundred strands to the rope, each of them weak when alone, when you tie the strands together, how much pulling power do you get?

NAT: I suppose a hundred times as much as any one strand.

SOCRATES: Wrong. It is far more than that. It is enough to pull a large boat. The cumulative value of clues that all point, however weakly, in the same direction increases geometrically, not arithmetically.

NAT: All right, but that is only an analogy, not an argument.

SOCRATES: It *is* an argument: an argument from probability.

And here is another weak argument from the physical world. If you saw real magic—not just stage magic, not just an optical illusion, but real magic, mind moving matter directly, like levitation, would you not conclude at least that simple materialism had been disproved and that that opened up the *likelihood* that spiritual souls exist, which were invulnerable to physical death?

NAT: I suppose so, but I have never seen any such magic.

SOCRATES: Then I shall show you an example of it right now. I shall levitate in front of your eyes, and you will not say it is an optical trick.

NAT: Then I will probably say it is a verbal trick. It depends on how you define levitation.

SOCRATES: Then I will let *you* define it.

NAT: OK, levitation is forcing the body to defy gravity and rise into the air simply by thinking it and willing it, not by hoists or lifts or any other physical aid from outside it.

SOCRATES: Good. I shall now levitate. (*Socrates gets off the log, stands up, and leaps high in the air for a second.*) See? I fulfilled your definition.

NAT: That you did!

SOCRATES: See? There is indeed the reality of magic, of mind over matter, of soul over body. I warrant you that no mere body, no corpse, has ever levitated, for nothing merely physical can defy the laws of physics.

NAT: That's not an argument; that's a joke.

SOCRATES: No, it is not. It shows the existence of something that is not merely physical and thus can defy physical laws. If it can defy gravity, it may defy death.

NAT: That's not magic. That's not levitation; that's just leaping. You didn't stay up.

SOCRATES: True. But it fulfilled your definition of magic.

NAT: But you can't make any other bodies defy gravity, only your own.

SOCRATES: Wrong again. Show me an object and I will move it by the power of thought.

NAT: All right. Here I am, a body on the other side of this log. Make me levitate against my will.

SOCRATES: A little harder than the first but still doable. Watch. (*Socrates gets up and lifts Nat into the air, then sets him down.*) I admit that I could not do that without the use of my magic wand, namely, my two arms. But magicians often use magic wands. They are mediators. They transfer the power of my spiritual mind and will, which are in my body somehow, into your physical body.

NAT: That's not miraculous. That's ordinary.

SOCRATES: I did not say it was miraculous, only that it was magic. Magic is extraordinarily ordinary.

NAT: For whatever reason, I do not think that "argument" will convince an unbeliever in life after death to become a believer.

SOCRATES: Nor do I. Yet, it shows *something*, and that something may be evidence for the reality of spirit and the *possibility* of immortality, though well disguised by the veil of familiarity.

NAT: So far you have no proofs at all. What about arguments from within ourselves rather than from the physical world outside us? They would seem to be stronger.

SOCRATES: They are. For instance, the one Plato gives us at the end of the *Republic*.

NAT: I thought that book was about politics. What's the connection with life after death?

SOCRATES: In this long and complex book, Plato is trying to demonstrate, above all, as his final conclusion, that justice is always more profitable than injustice for every individual soul, as well as for states; and to do that, he first shows that it is profitable for states. And at the end, after he has proved that justice is profitable in this life, as a kind of postscript he tries to show that justice is even more profitable after death, and so he has to show that there is life after death.

NAT: How does he do that?

SOCRATES: First, he defines evil as that which corrupts or destroys something good.

NAT: That sounds like a good definition to me.

SOCRATES: Then he shows that each evil is relative to a good, to the particular good it corrupts or destroys. For instance, ophthalmia for the eye, mildew for corn, rust for iron. He calls that intrinsic evil or essential evil or natural evil, as distinct from extrinsic or accidental evil.

NAT: Seems right so far.

SOCRATES: So if a thing is not destroyed by its own intrinsic, natural evil, it can't be destroyed by the evil of anything else. Rust does not kill corn, nor does mildew kill iron. Ophthalmia does not destroy hearing, nor does deafness destroy sight.

NAT: So far, so good. Go on.

SOCRATES: So if there were something whose essential and intrinsic evils can only corrupt it but cannot destroy it, so that that thing is indestructible by its intrinsic and essential evils, and if it cannot be destroyed by the evils of anything else, and if it cannot be destroyed by the good, since the good is not that which destroys good, then those three premises seem to prove that there is nothing that can destroy it.

NAT: And that thing is the soul?

SOCRATES: Yes. For the soul has its own evils, namely, folly and vice, intellectual evil and moral evil, lack of wisdom and lack of virtue. But no matter how much these vices corrupt souls, they do not destroy them.

In other words, there are only three ways in which anything, including souls, can be destroyed: by its own natural evil, or by the evil of something else, or by its good. We observe that the first does not happen, and we understand that the other two cannot, in principle, happen.

NAT: What a roundabout argument!

SOCRATES: Yes. In that way it is like Aquinas' argument that observing animals proves that human happiness cannot consist in the goods of the body because there is always some animal whose body is better than ours in some way, but our happiness is greater than theirs. A surprising argument. But the question is simply whether it is valid. Is there an ambiguous term, a false premise, or a logical fallacy?

NAT: I don't see one immediately, but I'll bet I could find one if I took the time. Next argument, please!

SOCRATES: There is the argument from the soul's simplicity. Souls do not have different parts, though they have many different powers. And what has no parts cannot be destroyed by pulling it apart. So if souls are destroyed, they must be destroyed in a different way than bodies are, for when bodies die, they fall apart. In fact, the whole self falls apart into two parts, the body and its soul, or its life. And then the body's functional systems fall apart: breathing and blood circulation and digestion and so forth. And then the actual organs and their cells and even their molecules fall apart. But that cannot be how souls die, if they do die.

NAT: But this argument does not prove that souls do not die, only that they do not die in the way that bodies die.

SOCRATES: Correct. But what other ways could there be, except annihilation? But nothing is simply annihilated in the universe.

NAT: Well, if souls are not parts of the physical universe to begin with, they are not subject to the laws of the physical universe like that law against annihilation.

SOCRATES: But if souls are not bodies or parts of the physical universe, they do not die when bodies in the universe die. Or even when the universe as a whole dies.

NAT: I see. That follows.

SOCRATES: So what other ways of dying could there be for souls?

NAT: Perhaps it is the body that pulls itself away from the soul rather than the soul that pulls itself away from the body at death. Perhaps the body is like the atmosphere, and the soul is like the breath, and when the atmosphere leaves, the breath dies. Perhaps souls need bodies as food, so to speak.

SOCRATES: But if the soul is the source of life, it is the other way round: the body needs the soul as the source of its life rather than vice versa.

NAT: Perhaps it works both ways. A synergy. A mutual dependence.

SOCRATES: I do not think that is possible for the very existence itself of anything. How can A depend on B for its existence at the same time as B depends on A for its existence? How could the art create the artist at the same time as the artist creates the art?

NAT: But that is exactly what happens in art. You are not an artist until the art appears.

SOCRATES: But that is a case of two different kinds of causality: the art *defines* the artist; it is his "formal cause". But the artist *creates* the art: he is its "efficient cause", its cause of the art's existence. Here we are talking about efficient cause only. No two things can possibly be the efficient cause of each other. If the effect depends on the cause, the cause is prior. But nothing can be prior to itself.

NAT: This is becoming too abstract and metaphysical for me. At any rate it does not mollify my doubt. Try another argument.

SOCRATES: How about this one? If we observe a power of the soul that cannot possibly come from the body, that would prove that the soul is not a body or part of a body or dependent on the body or on any part of the body, or a function of the body, would it not?

NAT: I think so.

SOCRATES: And that would indicate that it is not subject to the laws of the body.

NAT: Apparently so.

SOCRATES: Including the law of mortality, that whatever is born must die.

NAT: Unless that law is not only a law of bodies but also of souls. As Buddha said in the *Diamond Sutra*, "Whatever has a beginning, has an end."

SOCRATES: But there is no proof that there is any such universal law. The fact that it is true for bodies does not mean it is true for souls too.

NAT: What power of the soul are you thinking of in this argument?

SOCRATES: There are many. One of them is the power to objectify the body, to know the body as an object. No mere body can do that. To objectify X, I must be more than X.

NAT: Give me examples.

SOCRATES: The projecting machine in a movie theater that projects images onto the screen cannot be one of the images on the screen.

NAT: Give me a more mental or spiritual example.

SOCRATES: I can remember and objectify my past only because I am more than my past. My past is dead; my present is alive.

NAT: All right, the principle seems to be true universally. So because our souls can objectify our bodies, they must be more than our bodies, so they need not succumb to the law of all bodily things, including the law that whatever has a beginning must have an ending. Is that the argument?

SOCRATES: Yes.

NAT: But animals can objectify their bodies too. They know their bodies very well. But they are not immortal.

SOCRATES: They can know their bodies only because they have souls: animal souls even though not rational souls. Rocks can't do that.

NAT: But this argument is only going to prove that we, like animals, have souls—not that our souls are immortal.

SOCRATES: So far, yes. But we can bring the argument up a step by introducing self-consciousness, the ability to objectify not just our bodies but also our souls. We can be aware of our souls, think about our souls, judge our souls, and so forth.

NAT: Can't animals do that too?

SOCRATES: No. They can objectify their bodies but not their souls. They are conscious of the world and of one another but not of themselves as subjects.

NAT: How do you know that?

SOCRATES: Well, if they had self-consciousness as we do, they are very good at hiding it.

NAT: What evidence is there that we have it and they do not?

SOCRATES: Many distinctively human experiences, such as guilt. Animals cannot experience guilt, only shame.

NAT: How do we know that guilt is not just a kind of shame? Why are the two different in essence? They are both negative feelings.

SOCRATES: But shame is only social, while guilt is individual and private. In guilt I feel bad because I judge myself; in shame I feel bad only because I feel judged by others. You see, it is self-consciousness that makes the difference.

NAT: Wait. There is a logical problem here. Self-consciousness is a form of consciousness, right?

SOCRATES: Of course.

NAT: And in all forms of consciousness, there is a subject that knows and an object that is known, right?

SOCRATES: Right.

NAT: And the knower must always somehow be more than the thing known, other than the thing known. The knowing subject must transcend the known object.

SOCRATES: Yes.

NAT: For instance, the mind knows the senses, but the senses cannot sense the mind. The intellect understands the emotions, but the emotions do not know or even feel the intellect. And humans can understand animals in ways that animals cannot understand humans. And if there is a God, God could know me perfectly, but I could not know Him perfectly.

SOCRATES: Yes. That seems to be a universal principle.

NAT: Then how is self-consciousness possible? In self-consciousness, I know myself and thus transcend myself. Not only do I transcend my world and my body by the power of my mind, but I also transcend my mind and my soul, my very self. How can my self be more than my self? How can X be more than X?

SOCRATES: Perhaps the self is not simply the soul. After all, I call it "my" soul just as I call my body "my" body.

NAT: What is this "I"?

SOCRATES: Perhaps it is the subject that is not objectifiable.

NAT: But we are objectifying it right now in questioning it!

SOCRATES: But we cannot define it, as we can define body, soul, mind, and everything else in us, but not the "I" that "has" them all.

NAT: That is indeed mysterious. But we must be careful to explain the unclear by the clear, not vice versa. And it is very clear that it is logically impossible for X to be more than X, isn't it?

SOCRATES: Yes. But we do have self-transcending experiences, not only out-of-body experiences, but even out-of-mind experiences. Yet it is the mind that has those experiences. I see myself, I know myself, I even judge myself. But the judge has to be more than, and other than, the judged. How can I be more than myself?

Here is an astounding thing that we experience right now, in this life, that seems even more astounding than the existence of an afterlife. We seem to transcend the law of non-contradiction. Of course that is impossible; it is only a seeming. But it happens. We do have in us something that seems to be more than the self-that-we-can-know.

NAT: I thought you were a rational philosopher, Socrates, not a mystic!

SOCRATES: Why not be both, and be fully human?

NAT: So what is the argument now? How does the premise of self-consciousness logically prove the conclusion of life after death?

SOCRATES: It is not yet fully clear. Shall we try to formulate it more logically?

NAT: I fear it will take much time and effort. I would prefer to survey your other arguments first, and perhaps come back to this one when we have more time.

SOCRATES: As you please. But we have as much time as we want to have here on this log. You simply do not *want* to think about this formidable mental challenge now. For it focuses on the most mysterious word in our language, the word "I".

NAT: I admit it: I am lazy.

SOCRATES: I hope some of those who read this dialogue of ours are not as lazy as you are so that they try to formulate this argument more logically and explicitly. You know, courage is an intellectual virtue as well as a moral virtue: not to give up on the search for truth or the exploration of any argument, which is a road to truth.

NAT: I have not given up that fight, just postponed it. Tomorrow, perhaps.

SOCRATES: "Tomorrow, and tomorrow, and tomorrow ..."

NAT: Do you have another argument, whose premise is less mysterious?

SOCRATES: Yes. The premise of this further argument of mine is knowable by simple introspection: that our mind transcends our imagination—that we can know abstract, eternal, necessary, and unchangeable truths like $2 + 2 = 4$, or that we can know the measurable and definable difference between a figure with 104 sides and a figure with 103 sides even though we cannot imagine that difference with our inner senses.

NAT: How does that prove that we survive death? There seems to be a very long distance between that premise and that conclusion.

SOCRATES: The thinking we do abstractly is not dependent on the body and its sense experiences, right? The senses do not do abstract thinking, only concrete thinking. They see "red beet", but the mind abstracts the redness from the beet and conceives the process of making white things red. That is the origin of both art and technology, which animals cannot do, as we can. We see two rabbits and two rabbits and know they are four rabbits, but we also formulate the general principle that $2 + 2 = 4$ and thus we do mathematics. We need little or no sense experience for that. That is why there are child prodigies who can be great mathematicians but not great psychologists or great historians: because abstract thinking does not depend on experience. Does this all not seem evident to you?

NAT: I think so, but I do not see how this proves what will happen after death. What is the connection?

SOCRATES: The connection is that if this act of abstract thinking is independent of the body, it is independent of the body's limitations such as its mortality.

NAT: Oh, I think I see two problems with that argument.

SOCRATES: What are they?

NAT: First of all, abstract thinking is not totally independent of the body. We know by observation that if the brain is not working, we cannot do this abstract thinking, and the brain is part of the body. So even if this abstract thinking is not done by senses, it depends on the body's brain. A blow to the brain stops it.

SOCRATES: That is true. But it is possible that the mind that does abstract thinking is dependent on the brain only as long as it is in the body but not after it leaves the body in death.

NAT: You can't prove that there is such a state. You can only assume it, and that is begging the question, assuming the very thing you claim to be proving: that souls exist after death.

SOCRATES: I don't claim to prove that it is real. I just need to show that it is *possible*, that it does not contradict itself or any other truth we know.

NAT: So this argument of yours proves only the *possibility* of life after death, not its actual reality.

SOCRATES: Yes. It is quite possible that the mind is like a diver who cannot survive or move when he is far under the sea without a diving suit, but who can survive and move without a diving suit quite easily when he is not far under the sea. The fact that he needs a diving suit when he is far under the sea does not prove that he needs it in shallow water or on land.

NAT: So in this little analogy of yours, the diving suit is the brain, and the diver is the mind, and the sea is the body.

SOCRATES: Yes.

NAT: But we have no experience of being on land, of not being in the sea of bodies.

SOCRATES: Perhaps we do. Have you never heard of out-of-body experiences?

NAT: They may be illusions.

SOCRATES: But even if they are illusions, that does not prove that the land does not exist or that we will not someday live there. It is possible, is it not?

NAT: Yes.

SOCRATES: And therefore it cannot be ruled out as impossible, as your argument tries to do, your argument whose true premise is that in this life the mind depends on the brain for even its abstract thinking, but which then proceeds to the conclusion, which does not necessarily follow, that the mind must be equally dependent on the brain when it is outside the body.

And there are also some clues that even in this life the mind sometimes operates without the body, when the body and brain are dead.

Thus, even your premise is not true. There are well-documented cases of so-called near-death experiences or out-of-body experiences, when patients on an operating table were brain-dead for a considerable time, sometimes as much as twenty minutes, when the brain was not working at all. When they came back into their bodies, they reported accurately what the doctors and nurses had said while they were brain-dead. There is a whole institute at two major universities, the University of Connecticut and the University of Virginia, devoted to empirical, scientific studies of such cases. In these cases it is not just abstract thinking but even awareness of physical things that seems to survive the total loss of brain activity.

NAT: That's just occasional anecdotal evidence from a few exceptional cases.

SOCRATES: No, it's an empirical, scientific study of thousands of cases. In fact, there are literally millions of cases in your country alone where people claim to have had out-of-body experiences.

NAT: But they do not prove life after death.

SOCRATES: Why not?

NAT: Because all these patients, in order to report what they saw or heard when they were apparently brain-dead, were resuscitated. But if they were resuscitated, they were not dead, because death is irreversible. So by definition, this is not data from some other world, or from the land of the dead. They were not really dead if their life continued.

SOCRATES: Perhaps their experiences refute the assumption that death is irreversible. We can't just assume a definition to be correct and then dismiss the evidence that seems to disprove the definition. If we are open-minded to all the evidence, we must revise our definitions in the face of new evidence.

NAT: This argument seems to depend on the definition of a definition.

SOCRATES: No, it depends on empirical evidence. These people were thinking even when their brain was not working. That seems to prove that thinking is not wholly dependent on the brain.

NAT: Well, let's look at my second objection to your argument for the mind's survival of the death of the body. Your premise is our power to do abstract thinking with the mind. But even if I grant that premise, and even if that shows that the mind is independent of the body, and even if that independence is total, as in Descartes' dualism, and even if the mind is free from all the physical laws that pertain to the body alone, that does not necessarily mean that it is free from the laws that are common to both mind and body, such as the law of causality. And one of those common laws may still be that whatever has a beginning must have an ending. That may well be a law of everything in the universe. It is certainly a law of all physical things, even long-lived things like galaxies. You have not proved that it is not also a law of all spiritual things, all minds.

SOCRATES: Nor have you proved that it is. I am trying only to open doors, to open possibilities, not close them. I do not claim that these out-of-body experiences are proofs. But they are certainly relevant data, and the most obvious explanation of the data is that the soul is in fact still acting even when the body is not.

But let us move to still another argument, which is quite metaphysical. Would you agree that there are only two ways in which anything can either come into existence or go out of existence: as a whole or part by part?

NAT: Yes.

SOCRATES: And man dies because his soul and body are parts that come apart?

NAT: Yes.

SOCRATES: And the body dies because it decomposes into its parts?

NAT: Yes.

SOCRATES: But the soul has no parts. It has many faculties or powers and many activities, but it does not have many parts. You can't have half a soul. You lose a part of your body when you get a haircut, but not part of your soul. Isn't that true?

NAT: Yes.

SOCRATES: So the soul cannot die by decomposition. So the only way it could die is by being annihilated as a whole.

NAT: The logic would lead us to that conclusion, yes.

SOCRATES: Do we ever see anything in the universe either created or annihilated as a whole, totally, all at once?

NAT: No.

SOCRATES: Then how could a soul die?

NAT: By gradual diminishment as a whole. We see things diminish, like light. Why could the soul's life not diminish like a beam of light and finally go out entirely?

SOCRATES: Because light is not a whole. It is spread out in space and therefore has parts, and the parts can come apart, and the more they do, the more photons leave the light beam, the less light there is. But the soul cannot diminish in that way because it is not spread out in space and does not have parts.

NAT: Hmm ... I think that argument is inconclusive because light is not only made of discontinuous particles but also is a continuous wave.

SOCRATES: I think it is your analogy with light that is inconclusive, not my original argument. Even a wave, if it is not made of particles, is spread out in space, unlike a mind or a thought.

And here is another abstract and metaphysical argument from Plato's *Phaedo*. I have doubts about it, but it deserves at least a look. The "soul" means first of all the source of life for the body, that which gives life to the body, right?

NAT: Yes.

SOCRATES: And the principle of causality is universal, is it not? Nothing can give what it does not have.

NAT: Right.

SOCRATES: So for the soul to give the body life, it must have life by its very nature. And what has life by its very nature cannot lose it because nothing can lose its essential nature. Humans can lose health or wisdom or virtue or even an organ, but humans cannot lose humanity, any more than triangles can lose triangularity.

NAT: Yes ... no, wait. Perhaps the soul is not life by its very nature. Perhaps it, too, receives life from a higher source—perhaps God—before it passes life on to its body. And if God created it, God could also annihilate it, even though no force in nature could either literally create or annihilate.

SOCRATES: In that case, no force in nature at least could kill it, either by decomposition or by annihilation, and it would not die when its body died, since the body's life is only the effect of the soul rather than its cause. But it could die only when God, or whatever is the soul's own cause, ceased to give it life.

NAT: Yes. But that cause, whether it be God or anything else, cannot be predicted or guaranteed to give it life. So this is an inconclusive argument that depends on something like faith in God to love it and therefore give it life.

SOCRATES: Even so, in the natural order the argument seems to show that it does not die because its body dies.

NAT: No, it doesn't. Because that argument proves too much. Since animals and even plants have souls, though not with the power of abstract or rational thinking, this argument proves that even their souls are immortal.

SOCRATES: That is true. So the argument must begin not with souls in general but with specifically human souls. But if the same soul both reasons and gives life to the body, that is, if we do not have two souls, then I think we can reformulate the argument as Plato does. Let's see ... No, I see you nodding off again. When the hard work begins, you drift away. Let us hope that some of the readers of this dialogue are less lazy than you are. But I have one more argument, which I think will be the most interesting of all to you.

NAT: Why?

SOCRATES: Because it is not about the mind but about the heart and love. It is the argument from the premise that we observe in ourselves a natural desire for immortality, and, much more, for a totally happy immortality, some kind of Heaven, even though we cannot define it positively or imagine it.

NAT: That sounds very suspicious to me. How can you logically prove that a thing exists just because we desire it? Our desires do not change the nature of reality. No matter how much we love life and hate death, that has no power at all to change the fact that we die.

SOCRATES: Of course it doesn't. But that's not my argument.

NAT: What is it, then?

SOCRATES: We observe within ourselves many desires, do we not?

NAT: Yes, of course.

SOCRATES: And some of them are universal, that is, found in all of us, because they come from our very nature, while others are not universal because they come from things like advertisements or quirks of our appetites or experiences that are found in only some of us, not all of us. Those desires are innumerable, but our universal and natural desires are few.

NAT: What are some of these universal desires?

SOCRATES: Everyone desires to know rather than to be ignorant, do they not?

NAT: Yes, though some desire to lie and keep others in ignorance, and some do not.

SOCRATES: And would you not also say that all desire to receive both love and justice, even though some of us do not desire to give it to others?

NAT: Yes.

SOCRATES: And all desire to see beauty rather than ugliness.

NAT: Yes.

SOCRATES: And to have friends instead of loneliness.

NAT: Yes.

SOCRATES: And to have sexual pleasure and food and drink and sleep.

NAT: Of course.

SOCRATES: So we could classify desires into those that are universal because they are natural and those that are not universal because they are accidental.

NAT: Yes.

SOCRATES: And every desire has an object, does it not? We can't just "desire"; we always desire something.

NAT: Yes.

SOCRATES: Now, when we look at the objects of the accidental desires, we find that some of them exist, like expensive cars or political power or vacations by the sea, and some of them do not, like flying through the air like Superman or going to the Land of Oz.

NAT: Right. That's why the mere fact that we desire something does not prove it exists.

SOCRATES: But all the objects of our universal and natural desires do exist! Truth and justice and love and beauty and friendship and sex and food and drink and sleep.

NAT: Yes, they do.

SOCRATES: And what is the reason for the difference? Why do all the objects of the universal desires exist, but only some of the objects of the particular desires?

NAT: Because the universal desires come from our common nature, while the other desires do not, I suppose.

SOCRATES: Correct. And do we ever lose our essential universal nature?

NAT: No.

SOCRATES: Why not?

NAT: Because that would be a self-contradiction: a man who is not a man.

SOCRATES: Then if all our natural desires correspond to real objects, and the desire for immortality is a natural desire, it must correspond to a real object.

NAT: That does not prove everyone will get immortality, any more than the natural hunger for food means everyone will get food. Some starve.

SOCRATES: True. The argument only proves that it exists, not that you will get it.

NAT: That's cold comfort.

SOCRATES: But reflect on this: if no one gets it, the desire is meaningless. Nature did not give us any desires that could not ever be satisfied. If we found a race of living rational beings on another planet who did not live by eating food, they would not have any desire for food. If there were a race all of whom were females with no males, they would have no sexual desire toward males because males would not exist. Natural hungers and natural foods that satisfy those hungers are reciprocal and relative to each other.

NAT: True. But does that prove our souls live on after the body dies?

SOCRATES: It certainly seems to strongly point in that direction. If this natural desire did not correspond to any real object, that would disprove an otherwise universal law of nature.

NAT: But that is not a deductive argument, but one that depends on an induction, where you reason from the premise that every other natural desire corresponds to a real object to the conclusion that all of them do, and therefore this natural desire (the desire for immortality) also corresponds to a real object. It is not an argument from "all" to "some" but from "some" to all. It is inductive. So it is only probable.

SOCRATES: But even so, it is at least extremely probable. I think that is enough to satisfy most people's rational demands.

NAT: Oh, I think most people are not that dependent on reason and logic. I think most people believe in immortality not by reason but by faith, if they trust that their religion is not a human invention but a divine revelation.

SOCRATES: Well, that *is* a deductive argument, then, if you begin with a God who never errs and conclude that this teaching is not in error either. And that gives you a premise that is as strong as possible, if only you grant the truth of that premise. Even our best reasonings may err, but if there is a God who never errs, either by being deceived or by deceiving, and if he promised us life after death, as many believe, then we have a secure foundation for believing in the soul's immortality.

NAT: But that is not philosophy but religion. It depends not on reason alone but on a faith premise. So I think you have not quite yet proved immortality beyond doubt by reason alone. Of course, for anyone who believes the largest religion in the world, the supreme proof of life after death is not a philosophical argument but a historical event: the Resurrection of Jesus. The arguments for that, in turn, can perhaps be very probable, but, as with all historical events, not certain. So we still do not have a certain proof of immortality.

SOCRATES: But we have a reasonable "wager", as Pascal would put it, do we not? Especially considering what is at stake?

NAT: I will admit that, if you admit it is not a certain proof.

SOCRATES: Then although we began as opponents, playing opposing parts, we come to an agreement in the end.

Questions for Discussion or Personal Essays

1. Do you think there is a more important question than what happens to us when we die? If so, what is it and why is it more important?

2. Can we separate the religious, or faith-based, and the strictly rational aspects of the question of what happens to us when we die? If not, why not? If so, how?

3. Socrates takes for granted that what we are after death, if anything, depends on what we are before death. Do you agree that this is necessarily so or not? Why?

4. Is there any way a materialist or an epiphenomenalist could believe in life after death? If so, how?

5. Do you disagree with any one of Socrates' hierarchy of probable arguments?

6. How many and what sort of the things you believe rather than know with certainty do you think are based on authority?

7. What is the proper meaning of "authority"?

8. What other conclusions besides life after death do you think might be reasonably believed because of an argument from authority rather than any stronger kind of argument?

9. Were you surprised by Socrates' quotation of the medieval cliché that the argument from authority was the weakest of all arguments? Why or why not?

10. Which of the following two arguments do you think is stronger: (1) an argument based on authority when the authority is infallible but with only probable arguments for the premise of the infallibility of that authority, or (2) one based on reason alone, not authority, but with only probable arguments for its premise? Why?

11. Do you see arguments from the natural world below us as irrelevant, moderately helpful, or very helpful in concluding anything about the human soul? If, as Socrates claims, they are "clues", how do you evaluate the strength of clues? If clues are apprehended by intuition, how do you judge intuitions?

12. How can the "Primitive Farmer's Dead Ox" argument be relevant to the human soul and its possible immortality?

13. Evaluate Plato's argument in the *Republic* for immortality. (It is mentioned twice.)

14. If the many strands of separate arguments (say, twenty), converging together, add greatly (far more than twenty times) to the strength of their conclusion, as in a rope that pulls a boat, as Socrates claims, why can't this count for the Buddhist and Humean notion that the so-called self is only the illusion of many "strands" of consciousness or experience that is constructed by millions of acts of experience? What is the relation between quantity and quality here? How and when, if ever, can a sufficient increase in quantity become a new quality? Find analogies or examples or applications of the principle about the relation between quantity and quality elsewhere.

15. Is Socrates' labeling his "levitation" (leaping) and his "magic wand" (lifting) as "magic" a mere joke? If it's an argument, what does it prove?

16. Does Socrates' more elaborate version of Plato's argument for immortality from the *Republic* that comes here have more

force than Plato's simpler one mentioned in question 13? If so, why? If not, what good is the elaboration?

17. Do you see any controversial assumptions behind this argument?

18. How would a skeptic reply to the argument from the soul's simplicity better than Nat does?

19. If you do not understand Socrates' reference to the distinction between efficient and formal causes at the end of this argument, look them up under "Aristotle's Four Causes"; they are one of the most fundamental distinctions in all of philosophy.

20. If souls are immortal, are they the only exception to Buddha's law in the *Diamond Sutra*? If not, what others are there? If so, why do you suppose this should be so?

21. What is it in us that objectifies everything else, including not only our bodies but also our souls? Why is that question so difficult to answer? Who is the "I" we mean when we say "my" soul?

22. There is an apparent logical self-contradiction in the notion of self-consciousness, for the self that knows must be the same as the self that is known, unless it is a case of mistaken identity, but in all cases of knowing, the knowing subject must transcend the known object and therefore *not* be identical with it. How can this puzzle be solved?

23. Can you formulate a logical way of proving the soul's immortality from the premise of self-consciousness? If not, do you intuit that there may be such an argument? If not, why do you think Socrates does? Might the premise that "the knowledge of anything cannot be merely one of the parts of that thing" serve as the principle for that proof? If so, how?

24. Why does Socrates think that that argument (from abstract thinking to immortality) works to prove the immortality of the human soul? If an animal gave evidence that it could think abstractly and not just with the sensory imagination, would that prove its immortality? If so, can you formulate the argument more clearly than Socrates does?

25. Evaluate the analogy that the mind is to the brain what a computer user is to a computer. In what sense(s) is the analogy apt and in what sense(s) not?

26. Do you think that the fact of the dependence of the mind on the brain disproves the idea that the soul survives the death of

the brain and body? If so, why? If not, why not? Can the mind be dependent on the brain for its *activity* without being dependent on the brain for its continued *existence*? Why or why not?

27. Assuming the veracity of the data concerning out-of-body experiences, does this prove to you that the soul survives the death of the body and brain or not? Why or why not?

28. Socrates and Nat leave in limbo the argument from the soul's simplicity. (The conclusion is that it cannot die either by decomposition or annihilation.) Can you finish it, either to confirm it or refute it?

29. Evaluate the argument from desire.
    - Does it necessarily presuppose teleology?
    - What is the evidence for teleology?
    - Does it necessarily presuppose that "nature makes nothing in vain"?
    - What is the evidence for that?
    - If the argument proves the soul's immortality, does it also prove the existence of a desirable Heaven as well, even if we cannot define positively what that would be?
    - Does it prove the existence of a desirable God as well, even though we cannot define God either?

30. Is Pascal's "wager" (look it up; read it—the whole thing!) another argument for immortality? Or is it an argument just for "wagering" (i.e., *believing in*) immortality?

5

Cosmology: How Does Everything in the Universe Work?

In premodern times, the difference between philosophy and the special sciences, and the difference between their methods, had not yet been clearly formulated. As late as the eighteenth century, Newton still called his physics "natural *philosophy*". Many of the questions about the cosmos, or the universe, such as the age of the universe, the nature of the stars, the atomic structure of matter, and the history of prehuman life on earth, had not yet been answered by the natural sciences.

But not all the questions about the physical universe have been removed from philosophy and given to modern science to deal with. There are still very important questions in "philosophical cosmology", which means philosophizing about the universe we live in. There are also important questions in the philosophy of science, but that is about science itself, not about the universe.

One of the most important questions in philosophical cosmology is about the fundamental relationship between all things and events in the universe, namely, causality, or the cause-effect relationship. That is the topic of this Socratic dialogue.

NAT: Socrates, the last time we talked, we discovered a puzzle that seems more mysterious than anything else in the universe: the meaning of the "self" or "I" or "person"—perhaps identical with "soul" or perhaps not. When I try to think through other philosophical questions, I seem to make some real progress, even though I never quite come to an end that I can be totally satisfied with. But this question is a real stickler.

SOCRATES: So is that what you want to dig into again today?

NAT: No. (*Socrates breathes a sigh of relief.*) But I want to try an easier question, about the universe below us, or around us. We seem to know that universe much more adequately than we know ourselves. (And that is itself a puzzle: How can we know the things that are so far away from us, like other galaxies, better than we can know the thing that is the closest to us, namely, the self?) So I'd like to philosophize about the universe today, if that's OK with you.

SOCRATES: Fine. What question about the universe intrigues or puzzles you the most?

NAT: Its name. Why is it a "uni-verse" rather than simply a diversity? What holds it all together? What is the one behind this many?

SOCRATES: That was the first question that was dealt with by the philosophers before my time, the so-called pre-Socratic philosophers.

NAT: And what answers did they come up with?

SOCRATES: Most of the answers were about what all things were made of, such as water, air, fire, the infinite, numbers, being, atoms, or a mixture of all things in all things.

NAT: It seems obvious to us today that all those answers are only partially true, but none are the whole story. And it also seems obvious that that's a question for modern physics: What is matter? What is the stuff everything is made of? But I want to know something different: how all the things and events in the universe are related to one another. It is a single uni-verse, after all, a one-in-many or many-in-one, a system.

SOCRATES: It seems to me that you have asked a better question than those early philosophers did: not just what everything is made of but how they are all ingredients in a single system of things and actions. They were asking only about the static nature or content of things in themselves, but you are asking about the dynamic activity of things in relation to one another.

NAT: Yes. And I know physicists today say that there are four fundamental forces that hold all things together and move them: gravity and electromagnetism and the so-called strong nuclear force and the weak nuclear force. But I'm not competent to discuss modern physics. I'm looking for something more macrocosmic, not micro-cosmic; something more philosophical, something philosophy can deal with, not specialized physics. I'm not sure how to formulate my question, much less search for an answer. I guess it's this: What is the fundamental relationship among all things in the universe?

SOCRATES: I think what you are looking for is the meaning of cau-sality, or cause and effect. For that seems to be what relates every-thing to everything else, what connects every thing and event in the universe with every other thing and event in the universe.

NAT: Yes. And that's about both things and events because things are caused by events, like planets being caused by the cooling of gas clouds, and also events are caused by things, like the explosion of a supernova being caused by the supernova, the star itself. The things are like the characters, and the events are like the plot, and the history of the universe is like a very long play.

SOCRATES: That is a useful analogy. I think we need to add the strange fact that one kind of these actors or characters, namely, ourselves, is also able to ask philosophical questions, questions like this one, questions about the whole of which we are both parts and also observers of the whole, including ourselves.

NAT: And all these things and events began with the Big Bang, right? That was the first event, the initial cause of the subsequent events in the ongoing expansion of the universe, the first cause that set all the other causal events moving.

SOCRATES: Which raises the question whether that event also had a cause.

NAT: In any case, it's causality that connects all the events in the universe. For within that story, that plot, that history, that cool-ing and solidification throughout the universe, and, at least on this planet, the evolution and history of the only species that transcends the whole universe by questioning it and knowing truths about it—within that cosmos, down through all of time, everything that happens, happens for a cause, for a "because", for a reason: stars form, and planets revolve, and life appears, and humans live and die and hunt and eat and reproduce and produce civilization, and marry and fight and contract diseases and invent inventions, and culture, and philosophies. We are here on this log because of all those incredibly complex events that caused us to be here. We are star stuff having attained self-consciousness. And if everything that happens has a cause, so does the universe and ourselves and our actions, including our philosophizing.

SOCRATES: Well, yes, causality is certainly true for every *physical* thing and event, anyway. Although some philosophers say that thinking and choosing transcend the laws of causality, because they are free rather than determined.

NAT: But even thinking and desiring and emoting have causes. And even if those events are not physical, yet some of the causes of those nonphysical events are physical, as when a slap in the face causes anger, or when empirical results of a laboratory experiment cause the scientist to think a new theory to account for the new data. And some of the causes of those mental events are mental, as when a train of thought or a process of thinking causes a new thought or changes someone's mind. For thinking, too, is an event in time. And all events have causes. Nothing just happens for no cause or reason at all.

SOCRATES: This certainly seems to be true. So what question does that raise in your mind?

NAT: The first one it raises is this: If all events have causes, does that mean there can be no such thing as free will or free choice, including both choices to act and choices to think? If all our choices, too, are caused, how can they be free? But if they are not free, how can we praise or blame people for them? And how can we command or counsel people to make the right choices if they are not just *influenced* or *conditioned* but totally *determined* by their causes? We don't do any of those things to machines, even the most complicated machines. And how can we speak of justice, or of what ought to be done as distinct from what is done? If there is no free choice, if everything is determined and not free, all moral language seems to be pointless.

SOCRATES: That is a strong argument for free will, or free choice.

NAT: But if there *is* free choice, if we are not merely links in a chain of causes, or dominoes in a row, or parts of a cosmic machine, then it seems there is something that happens that is not caused, so that the law of causality is broken. One of those links in the chain, in the long row of dominoes that is the history of the universe— the link that we call ourselves—escapes the chain, or the dominoes.

But that makes no sense either. Everything that happens has to have some reason why it happens, even our free choices. They can't just pop into existence without a cause any more than physical events can.

So we seem to have here a real dilemma. We don't want to give up either free will or the principle of causality. Yet they seem to contradict each other. What do we do about that?

SOCRATES: We look at each one of those two things more carefully to try to see why they do not contradict each other—as Augustine and Boethius and Aquinas and other religious philosophers did with free will and divine predestination, which seems to be a supernatural or supercosmic determinism rather than a natural and cosmic determinism.

NAT: All right. Well, perhaps the solution is really very simple. From the point of view of causality, I see no reason why there can't be two kinds of causes, free and unfree. It's true to say that some of the events that happen in the play that is our lives are caused by the setting and are not free, like thunderstorms and diseases and loose rocks falling from the wall, while other events are freely chosen by the characters in the play, for instance, one person throwing a stone at another.

SOCRATES: Is the problem solved that easily?

NAT: Now that I think about it, it's not that easy. I see a problem with that. It's true, but it doesn't solve the problem, because that explanation works forward from free choices, how they work freely to cause their effects, but it does not work backward to their prior causes, so to speak. What I mean by that is this: Suppose I choose to murder someone. The murder is the cause and the death of the victim is the effect. And the *effect* happens unfreely and necessarily: once I shoot him, the victim dies necessarily. But the *cause* happens freely: my choice to murder does not happen necessarily, as my victim's death does, but it happens freely. That's why I'm blamed for the murder. So how does it work backward? If my free choice is caused, how can it be free? But if it has no cause, that seems irrational.

So the problem isn't solved that easily. I just showed that free will is problematic from the viewpoint of the law of universal causality, but universal causality is just as problematic from the viewpoint of free will. From the viewpoint of free will, it seems that the causal chain that determines everything else has to be broken if our choices are free. But how can the causal chain be broken? How can anything happen without any cause at all? That's not what free choice means. It's not the "pop!" theory. Free choices don't just happen without any reason any more than physical events happen without any reason. So let's see ... perhaps the difference between a free choice and all other events is simply that *we* are the causes of our free choices. But what is that "we"? Is there a "me" that causes "my" mind to think and "my" will to choose? If so, what is it? Who or what is the self that owns "my" mind and will? That's the question we raised but did not answer in our conversation about human nature. And even if there is a "me" that causes my free choices, the same problem appears there; it's just put back one more step.

Let's see if our experience helps us here. The causality that we experience happening in our souls or minds or wills seems to be somehow a different kind of causality than the kind that we experience happening in mere bodies out in the cosmos. The causality that works in our free choices, however it works, is the kind of causality that does not remove our free will, as purely physical causality does, such as a blow to the head. Maybe that's the difference between efficient causality and final causality. But no, final causality applies to things without free will too: the physical growth of a baby into an adult, for instance.

SOCRATES: I follow your analysis so far, and I think it's true. So how do you think we should explore that difference between two kinds of causality?

NAT: By looking more carefully at a real example of this nonphysical causality. For instance, a teacher freely choosing to suggest an idea to his class, an idea that his students are free to accept or reject so that their acceptance or rejection is theirs, not his—it is caused by them, by their free choice, and yet the teacher was also a partial cause of their new state of mind. But not a total one, not the only cause, because that would leave his students unfree. The students have to choose to be open-minded to the new idea; they have to be teachable, and that is a free choice on their part: a free choice on the part of the effect to receive the cause, to let it in, to let it happen in the mind, at least to be there to look at, whether the idea is eventually accepted or rejected.

So even if we don't clearly understand *how* that free causality works, we know that it does in fact work, and that it works only on the spiritual level, not on the merely physical level. That's not solving the dilemma yet, but it's a beginning.

SOCRATES: But both of these very different kinds of causality are called "causality". So what is it that is common to both? What, exactly, is causality in general? We have not yet defined our key term.

NAT: How would you define it?

SOCRATES: I will not define it.

NAT: Why not? Do you think it is not definable?

SOCRATES: No, I want *you* to define it.

NAT: And how do I go about that? Just toss off a couple of words that feel good?

SOCRATES: Why not begin with how we all do use the word?

NAT: That sounds right. Well, let's see. We say that A is the cause of B if A somehow makes B either to be for the first time, like a man and a woman procreating a baby or an artist creating a work of art, or to change, to become something different, like hunger causing a baby to cry or a sculptor causing a shapeless stone to take on the shape of a man's face. So a cause either brings its effect into existence, like an author writing a book, or brings it into a new state, like an arrow piercing a man's heart or a thought entering a man's mind and moving him to act.

SOCRATES: Very good. That does indeed seem to be what we mean by "cause". It also distinguishes a cause from the merely observed sequence of a before and an after that may or may not be a real causal relation.

NAT: And another thing that makes it complicated is the fact that usually there are many causes of an effect, not just one. For instance, the causes that brought about my existence include not only my parents but their parents too, and all our ancestors, and also, indirectly, all the things that allowed them to exist, such as the Big Bang and the cooling of the planet, and the evolution of life forms, and the life history of each of my ancestors, and even little coincidences like the spur-of-the-moment suggestion of my great-grandfather's friend that he meet and date the girl who became my great-grandmother. The network of causes is immensely complex, but it seems to tie all things together.

SOCRATES: Like a cosmic plot.

NAT: So does that mean there must be a cosmic plotter? Is this an argument for the existence of something like God? And if all events are contingent, or dependent on their causes, does that mean there must be a first, uncaused cause that makes the whole chain of dominoes move, both the physical and the nonphysical? Does the Big Bang require a Big Banger? And does that apply to our thoughts and choices too?

SOCRATES: That is a question we ought to address some other time. It is a different question, and a very big one, and we don't have time for it today. For we have not finished with causality itself yet.

NAT: What questions about causality did we leave unanswered?

SOCRATES: Well, one of them might be whether you are certain of the principle of causality itself, that nothing can ever come into being or change without a cause.

NAT: But no one doubts that. No one thinks that some things just pop into existence for no reason at all. Only someone who is literally insane could believe the "pop!" theory. If a large blue rabbit suddenly appeared on my head, you would *not* say, "Ah, yes, I am not surprised by that; large blue rabbits simply happen." You would want to know why it happened, what made it happen. And that is true not only for things that are unpredictable or surprising, like large blue rabbits, but also for things that are predictable and unsurprising, like the sun melting snow or parents having children.

SOCRATES: You have observed the fact that we all have and use this concept in our thinking. But you have not proved that it corresponds to the cosmos, to objective reality. Perhaps it is just our way of explaining things. Perhaps this concept is not received and copied from the universe but actively shapes it, imposes itself upon it like a cookie cutter cutting the cookie dough into pre-formed shapes.

NAT: Why do you raise that strange-sounding question?

SOCRATES: Because that is the challenge that both Hume and Kant, in different ways, throw down to this concept of causality. And whether they are right or wrong, they are probably the two most important and influential and intelligent of modern philosophers.

NAT: That surprises me, because that subjectivizing or psychologizing of causality seems to make the issue less clear, not more.

SOCRATES: Why?

NAT: Because if causality is only in our own minds and not in the real world, how come our science works so well, and even our common sense and our philosophy, all of which are dependent on that concept? Who would deny that one thing really causes another? The alternative to that seems to be the "pop!" theory.

SOCRATES: No, neither Hume nor Kant believe in the "pop!" theory.

NAT: Well, then, what do they believe about causality and what led them to doubt that it's an objective reality? What premises led them to that strange conclusion?

SOCRATES: Two different premises. With Hume it was his "hard empiricism". He believed that our only access to the real world was through our senses and that all our ideas were dependent on our sense impressions, in fact were pale and abstract copies of our vivid and concrete sense impressions. But there is no sense impression for causality itself. It has no color, shape, size, mass, or quantity of physical energy. It is an idea that is not a copy of any sense impression. Therefore, Hume concluded, it is only our mental habit, not an insight into how things in the real world actually work. We see birds and eggs together so often that when we think one idea, we also think the other. But there's no logical necessity that leads from the idea of a bird to the idea of an egg, as there is a logical necessity that leads from the idea of 2 + 3 to the idea of 5.

NAT: But then all explanations of the real world by this concept of causality can't claim to be known to be true. But that delegitimizes not only philosophy but also science and common sense. All three of those human enterprises depend on the idea of causality being objectively true. Hume reduces all sciences to psychology.

SOCRATES: Yes. Hume ended in skepticism. We can be certain only of "relations of ideas", not of "matters of fact".

NAT: But skepticism is self-contradictory! We saw that in our first conversation. How can it be true that there is no truth? How can it be an objective truth that we can't know objective truth? How can we be certain that we can't be certain? How can we know that we don't really know?

SOCRATES: I don't know.

NAT: You're kidding, right?

SOCRATES: Maybe.

NAT: That's funny, but it's not an answer.

SOCRATES: Actually, it is. That "maybe" is Hume's answer to the self-contradiction argument against skepticism. He does not say we know that we know nothing with certainty, but he reduces all our knowledge to probability and practicality, what works. He does not deny knowledge, only certainty. He says that we have knowledge of the real world through our senses, but it's only probable, not certain. For instance, it's very probable, but not certain, that the sun will come up again tomorrow.

NAT: And I suppose he's certain of that? That it's not certain, but only probable?

SOCRATES: No, that's only probable too.

NAT: And his premise, the premise of hard empiricism, that every concept we have is only a pale copy of some sense impression—that's his first premise, right, from which all these very problematic and counterintuitive and skeptical or semi-skeptical conclusions follow?

SOCRATES: Yes.

NAT: Does Hume prove that premise?

SOCRATES: Only by observation, by outer and inner sensation or introspection.

NAT: What if I say my introspection reveals something more, something like Descartes' "I think, therefore I am", something more abstract and spiritual? Is it simply David Hume's inner vision versus Nat Whilk's?

SOCRATES: No, he argues.

NAT: How?

SOCRATES: He says simply that if you claim to have some idea that is not a copy of a sense impression, tell me what it is and I will show you how it is in fact derived from a sense impression. If I cannot do that, you win. If I can, I win. For instance, the fantastic idea of a golden mountain presupposes sensations of gold things and of mountains, and then rearranges them. Even the idea of God presupposes experiences of good qualities or perfections and then simply extrapolates them to infinity.

NAT: How does he account for the idea of causality, then?

SOCRATES: As a mental habit, a kind of rut in the mind caused by repeated observation of the same pattern occurring over and over again.

NAT: And how does he account for mathematics? Is it only probable that $2 + 3 = 5$?

SOCRATES: No. But he sees mathematics as telling us nothing about the real world, just about numbers. The number two is not a thing, like one of two ducks.

NAT: But mathematics tells us truths, like $2 + 2 = 4$.

SOCRATES: That is an equation. Mathematics is about equations, and equations are tautologies, self-evident propositions. They are reversible, unlike ordinary sentences. They don't say "is" but "equals". Their predicates add nothing to their subjects. They tell us nothing about how things are in the world. If they claimed to do that, they would have to be verified or falsified by sense observation. We know that two of anything plus two more of that same thing must always be four of those things. For instance, two ducks plus two ducks are four ducks. But we need sensations to tell us whether there are any ducks, and what they are. Mathematics and logic are about what Hume calls "relations of ideas", while empirical propositions are about "matters of fact". To deny a matter of fact is never self-contradictory, while to deny a "relation of ideas" is. It's not self-contradictory to say that ducks don't exist, even though it's not true. But it's self-contradictory to say that two ducks plus two ducks is not four ducks. It's also self-contradictory to say that two unicorns plus two unicorns is not four unicorns.

NAT: Well, then, if every idea is either empirical or a tautology, what about the idea of me? Where does Hume say the idea of a self comes from? It's not a "relation of ideas" or an empirical matter of fact.

SOCRATES: He denies that there is any such thing as a substantial self.

NAT: I thought you said he was intelligent. Even the insane know they exist.

SOCRATES: The idea is indeed radical, but he argues for it. He says that when he looks inside himself, all he sees are two kinds of thought processes: either the abstract thinking that produces "relations of ideas" or the perception of some "matter of fact" that can be verified or falsified by observation, which includes not only the outer sensing but also the inner sensings that we call imagining and feeling. And he sees no self there, only those two processes of mental activity. You can see or imagine a body, but you can't see or imagine a self or a soul or a spirit or a mind. What shape is it? So he says there is no real substance behind these activities, no noun behind those verbs, no processor behind those processes.

NAT: But how can there be a process if there is no processor? How can there be acts if there is no actor? Where did we get the idea of a substantial self from?

SOCRATES: He says we invented it just as you did right now, inventing the idea of an actor from our observation of an act. But we never observe this acting self, the substance that *sub-stands*, that "stands under" its actions as a foundation stands under a house. And Hume applies this to physical things as well as selves or minds or souls. There are no substances. "Substance" means "that which stands under" either actions or properties. We observe the actions of a duck and the properties of a duck, but we do not observe the thing that we say possesses these properties.

NAT: And actions too, as well as properties, right? He denies that there are substantial actors that cause these actions?

SOCRATES: Yes.

NAT: So he denies that birds really cause eggs.

SOCRATES: He denies that we can know that that is a matter of fact. We see the birds and the eggs but not the causality.

NAT: Then all nouns mislead us, but verbs and adjectives do not.

SOCRATES: I think that is what he would say if he translated his epistemology into linguistics, yes.

NAT: So there is no such thing as a human being. We are not beings. Hume himself is not a Humean being.

SOCRATES: A pun does not constitute an argument.

NAT: But for him there are no real beings. There is no being. The word is a mistake. "Being" as a noun is a meaningless word for Hume.

SOCRATES: Yes. Hobbes had said the same thing, earlier, as a deduction from his epistemology of hard empiricism.

NAT: So things in the cosmos are not really things, and they are not really connected by cause and effect. Both of those concepts—substances and causes—are just subjective, mental habits, conceptual ways in which we order our experiences. The world is not really held together by causality.

SOCRATES: That's right. He said each thing or event is separate, like an atom.

NAT: That would be a very convenient philosophy for a criminal to use: "I didn't really kill that man or rape that woman; that's just how your mind has to think." That's ridiculous! How does he account for morality then?

SOCRATES: He says it's subjective; it's a feeling. Morality becomes part of psychology. We impose our moral feelings on the facts, like looking through colored eyeglasses at a colorless world. There are no moral facts.

NAT: But the same premises of extreme empiricism that make morality merely subjective also make science merely subjective, because physical causality performs the same function in the material world as moral responsibility performs on the spiritual level: it links things and events together and makes the universe truly a *uni*-verse, a single system of relations between diverse things.

SOCRATES: That is correct. You understand him accurately.

NAT: My first instinct is to think that he is playing a game with us.

SOCRATES: What do you mean?

NAT: Well, his premise is his radical empiricism. And that premise is not a tautology, not self-evidently true, like $2 + 2 = 4$. There are arguments both for it and against it.

SOCRATES: I think that is true.

NAT: And he deduces from that premise, by apparently very tight logical arguments, conclusions that are very obviously false to me and, I think, to most people.

SOCRATES: That is also true.

NAT: So I suspect he is playing an elaborate game with us. It is a "reductio ad absurdum" argument, a refutation of a premise by showing that it necessarily entails an absurd conclusion, which is his skepticism.

SOCRATES: He does not think that conclusion is absurd.

NAT: But it is. At least, the falsehood of his conclusion (of his skepticism of both science and morality) is much more obvious than the truth of his premise of hard empiricism. His skepticism of science, with its explanations by cause and effect, and of morality, with its judgments of good and evil, are obviously absurd, and they logically follow from his premise of radical empiricism, so what he's really doing is showing that his premise must be wrong, not that his conclusions must be right.

SOCRATES: I think you are wrong here about what he intended to do. He pretty clearly believed his conclusions.

NAT: Well, then he accomplished, in this reader, at least, the exact opposite of what he tried to accomplish. He accomplished a refutation of radical empiricism.

SOCRATES: Why do you say that his skeptical conclusions are absurd? Merely because they are unpopular?

NAT: No, because they are unlivable. Even if I cannot refute those conclusions in theory logically (and by the way, I hope I *can*), I cannot live them, and neither can he, I think.

SOCRATES: Oh, he admitted that. He says that he has to leave his philosophizing room and go into the next room to play billiards with a friend in order to reenter human life and human relations.

NAT: How can he justify such a schizoid life?

SOCRATES: I think he would say that the human house is large enough to have two very different rooms in it.

NAT: That may be true of the Humean house, but it is not true of the human house. How can we live so differently from what we think? What good is philosophy if it does not help us live but contradicts the way we have to live?

SOCRATES: Hume saw philosophy as something very different than you and I do. We both see it as the love of wisdom.

NAT: Which is something existential and personal and practical and livable.

SOCRATES: Yes.

NAT: You mentioned Kant in relation to Hume. What was his reaction to Hume, especially to Hume's denial of real causality?

SOCRATES: He credits Hume for awakening him from what he called his "dogmatic slumber".

NAT: Did he, too, despair of reason as Hume did and embrace skepticism, or probabilism?

SOCRATES: No, because he redefined reason, not as a copy of the real universe, but as that which the universe copies. He called that his

"Copernican revolution in philosophy". What Hume said about causality—that we imposed the idea on the world, not the world imposing it on us—Kant said for all logical categories, and for the physical categories of time and space, and for the metaphysical categories of self, world, and God. He said we can't know that they are real in themselves, just that we have to think that way. We can't know things in themselves, only things as we have subconsciously shaped them by our thought. Truth is more like the conformity of things to thoughts than the conformity of thoughts to things.

NAT: So Kant is even more of a skeptic than Hume, since Hume at least gave us probable knowledge of the real world, or things-in-themselves, and Kant gave us none.

SOCRATES: Kant didn't think he was a skeptic. He thought he had *rescued* reason from Hume.

NAT: Why?

SOCRATES: Because Hume assumed, like everyone else before him, that reason's job was to discover the real structures of reality, and on that assumption Hume then went on to say that reason was able to do that only in the empirical, sensory realm and only with probability, never certainty. But Kant said that reason was doing its job perfectly well because its job was not, as everyone before him, including Hume, had assumed, to discover the world but to create the world—not its existence, of course, since we are not God and did not create the universe, but its structures, its intelligibility. He said we could not know things-in-themselves, things as they are outside our minds, independent of our thinking, because we were not *supposed* to know things-in-themselves, but only to structure appearances.

NAT: But that seems even more skeptical than Hume. And if it is, then it is refutable by the same argument we used to refute skepticism in our first conversation: it is self-contradictory.

SOCRATES: How would that self-contradiction argument apply to Kant?

NAT: If Kant is right about what he calls his "Copernican revolution"—if he is right that *that* is the way things are, that that is the real, true relation between reason and reality rather than the way people thought it was before his Copernican Revolution—then in knowing that, he is knowing a thing-in-itself, an objective fact.

Is it an objective truth that we cannot know objective truths? Is it a real thing-in-itself that we cannot know real things-in-themselves?

SOCRATES: That does seem self-contradictory. As another, later philosopher, Wittgenstein, argued, in order to draw a limit to all possible human thought (as Kant tried to do), it is necessary to think both sides of that limit. But now we're getting back into epistemology. I thought we were doing cosmology today and focusing on the idea of causality.

NAT: All right, but I think I see the same self-contradiction in Kantian cosmology as I do in Kantian epistemology, and it's about the idea of causality.

SOCRATES: What is the self-contradiction?

NAT: Kant says that we can't know a thing-in-itself, a thing as it is independent of our knowing of it, right?

SOCRATES: Right.

NAT: So we can't know that causality is an objective reality, right?

SOCRATES: Right. He says it's a necessary and universal category, an idea that we use to order the world.

NAT: So he says that it is our idea of causality that makes or shapes or causes the order we see in our world, right?

SOCRATES: Right. The idea of causality is not the only such idea, but one of them.

NAT: But "shaping" is a causal relationship. The shape of the cookie cutter causes the shape of the cookie. So for Kant there is a real causal relationship between our idea of causality and the world we perceive, but the relationship is the opposite of what we used to think it was. We determine the world; the world does not determine us.

SOCRATES: Yes, that is what he means by his "Copernican revolution in philosophy".

NAT: But that's still a causal relationship, though it's the reverse of the one we thought it was before Kant. So we do know a real causal relationship, then: the real causal relationship between reality and the idea of causality. It's the opposite of what we used to think it is, but we know it, if we accept Kant's philosophy.

SOCRATES: Yes, in the sense that we have to think it. It's true.

NAT: So we know that truth, that fact, that real situation, that real causal relationship between reality and the idea of causality, that thing-in-itself, that objective truth.

SOCRATES: Yes.

NAT: But Kant said we can't do that. We can't know any things-in-themselves.

SOCRATES: Yes, he says that.

NAT: So he is contradicting himself.

SOCRATES: It seems so.

NAT: I am disappointed. How can two of the most brilliant philosophers who ever lived both be so unbelievable?

SOCRATES: I do not know the answer to that question. I am a philosopher, not a psychologist.

NAT: Well, then, suppose we set both Hume and Kant aside.

SOCRATES: Hume are we setting aside now?

NAT: Are you saying we Kant do that?

SOCRATES: No, but I think we might ask Hume else we should consult to understand causality then.

NAT: And who else would that be?

SOCRATES: Let's try Aristotle, for he is the paragon of common sense.

NAT: And what did he say about causality?

SOCRATES: He distinguished four causes, or four kinds, of causality, four dimensions of it. Both Hume and Kant were considering only one of these four kinds, what Aristotle called the "efficient cause", by which he meant the origin or maker of a thing, or of the actions or changes or movements of it. That was what we agreed to mean by causality at the beginning of this conversation. Aristotle would have said that that definition was too limited.

NAT: What are the other three kinds of cause?

SOCRATES: One is what he called the "final" cause, which is the end or goal toward which the thing naturally moves, as an acorn grows into an oak tree by its own nature, or as a battle is directed, in this case not by itself but by the intelligence of the general, toward the end of winning a war. Even things without intelligence not only move but move to specific ends. The efficient cause supplies the power, but the final cause supplies the direction. For instance, we say a volcano is erupting because of the pressure underground—that's the efficient cause, the push, so to speak—but we also say that the lava is coming down the slope because it is being moved by the earth's gravity—that's the final cause, the pull. Or when we drive a car down a road, the engine and the gasoline supply the efficient cause, and our steering supplies the final cause, the direction. Some final causes are known and willed by human reason and some are not, such as the growth of a plant or an animal, or the pull of gravity. But both move in an order toward a natural end.

NAT: Even the lava? There's no life there, no growth from within.

SOCRATES: Yes, even the lava. If we build a wall against the lava's descent from the top of the volcano, the wall is a force of defense against the lava's force of offense, which is the tendency to move toward its natural end, which is the mass of whatever body is attracting it, in this case the earth. That's why heavy objects fall rather than rise.

NAT: So why do we always think only of the efficient cause when we use the word "cause" today, and not the final cause?

SOCRATES: I think there are two reasons. One is that final causality is not part of modern science, because the scientific method has no way of detecting or measuring final causes, so it simply does not deal with them. That dimension, the end or purpose, is "seen" or grasped by an act of intellectual intuition, not by either the senses alone or mathematical measurement and calculation. But science works so well partly because it deliberately limits itself to those two kinds of knowing. It's like laser light: its narrowness and concentration are the key to its power.

The other reason is that final causality is controversial today, as it was not in the past, because it seems to imply intelligence and design in the universe, and thus a universal designer, which would be at least something very like a God. And science is not equipped to deal with religion, either to prove it or to disprove it. We want to keep the two safely separate.

NAT: Oh, that opens up a big can of worms. I don't see why final causality is religious rather than scientific.

SOCRATES: Neither did Aristotle.

NAT: It's not religious faith, only logical reason, to say that design implies some kind of designer, some kind of intelligence, whatever it is. And also that the intelligence that designed the universe is at best only partly known by us, and beyond the power of science to know because it's not part of the universe that science knows, any more than the painter is a part of the painting, or the architect a part of the building, or the novelist a part of the novel.

SOCRATES: Do you see the argument for a superhuman mind behind the universe being valid not just in the order of final causality but also of efficient causality?

NAT: I think so. The Big Bang, which would be the first event, seems to imply some kind of Big Banger, and not because of any religious faith or religious claim but simply because if the principle of causality is true, nothing happens without a cause, and the Big Bang really happened, so it has to have a cause. So both the cosmic chain of efficient causes and the cosmic pattern of final causes seem to be scientific evidence for some kind of universe-transcending Cause in both kinds of causality. But science can't explore that Cause, only its effect. Science can explore only the visible, measurable universe.

SOCRATES: Would you say this is a proof for the existence of God?

NAT: Not if you mean the God of any one religion. We are doing philosophy, not religion, here in Socrates University, here on this log.

SOCRATES: But it seems that strictly philosophical argument leads to the God of religion, doesn't it? Your argument about efficient causality—that the Big Bang seems to demand a Big Banger—and your argument about final causality—that cosmic design seems to demand a cosmic designer—seem to logically entail a Creator and Designer of the universe. If so, then what else do you think mere scientific and philosophical reason can tell us about God, besides that God exists and is the cause of the universe? Does the logic lead from science to religion?

NAT: I don't know. That's another big can of worms, an important question. So important that I think we need a whole other conversation about it.

SOCRATES: Which we shall have later.

NAT: Tell me, Socrates: Do you think the main reason most modern philosophers and scientists do not believe that final causality is real is their fear that it seems to involve something like a God?

SOCRATES: I don't know. I'm a philosopher, not a psychologist, Nat. I don't judge personal motives, only logical arguments.

NAT: Well, let's get back to our exploration of causality. What were the other two kinds of causes according to Aristotle?

SOCRATES: A third kind of cause is what he called the "formal" cause. It is the thing's essence.

NAT: That sounds mystical. Or else it's just a fancy name for perfume.

SOCRATES: No, it's not mystical; it's rational, if "reason" means more than what computers can do. In fact, it's commonsensical. A thing's essence is simply its necessary and unchangeable inner identity, as distinguished from its external relationships to other things and its changeable, accidental properties. For instance, the dogginess of the dog as distinct from how old or how clean it is, or the humanity of the human as distinct from the age or race or gender, or the wateriness of water as distinct from how much of it there is or how hot it is.

NAT: That's common sense, but it doesn't sound like science. How can science identify essences?

SOCRATES: The strictly scientific method can't. Essences appear to the understanding, not to sensation or mathematical calculation.

NAT: I think they do appear to sensation. If some visible property in a thing changes, it's an accident. If not, if it never changes, it's part of the essence.

SOCRATES: I don't think that's necessarily true. Suppose a property never changes but *can* change. For instance, no human being has ever been more than thirteen feet tall. But that height limit is not the essence, and it may happen someday that a human being grows that tall.

NAT: So how do we identify essences?

SOCRATES: Not just by sense observation of what is so far constant, but by a kind of intellectual imagination. We can imagine a man more than thirteen feet tall who is still a man, but we can't imagine a man without a body or without a mind who is still a man.

NAT: You mean by "imagination" not just picturing in your mind something you perceived with your senses but conceiving a meaningful concept, right?

SOCRATES: Yes.

NAT: I see. And I agree that we can make that distinction between the essential and the nonessential in our minds. But why must that be true of reality and not just our convenient way of organizing our ideas?

SOCRATES: For a very practical reason. If we can't distinguish essences from accidental properties, we're open to really stupid and destructive confusions like racism, which sees different races as essentially different species. Racism exalts the accidental difference of race into something essential. Or we could reduce the essential difference between humans and animals to an accidental difference like degree of intelligence, and thus either deny that we have reason and free will or affirm that animals have those powers too.

NAT: I see.

SOCRATES: But understanding and identifying essences is not done by scientific method thinking. It's neither pure logical or mathematical calculation, such as a computer can do, nor registering empirical sense data, which a camera can do; it's done by an intellectual intuition, which only persons can do, and not computers or cameras. Thinking by the scientific method is not like ordinary light but like a spotlight, or like laser light. It's narrow and concentrated into thinking about only these two things, or rather these two dimensions of things, namely, quantities rather than qualities and appearances to the senses rather than to the intellectual intuition, the understanding. That narrowness is what makes laser light so much more powerful than ordinary light. But ordinary light is more important for ordinary living. We can't live without ordinary light, that is, intuition and common sense and wisdom and the love of wisdom, which is what philosophy is supposed to be. But we can live without the scientific method.

NAT: Can we?

SOCRATES: Of course we can. Because we did just that for thousands of years.

NAT: That's true, but we live much better and much easier if we have science and its products in technology. When you're in pain, you want good medicine and medical technology.

SOCRATES: Yes, of course, but you also want good philosophy.

NAT: Do you? When you are in pain?

SOCRATES: Yes, because you want to have good reasons for wanting the medicine and technology. And those reasons stem from wisdom, from understanding yourself and your real needs and what is really most valuable. For instance, you believe that health is more valuable than money, and therefore you pay big bucks for an operation. If we don't understand what's essential to our own nature, how can we live wisely?

NAT: We can't. You're obviously right. I guess many geniuses miss what is obvious.

SOCRATES: And if we lack that wisdom, the wisdom to distinguish the essence from the accidents, we might be so foolish as to try to change our essential nature, for instance, to escape our bodies, as the so-called transhumanists want to do.

NAT: That sounds like they want death.

SOCRATES: No, they want immortality. They want to extract the mind from the body and make it into computer software.

NAT: That's not immortality for *me*. I'm not software!

SOCRATES: Or we might want to change our essential nature in the opposite way, by trying to escape our rational minds—for instance, by hallucinogenic drugs or simply trashing reason itself, as some kinds of that very fashionable philosophy called "postmodernism" want to do.

NAT: OK, so that's three kinds of cause we've looked at now: the efficient cause, the final cause, and the formal cause. What's the fourth kind of cause?

SOCRATES: The "material" cause. The formal cause is what a thing is made into, and the material cause is what a thing is made out of, its raw material. Take a wooden house. Its efficient cause is the carpenter who makes it. The final cause is to shelter a family. The formal cause is that it's a house rather than a bridge or a chair or a statue. The material cause is wood. So the two internal or intrinsic causes are the form and the matter, the formal cause and the material cause; and the two external or extrinsic causes are the origin and the end, the efficient cause and the final cause. It's a very handy scheme to classify and distinguish the four kinds of questions anyone can ever ask about anything.

NAT: If it's so commonsensical and so useful, why isn't it popular among philosophers today?

SOCRATES: That question opens another can of worms: cultural history. I think the two main answers are that science works best when it confines itself to efficient causes and material causes, and that final causes seem to imply something like God, and that seems to involve religion.

NAT: So our whole cosmology, our whole "big picture" of the cosmos, our whole attitude toward the universe, is determined by our love of this new invention of ours, the laser light of the scientific method, and by our fear of religion? By technophilia and theophobia?

SOCRATES: Well, as I said, I am not a psychologist who reads subconscious motivations.

NAT: But according to Plato you did treat great questions like love in the *Symposium* and great questions like God in the *Euthyphro* and the *Apology*.

SOCRATES: Let us explore them some other day.

Questions for Discussion or Personal Essays

1. Have modern science and the scientific method rendered Aristotle's idea of the Four Causes obsolete? If not, why does it seem to many people that they have? If so, why does it seem to both Socrates and Nat that they haven't?

2. Can you think of another candidate for the position of "the fundamental relationship between all things and events in the universe" besides causality?

3. Why might it *not* be as obvious and universally agreed, as both Socrates and Nat assume, (1) that there are only three possible levels of reality, namely, ourselves, the universe that is less than human minds, and whatever may be greater than human minds, and (2) that the three different levels of difficulty and mystery correspond to the three different levels of perfection or reality?

4. How did Aristotle's Four Causes enable him to classify all previous philosophers? Research this question in the book labeled little alpha (lowercase alpha) in his *Metaphysics*.

5. Another research question: How do the four realities that Plato thought were eternal in his dialogue *Timaeus* constitute an example of Aristotle's Four Causes?

6. How might the Four Causes help you outline an original essay on arguable topics like drug addiction, immigration law, the war on terrorism, the problem of evil, or transgenderism?

7. Is it an unwarranted extrapolation to see the Big Bang as needing a cause just as every other event that happens after it also needs a cause?

8. How, other than inductively, by piling up sensory experiences into a generalization, would you prove that the principle of causality ("every event, every change, must have some cause") is necessarily true? If only by generalization, can that inductive evidence render the principle not just probable but necessary and certain? If by deduction, from what premise(s) could you deduce it? (This is a very difficult question!)

9. What seems to be the difference between physical and spiritual causality? (Don't just say "free will"; try to think through how that works causally.)

10. If you had to choose between denying free will and denying the principle of causality, which would you deny and why?

11. Can you prove that free will exists by freely choosing to believe in it? Is that like proving that King Arthur existed by exhuming his corpse? Is it like Descartes proving his existence by thinking about it ("I think, therefore I am")? If so, what is common to these three examples? If not, how are they different?

12. What, exactly, *is* causality, or the cause-and-effect relationship? Don't just use a synonym; explain how it works.

13. Nat notes that usually there are many causes for an event, not just one. Can you think of any case where there is one and only one?

14. Why do you think we spontaneously and universally reject the "pop!" theory? Or do we?

15. Do you see any way of keeping Hume's premise of empiricism and avoiding his skepticism of causality? If so, how? If not, do you see that as refuting empiricism or as refuting causality? Why?

16. Is causality empirically observable? If so, how? If not, aren't Hume and Kant right in saying that it is not in things but only in ideas? If not, why not?

17. Are ideas subject to the principle of causality? Can one idea cause another idea? What is the relation between an idea and the act of thinking an idea?

18. Hume argues that we have no empirical evidence for the reality of substances (things, entities that have, or stand under, visible properties). Can you refute his argument against substances (both physical and spiritual or mental, and thus including

minds or selves, which are not empirically perceivable) without abandoning his premise of empiricism? Would the distinction between Hume's "hard empiricism" and Aristotle's "soft empiricism" that was discussed in the second dialogue help? If not, why not? If so, how? What does Aristotle add to the epistemological map of human knowing that Hume does not, and what is the evidence for the truth of that addition?

19. Common sense unequivocally affirms the existence of self, substances, and causality. Does common sense have more authority than apparently valid logical arguments, or less? Which of these two, common sense and instinctive intuition or logical arguments, has rightful authority over the other and why? (You might research Thomas Reid, Hume's fellow empiricist but critic, as giving the opposite answer to that question from Hume's answer.)

20. Nat suspects that Hume's argument from radical empiricism to skepticism of causality, substance, and self may be a "reductio ad absurdum" argument. Explain the logical strategy of that kind of argument and evaluate Nat's reason for thinking that Hume's argument disproves his empiricist premise rather than proving his skeptical conclusion. Explain the logical parallel with Dostoyevsky's argument for the existence of God: "If God did not exist, everything would be permissible" (implying that obviously not everything is permissible; therefore, God exists) and Sartre's recasting that argument using the very same premise but implying that since God does not exist, everything *is* permissible). Both arguments can go either way, that is, either as a "reductio ad absurdum" proof of the falsity of the premise or as a proof of the truth of the conclusion. Which way is more convincing in each of these two cases (Dostoyevski's and Sartre's) and why?

21. How persuasive as an argument against Hume's theory is the fact that he cannot live it (remember the two rooms in his house)? If logic leads you to one conclusion and life leads you to the opposite one, what do you do and why? What are your options, and which do you think is the best one? Why is that the best one?

22. Do you see Kant's fundamental idea (his "Copernican revolution in philosophy") as universally true, universally false,

or true in some ways or some cases (which?) but not others (which?)? Why?

23. Evaluate Nat's and Wittgenstein's argument that Kant contradicts himself.

24. Does Aristotle's distinction between the four kinds of causes solve this problem by saying that Kant is right about formal causality but wrong about efficient causality? Why or why not?

25. How do final causes fit into the controversy about Kant's "Copernican revolution"?

26. Is Socrates' proposal to trust and use both science and the scientific method (the "laser light" or "spotlight") and philosophy and common sense (the "floodlight" or "big picture") essentially the same as Hume's two rooms? If not, why not?

27. Do you see other causes than the two that Socrates points out (technophilia and theophobia) for modernity's skepticism of final causality?

28. If all the problems of philosophy are closely related to one another, as seems evident every time Nat notes another "can of worms", is it more useful to take them one at a time or to deliberately take them together as a "package deal"? Why? Is there a third possibility?

6

Metaphysics: What Does "Real" Mean?

Many people today have a misconception about metaphysics: it identifies metaphysics with the occult or the mystical or the supernatural, since "meta" means "beyond", so that "metaphysical" seems to mean "beyond the physical". But metaphysics goes beyond physics without leaving it behind; it is "beyond" in scope or universality; it asks questions about everything that is real. Are there any universal laws or truths about all that has being?

That question is apparently the most universal question we can ask—about not just one kind of being or one dimension of being but about being as such. And thus it seems to be the most abstract question possible. If it leaves all concrete specificity, particularity, definability, and limitations behind, it seems to attempt to think about everything in general and therefore nothing in particular. This leads to a second, much subtler misunderstanding, and many modern philosophers have succumbed to it and thus shunned metaphysics. What can you say about "everything"?

Maybe a lot. Maybe being, like thought, has its own internal structures and is not just a totally empty non-concept. And maybe there are important differences about what being means, differences about being in general that will have logical consequences everywhere concerning particular beings or ways of being. Is being essence, existence, substance, oneness, intelligibility, identity, authenticity, or what?

And everyone asks a metaphysical question, even those who avoid the two misunderstandings we've discussed, when they ask whether anything is real or unreal. There are philosophers who think there is no reality, no objective reality, to causality or substance or plurality or unity or matter or spirit or even a self. And obviously, questions about the reality or unreality of God, souls, life after death, or absolute moral goods are important, meaningful questions, such that their answers make immense differences to both one's thought and one's life.

NAT: What is our topic for discussion today, Socrates?

SOCRATES: Let's begin with that snake.

NAT: Snake? What snake?

SOCRATES: The one next to your right shoe.

NAT: Oh! Bummer! But what does that snake have to do with philosophy?

SOCRATES: You'll see if you pick it up.

NAT: No way. I hate snakes!

SOCRATES: Then *I* will. (*Picks it up. It does not move.*) Now tell me what you notice about this snake.

NAT: Oh, it's only a toy. It's not a real snake.

SOCRATES: Right. Now tell me one more thing: What do you mean by "real"?

NAT: Oh, I see. It's a philosophy lesson.

SOCRATES: Yes. The division of philosophy that deals with questions like that is called metaphysics.

NAT: I thought metaphysics was about the supernatural and stuff like the occult.

SOCRATES: That's what metaphysics is about in California bookstores, but that's not what it means in the history of philosophy.

NAT: What is it about in the history of philosophy?

SOCRATES: It's about being.

NAT: The "meta" in "metaphysics" means "beyond", right?

SOCRATES: Right.

NAT: So metaphysics is about stuff that goes beyond the physical. Spirits and the spirit world, right?

SOCRATES: Wrong. It goes "beyond" the physical in *scope*, or universality. It doesn't leave the physical behind. It doesn't leave anything behind. It's about all being, not just physical being and not just spiritual being. It's about what it means to be, to be real, to have being. Not this kind of being or that kind of being but being itself, being as such, being qua being.

NAT: Hmm, I have a problem with that. What can you say about "being"? I haven't seen any news about "being" in the papers lately. I suspect metaphysics is about empty abstractions. When I think of being as such or being qua being, I get the picture of a whiff of smoke or a vapor dissipating and disappearing into space.

SOCRATES: That's almost exactly what Nietzsche said about it. But that's not what Plato, Aristotle, Augustine, Aquinas, Descartes, Spinoza, Leibnitz, Kant, Hegel, Sartre, or Heidegger said about it.

NAT: What did they say about it?

SOCRATES: Do you have at least a year of your time to keep sitting on this log and listening to my answer?

NAT: OK, let me change my question. How can anyone say anything meaningful about all of being? *Everything* is *some* kind of being. We want to know *what* kind. The word "being" tells us nothing. It's the most unhelpful, unspecific word in the language. It's supremely abstract, abstracted from all information. It has no distinctive subject matter.

SOCRATES: I understand your objection. But perhaps it has a distinctive point of view on its nondistinctive subject matter.

NAT: What does that mean? Give me an example.

SOCRATES: Well, let's look at a typical metaphysical question that was made famous by Heidegger, though it originated in Hegel. Heidegger asks essentially, "Why is there anything at all rather than nothing?"[1] That's a question about everything without distinction, but it's a distinctive question.

NAT: It's certainly not one we ask every day.

SOCRATES: And it's about the most important distinction of all, the distinction between being and nonbeing, or being and nothing, or existence and nonexistence.

NAT: Is that really an important question?

SOCRATES: Let's see. How do we describe a really important question? "It's a matter of life or death", right?

NAT: Right.

SOCRATES: And that's pretty close to "it's a matter of being or nonbeing", isn't it?

---

[1] Martin Heidegger, *Introduction to Metaphysics*, trans. Gregory Fried and Richard Polt, 2nd ed. (New Haven, Conn.: Yale University Press, 2014), 1.

NAT: I think I'm getting confused already with these theoretical abstractions.

SOCRATES: Well, then, let's get very practical and concrete. Do you like horses?

NAT: Yes, I do. But what does that have to do with metaphysics?

SOCRATES: Tell me, which would you rather have, one horse or a hundred horses?

NAT: A hundred.

SOCRATES: And would you rather have one real horse or a hundred unreal horses that exist only in your thought or imagination?

NAT: One real one, thanks.

SOCRATES: And how large is the difference between one and a hundred?

NAT: That's a big difference. The difference between one and a hundred is ninety-nine.

SOCRATES: But from your answer to my question of whether you would rather have one real horse or a hundred unreal horses, I see that that very big difference isn't as big to you as the difference between being and nonbeing. You'd prefer a hundred real horses to one, but you'd prefer one real one to a hundred unreal ones.

NAT: I see. You're teaching me the difference between real existence and mere thought, or between real being and mental being, or between *whether* a thing (like a horse) is and *what* it is, or between existence and essence. Even fictions have essences, or are essences.

SOCRATES: Yes. So let's do some metaphysics about that big difference.

NAT: But I see a logical problem with metaphysics. You're a stickler for defining your terms, right?

SOCRATES: Yes. I have this little quirky prejudice of mind: I like to know what things are. I like to know what I'm talking about before I talk about them.

NAT: I know a little logic. And I know that the best way to define a term logically is to tell its genus and its specific difference, right?

SOCRATES: Right. First you give the larger class it fits into and then you give its distinctive feature that sets it off from other members of the class. For instance, man is defined as the animal with reason; democracy is defined as government of and by and for the people; triangles are defined as enclosed plane figures with three sides.

NAT: And metaphysics is about being, right?

SOCRATES: Right.

NAT: But you can't define being. Because there's no genus for being, no larger class that being fits into, no kind of being that being is one kind of. Being is one kind of ... what?

SOCRATES: You are quite right. Being has no genus. So it can't be defined in the usual way. Yet, as we just saw in our conversation about the horses, it makes a difference, and we understand that difference, and we understand how to use the word. And we also saw that it's not a trivial word, but an important word. It matters; it makes a difference.

NAT: Yes.

SOCRATES: So what do you think we should do about those two facts—that we can't define it and yet we do understand it and its importance and we know how to use it?

NAT: What do you think?

SOCRATES: I think you should tell me what *you* think. There are only two possibilities for our investigation of being: Should we try to understand it or not? Should we give being to our attempt to understand being, or should we not? "To be, or not to be—that is the question", as Hamlet said.[2] He was questioning his life, contemplating suicide. We are questioning the life of metaphysics. Shall metaphysics be or not? Should we assume that it is impossible and give up before we try, or should we not give up but make the attempt? What do you say?

NAT: I say "let it be." Let metaphysics be.

SOCRATES: You stand in a rather grand tradition there.

NAT: Because so many great philosophers also did metaphysics?

SOCRATES: That's one reason. Another is that every artist did that to his art. Dante said, "Let my story be!" and gave us *The Divine Comedy*. Tolkien said, "Let hobbits be", and we had *The Hobbit* and *The Lord of the Rings*. And not only that, but your "let it be" is the phrase the Bible says God spoke when He created the universe with everything in it, including, eventually, yourself. So you are echoing three kinds of creators here.

NAT: Thanks for the compliment. But what can you say about being? Everything is some kind of being. What can you say about everything?

[2] Shakespeare, *Hamlet*, act 3, scene 1, line 56.

SOCRATES: Let's see. Do you think that the principle of causality is true for *all* being?

NAT: It seems so.

SOCRATES: Why?

NAT: Because nothing happens without a cause, and it seems that nothing *can* happen without a cause.

SOCRATES: So all events have causes.

NAT: Yes.

SOCRATES: Is every being an event?

NAT: I think so.

SOCRATES: Events are changes, aren't they?

NAT: Yes.

SOCRATES: So if there's anything that doesn't change, then that's not an event, and so it doesn't have to come under the law that all events need causes. So perhaps such a being does not need a cause.

NAT: That's logical. But what could that be? Do you mean God?

SOCRATES: Well, that's the obvious instance. But there may be others.

NAT: What?

SOCRATES: Perhaps many gods. Or eternal, unchangeable truths like $2 + 3 = 5$. Or Platonic Forms, the Ideas, essences like beauty itself or justice itself.

NAT: But those are only ideas. Ideas aren't real. The idea of a hundred horses isn't a real horse.

SOCRATES: No, but Plato's Ideas with a capital *I*, Plato's Forms, aren't ideas in our changing minds; they're not subjective opinions but objective essences, objective truths, that don't change and that judge our changing minds.

NAT: Why did Plato think they must be real and not just mental?

SOCRATES: Plato's argument for them is really very simple: if justice, for example, is not any kind of objective reality, any kind of real being, but only our subjective ideas and opinions, then how can anyone be wrong about it? How can we judge the tyrant's idea that justice is nothing but power, that might makes right—how can we rightly judge that idea to be wrong if it's not wrong *about* something real, if it's not a failure to know the reality of justice, real justice, which does not exist merely in the tyrant's mind or in anyone else's mind, but which judges some minds as right and other minds as wrong?

NAT: Well, the Sophists said that these Ideas like justice didn't really exist, and that there was no such distinction between being and seeming, or reality and opinion, and that all our thinking was just a matter of subjective opinion, that we invented the rules of justice and morality as we invented the rules of a game. Didn't one of them say that "man is the measure of all things"? And don't most of our pop psychologists and commencement speakers say you can be whatever you think you are and whatever you want to be?

SOCRATES: Yes. We have many sophists today.

NAT: So why don't we have sophist jokes instead of lawyer jokes?

SOCRATES: Perhaps it's because Hitler was right about people being more gullible to big lies than to the little lies lawyers tell. We'll have to look at the question about the objective reality of *moral* values or truths or laws or principles when we study ethics. For now, let's take a less controversial example, something that's not moral. Let's take mathematics. If I say that 2 + 3 = 6 or that squares can have five sides, is that just a matter of my opinion or a matter of somebody else inventing the rules for me? Or is that a matter of truth that's objective to all minds, and universally knowable by all minds, and which judges all minds, and which cannot be changed, as fictions can?

NAT: Obviously, the latter. We bump up against those truths with our minds just as we bump up against walls with our bodies. We discover them; we don't invent them. But they're just *mathematical* truths.

SOCRATES: Well, then, might there not be such truths outside mathematics too?

NAT: For instance, physical truths like gravity and the truth that you can't walk from Chicago into the Atlantic Ocean by going west, you mean?

SOCRATES: Yes, but those are only physical truths; I was thinking about metaphysical truths, truths that are absolutely universal. For instance, the truth that everything that exists, everything that is, everything that's real, everything that has being, is *intelligible*, is knowable by some mind. Everything has intelligibility; everything has some meaning. There's nothing that is simply and absolutely unknowable and unintelligible to all minds, including a perfect mind, if there is one.

NAT: Let me think about that for a minute.... You know, that's true. And that's remarkable! We can't point to any corner of the universe, or any dimension of reality, that the mind can't explore at all, or some area of human life that we can't know or say anything at all about, whether it's right or wrong, good or bad, true or false, or anything else. The idea that there is something that is totally and literally knowable and unthinkable—is unthinkable. It's a self-contradiction. We can't think the unthinkable!

SOCRATES: I think you are right, but I'm playing devil's advocate here: Why isn't this fact—that there can't be anything that's unthinkable—purely negative and not any positive knowledge at all?

NAT: Because a negative has to have something positive to exclude. It makes no sense to say we can know "everything except——" and then say nothing. You have to say "everything except God" or "everything except yourself" or "everything except metaphysics" or "everything except black holes", and that exception has to be positive.

SOCRATES: Good thinking, Nat. But—just to keep playing devil's advocate—why couldn't this meaninglessness or unintelligibility be like a dark cloud that resists and obscures all light?

NAT: Because that's only physical darkness. That can be defined and circumscribed by a mind. There's no mental equivalent to that darkness. And even if there were a totally dark and unknowable cloud, the cloud would be knowable *as a dark cloud*. It would have edges, to distinguish it from the light, so it would be definable on the outside, so to speak, even if not on the inside.

SOCRATES: So there seems to be at least one principle that is true of all being, one principle that is metaphysically universal: that all being is intelligible, in principle, somehow, by some mind, at least a perfect mind. Is that the only one? What else can we say about everything real?

NAT: Well, let me think. I think that anything that's real would have to be related in some way to other things. Even the darkness is related to the light as its opposite. Everything is different from everything else; it is other than everything else in some way: bigger, smaller, better, longer, stronger, on top of, behind, the cause of, the effect of, part of, the connection between ... whatever. Everything is related to everything else in many different ways.

Everything finite is related to other finite things, and even if there is something infinite, it's related to the finite as other, as noninfinite. Nothing is totally separate and not related to anything else in any way at all. So we've got at least two universal properties of all being: intelligibility and relation.

SOCRATES: You are very quickly becoming adept at metaphysics. Can you think of any other such properties?

NAT: Well, how about this one? Every whole is greater than any one of its parts. That's true of individuals and of groups, of matter and of thoughts, of numbers and of supergalaxies, of nature and of art.

SOCRATES: That's three universal properties or principles of all being so far.

NAT: And here's another thing: everything is good for something, has some kind of value. We can desire it for some reason or another; we see something in it that's useful or desirable in some way, just as we see some intelligibility in it. Even evil things are good in some way; they have to have some good in them to attract us to them. A murderer has to be a good shot.

SOCRATES: Anything else?

NAT: Well, if being, or existence, is accidental to a thing, then it needs a cause. It's contingent. Its essence does not include existence. That's why horses exist and unicorns don't. But if being is essential to anything, it doesn't need a cause. It's a necessary being, not contingent.

And here's another property: there are merely mental beings, like fictional people, and real beings, like real people, and they are not the same. Some real beings like us can cause mental beings—fictions—to come into being, just by thinking them up, but merely mental beings can't cause any real beings to come into being.

SOCRATES: So we can do metaphysics after all. You just discovered six universal properties of all being. You are a budding metaphysician.

NAT: Wait a minute. I'm not sure we're saying anything about being, about reality, when we say things like that. They sound like tautologies, which are only ideas—two words or sets of words that we use to mean the same thing, so we put an equal sign or an "is" between them. Maybe this is all just mental, a trick we play on ourselves or a game we play with our ideas.

SOCRATES: So you're saying that maybe it's not really objectively true that everything real is knowable and desirable and related, and that maybe someday, somewhere, we'll find some real being that's a real whole that's smaller than its real parts even though in our thoughts that can't be?

NAT: No, that's not only unthinkable but also undoable, unrealizable.

SOCRATES: So there are objective truths that are true of all being. So metaphysics is possible.

NAT: Then why do many modern philosophers say it's impossible? We just did it.

SOCRATES: Well, some philosophers, like Hume, say we can't transcend our sense experience of particular things and reach universal truths that we know with certainty to be objectively true. Their "hard empiricism" in epistemology makes metaphysics impossible.

NAT: But we just did it. So we refuted them.

SOCRATES: It's not that easy. And others, like Kant, say that we can't know things as they are in themselves but only the appearances that we are unconsciously constructing and forming by imposing our mental categories onto that unknowable reality, like cookie cutters shaping cookie dough.

NAT: His "Copernican revolution in philosophy"—I remember that. I thought we refuted that when we argued about epistemology.

SOCRATES: Maybe we did and maybe we didn't. It's not that easy.

NAT: But even if we can do metaphysics, it seems to be just a set of self-evident platitudes and "of courses". Of course the whole is greater than any of its parts, and of course everything is related to every other thing at least by the relationship of otherness. It seems like a set of tautologies. How can it be interesting and controversial?

SOCRATES: Oh, there are plenty of controversies within it.

NAT: Like what?

SOCRATES: Well, for instance, materialism is a metaphysic that claims that everything real is material and that minds and souls and spirits and anything else that's supposed to be immaterial are unreal. That's pretty controversial. Some philosophers agree with it, and some don't.

NAT: Yes, that is metaphysics, isn't it? And it's controversial because many scientists are materialists, because they can explain the mind pretty darn well by matter nowadays, by what they know about how the material brain works.

SOCRATES: Do you remember how you refuted them back when we were exploring epistemology?

NAT: Yes. They argue that every so-called spiritual event—understanding, feeling, desiring, choosing, reasoning, even religious experience—can be fully explained by some physical or chemical or electrical event in the brain. They can identify a body event for every mind event. But that doesn't prove there are no mind events. I can identify an ink event for every word event in a book, or a sound event for every word event in a conversation, but that doesn't mean that a book is nothing but ink or a conversation is nothing but sound waves. Those events have different dimensions; some of them are physical and some are not.

Besides, materialism is self-contradictory, because materialism is an "ism", a philosophy, an idea. It's not made of atoms; it's made of ideas. Ideas aren't made of matter. And if ideas don't exist, then materialism doesn't exist either, because it's an idea.

SOCRATES: It's not that easy.

NAT: You keep saying that.

SOCRATES: I do, don't I?

NAT: What other reasons do philosophers have for not doing metaphysics?

SOCRATES: Well, many philosophers are nominalists. Nominalism claims that universal terms are only words or concepts, only mental, not real; that everything that's objectively real is singular or individual or particular, and that our mind invents classes of things that we see as resembling one another more or less, so we call them essences or natures or forms or qualities or species. But they say that these "universals" don't exist outside our minds, either as separate eternal essences, as Plato thought, or as ideas in the mind of God, as Augustine thought, or as the universal essential forms of particular things that are members of real species, like justice and triangularity and humanity, as Aristotle thought.

NAT: But nominalism is not only unlivable but also logically self-contradictory.

SOCRATES: Why is it unlivable?

NAT: It's unlivable because if none of our universal categories are real but are only the inventions we make to order things in our minds,

then order is invented, not discovered, and there's no real order
that's universal in the real world, so we're each living in our own
invented worlds. That's not how science works. It looks for formulas, and formulas are universals. Like energy equals matter times the
speed of light squared, or force equals mass multiplied by accelera-
tion. And if moral values, moral universals like justice, are only our
classifications of human actions, if they're only how we choose to
classify them, then there's no universal objective standard to appeal
to when we make moral judgments, and justice dissolves into personal opinions and desires.

SOCRATES: We shall have to take up that last point when we discuss ethics. And why do you think nominalism is logically self-contradictory?

NAT: Because if universals are not objectively real, independent of
our minds, then there can be no universal objective truths, independent of our minds. But then *that* is a universal objective truth!

SOCRATES: So nominalism leads to skepticism of all universal truths.

NAT: Yes. And skepticism is self-contradictory. We saw that already
in our earlier conversation.

SOCRATES: So you really think it's that easy?

NAT: Yes, I do. And the practical consequences are even worse. If
there are no real universals, then human nature is not a real universal either, so there's no essential equality and no universal rights.
And if every individual is essentially different from every other
individual, then there's no basis for universal laws except "majority
rules". But what if the majority votes for tyranny or cannibalism
or collective suicide?

SOCRATES: Which of your two criticisms of nominalism do you think
is stronger, the practical one or the logical one?

NAT: Well, the logical one is logically stronger, and the practical one is
practically stronger. The most unanswerable argument is the logical
one, but the practical argument is the one we need the most. I can't
choose between those two standards. They're both necessary.

SOCRATES: I think that's an excellent answer, Nat.

NAT: But it's not that easy, right?

SOCRATES: Actually, I was *not* going to say that again. I thought your
answer was the best one possible.

NAT: Then what if logic and practice conflict? What if logic seems to
prove one thing while life and practice demand another? Which
has the trump card?

SOCRATES: A very good question. And it divides philosophers. Hume, for instance, who admitted that his philosophy was unlivable, still believed it to be true because of his logic. And so did Parmenides, who thought he had logically proved a very different philosophy than Hume's: that change was an illusion because it was logically impossible. Zeno's famous paradoxes tried to prove that Parmenides was logically correct. On the other hand, existentialists and pragmatists and phenomenologists argue that experience always comes first and has to judge theories.

NAT: But that's a question of epistemology or method rather than metaphysics, isn't it?

SOCRATES: No, it's about metaphysics too, because it's about whether being includes universals, as Hume denies, and about whether being includes change, as Parmenides and Zeno deny.

NAT: So how would you counsel someone like Hume or Parmenides if he came to you with the problem of this conflict between the metaphysics your reason gave you versus the metaphysics your experience gave you?

SOCRATES: The first thing I'd say would be never to give up on either your reason or your experience. Rational theories have to be tested by experience, but experience has to be understood by reason. If you seem to have good reasons for believing an idea and also good reasons for not believing it, the first thing you have to do is to think again. Because truth can't really contradict truth. You must be misunderstanding something. Nothing can both be and not be in the same way at the same time. Two ideas that really contradict each other can't both be true. Keep thinking until you see which one is less than true. Sometimes, both reasons, both arguments, may be weak, either because a term is misunderstood or ambiguous, or because there's a false premise, or because the logic is not conclusive and the premises don't really prove the conclusion. It's usually the first of those three things, so we usually have to make distinctions to clarify the meaning of the terms. That's true in every field, not just philosophy, and in philosophy it's true in every division, not just metaphysics.

NAT: What strikes me in what you say is that we really are sure of the fact that two ideas that really contradict each other can't both be true. What I find striking is not the fact itself but how we know it. How do we know that? We can't prove it, because every proof presupposes it. But it can't just be a rule we will into existence, like the rules of a game, because those are changeable, and we can't change this one. We can ignore it, but we can't both ignore it and not ignore it at the same time—and that's the law of non-contradiction. We can disobey it, but we can't both disobey it and not disobey it at the same time—and that's the law of non-contradiction again. And even if we did will it into existence, we can't both will it into existence and not will it into existence at the same time—because that law precedes and structures everything we do.

SOCRATES: Do you think it might be just the way we all have to think because it's the structure of our minds rather than the structure of objective reality?

NAT: No, it can't be just the way we all have to think, because it's just as universally true of objective reality as it is of ideas. In the real world there is no exception to it. It's not just a verbal tautology, like eggs are eggs or X is X; it's real. It's the nature of reality. It's metaphysical.

SOCRATES: Why? Why do you think that law is true universally, of all being as well as all thinking?

NAT: Well, let's see. It's either based on nothing or on something. And it can't be based on nothing; it can't just be utterly without reason. And that something that it is based on has to be either subjective or objective. But it can't be just subjective, like our desire or our will or our choice or our need for order or our feelings. I think I already proved that. So it's got to be something objective. And I can't find any objective reality in the outer universe of matter or in the inner universe of thought that's as necessary and unchangeable as that principle is. So it must be based on something else that's neither our thought nor the universe. We have to call it something like "the absolute", or "the way things are". But it's not us and it's not the universe. So it seems to have something to do with God, or with some real Absolute.

SOCRATES: You think very logically, Nat.

NAT: Thinking logically doesn't help me avoid deep puzzles like this. In fact, it puts me into them and forces me to confront them.

SOCRATES: I found the same thing in my experience, Nat. That's why I was so skeptical of all easy answers. Especially skepticism, which is the easiest answer of all.

NAT: What about the question, Why is there anything at all rather than nothing? That's another one.

SOCRATES: Another what?

NAT: Another metaphysical question that has no easy answer. When I go through the same either-or logic again and I eliminate all the easy answers, I don't know what I'm left with.

SOCRATES: Let's see. Go through the logic again.

NAT: Well, either there is an answer to the question, Why is there anything at all? or there is not; either there is a reason for everything that is, or there is not. And if not, then either there is no reason for anything at all, which is ridiculous, because we know the reasons for most things, or there is no reason for just this one fact—that things exist—even though there is a reason for everything else. But how could there be a reason for everything else except that one thing? How could there be no reason for the very existence of all the things that all have their own reasons for existing? What would make that one thing different? How could the origin and basis of all rationality and intelligibility be irrational and unintelligible? How could light depend on darkness? It makes no sense. And even if just this one thing had no reason, there must be a *reason* why it had *no* reason, while everything else did have a reason. It couldn't be just an accident. So if it had a reason why it had no reason, it would have a reason too.

SOCRATES: I follow you so far, believe it or not. Go on.

NAT: So everything has to have a reason—a reason why it exists rather than not. I think I've proved that. That reason has to be either subjective or objective, and I think the same arguments that proved that the law of non-contradiction couldn't be just subjective proves that this—the reason why there is anything rather than nothing—also can't be just subjective. So it must be objective.

SOCRATES: So far, so good. What is your next step?

NAT: Well, for any being, either something else must be the reason it exists, like parents being the reason children exist and authors being the reason books exist, or else it itself is the reason it exists.

SOCRATES: Those seem to be the only two possibilities, yes.

NAT: And if it's something else, that just throws the question back one more step: Why does that "something else" exist? And that works for every possible "something else". No one part of the whole of existence can be the reason for the whole of it, only for some other part of it.

SOCRATES: That also makes sense.

NAT: But the only other alternative to the "something else" is to say that there is something that is itself the reason it exists.

SOCRATES: Our logic has forced us to that alternative, it seems.

NAT: But that makes no sense.

SOCRATES: Why not?

NAT: Because nothing can cause itself; no building can be its own foundation. Nothing can exist before it exists.

SOCRATES: That also seems to be necessarily true, at least for efficient causes. It might not be true for formal causes. A God can't be the efficient cause of Himself, but if His essence is existence, He is the formal cause of Himself, because the formal cause is the essence. It's an intrinsic cause, not an extrinsic cause. So even God would have to have a reason why He exists rather than not, but that reason would be not something else, extrinsic to His essence, but would be His essence. So His essence is one with His existence.

NAT: That makes sense. But I still have a problem with that: if you say that God is the reason for everything, I ask, Then what is the reason for God? No matter what being, or what kind of being, you put forth as the reason for everything, it won't work, whether it's a particular or a universal. A particular being can't account for all beings, for being as such. A concrete particular can't account for the universal. A part can't account for the whole. But if it's a universal rather than a particular that is the reason for all the particulars, that won't work either, because universals are abstract, and abstract universals can't account for concrete particulars. The laws of mathematics are abstract universals, but they can't account for a cent of my real money. Only work, or gifts, or other money, or some other concrete cause can explain a concrete effect like my money. So the same must be true of the universe. Universal abstract laws don't explain why concrete particular things exist.

SOCRATES: Well, let's not call this thing that we're looking for either "God" or "universal law" or anything else. Let's just call it "X". X must be real, but it can't be a concrete particular thing, one among many, and it also can't be an abstract universal, because it has to account for concrete particular things. So it couldn't even be a necessary law like the law of non-contradiction, because that's only a law, a principle, a truth, not a real being.

NAT: Right. So I'm stumped again. Where do I turn now?

SOCRATES: Let's review logical principles to orient ourselves. Logically speaking, there are three acts of the mind: understanding the meaning of a concept, judging a proposition to be true, and reasoning to a conclusion, proving that if the premises are true, the conclusion necessarily follows. That first act of the mind, understanding (its technical term is "simple apprehension") is an answer to the question, *What* is it? Its object is an essence, a nature, a "what". The second act of the mind, judgment, is an answer to the question, *Is* it? Its object is an act of existence. And the third act of the mind, reasoning, is an answer to the question, *Why* is it? Its object is a cause of some kind. Right?

NAT: Right.

SOCRATES: And we're trying to find the answer to the question, *Why* is it? for everything. Why is there anything at all rather than nothing? So that's the third act of the mind and the third question, right?

NAT: Right.

SOCRATES: Let's look at the difference between the thing we're looking for in the first act of the mind and the first question, and the thing we're looking for in the second. When we ask, What is it? we're asking about its essence, or its nature, right?

NAT: Right.

SOCRATES: And when we ask, Is it? we're asking whether it really is, whether it exists or not, right?

NAT: Right.

SOCRATES: So everything that exists has some essence, some nature, some "what", right?

NAT: Right.

SOCRATES: So what is the relation between a thing's essence and a thing's existence?

NAT: None, that I can see. The essence of a unicorn is just as good an essence as the essence of a horse, but unicorns don't exist and horses do. So there's no answer to the question why things exist—no answer to be found in their essence. That's why we need to ask for the cause, or the reason why the thing exists, and that's why we asked the question, Why does anything at all exist? It doesn't have to, by its essence. It's contingent, dependent on its cause.

SOCRATES: Suppose this X was different. Suppose its very essence was to exist.

NAT: Is that logically possible?

SOCRATES: I see no logical self-contradiction in it. Do you?

NAT: But what could that be?

SOCRATES: Well, it would have to be Being Itself.

NAT: That sounds like an abstraction.

SOCRATES: Perhaps it's God. God is not an abstraction. Divinity, or divine perfection, is the abstraction. The Creator of everything real has to be a reality.

NAT: That sounds too concrete and particular. You said "*a* reality", not "reality". If God is *a* reality, God is a particular, even if He is a unique particular. And that forces us to ask, What caused God, then? Nothing can bring itself into existence, not even God, because nothing can exist before it comes into existence.

SOCRATES: That's true. But why couldn't this God be not self-caused but uncaused? Why couldn't it exist because that is its very essence? Unconditioned, uncaused, unlimited Being Itself.

NAT: That still sounds pretty far from what people mean by "God".

SOCRATES: Well, there is one religious tradition that sounds very close to it. The God of the Jews supposedly told his prophet Moses that his true, eternal name was simply "I AM." He didn't add a predicate, an essence. That sounds suspiciously like "Being Itself". As if he's saying, "My essence is simply existence itself, unlimited by any finite essence."

NAT: But that's religion.

SOCRATES: No, it isn't. It's philosophy. It's metaphysics.

NAT: But it's about God.

SOCRATES: So what? Philosophy is about everything. At least metaphysics is. It excludes nothing except nothingness. There was a poet during the Enlightenment, Alexander Pope, who wrote, "Know then thyself, presume not God to scan; / The proper study of mankind is man."[3] Metaphysics says that the proper study of mankind is everything.

---

[3] Alexander Pope, *An Essay on Man*, epistle 2, canto 1, lines 1–2.

NAT: So philosophical theology can be part of philosophy.

SOCRATES: Why not?

NAT: Because philosophy isn't religion.

SOCRATES: Right. Why not?

NAT: Because it's purely rational. It appeals only to universal reason, not personal faith.

SOCRATES: Right. In contrast, religion is personal. It's a relationship. Faith is something we choose to do or not do. We'll need a whole other conversation to talk about that, that is, to talk about religion and evaluate it by philosophical reasoning.

NAT: But God is not just "AM", or "am-ness". He is a Speaker who says "*I* AM." How can I-ness and am-ness be identical? How can the subject and the object be identical?

SOCRATES: I'm afraid you will have to find a mystic to answer that question. You see, you're only a very intelligent and passionate beginner, and I'm only a philosopher, an intellectual midwife, and getting that baby out ...

NAT: Let me guess: it's not that easy.

Questions for Discussion or Personal Essays

1. Why do you think most people are skeptical about the possibility of doing metaphysics?

2. What is unique about the concept of "real" or "existing" or "being"?

3. Are the three words in question number 2 identical? If not, how are they related?

4. What is the point of Socrates' example of comparing one real horse to a hundred merely thought-about horses? Is that point always true? For example, compare one real toenail to a hundred fictional persons.

5. Socrates says that being cannot be defined. Why? What do you think is the closest we can come to defining it?

6. How can we understand a term we can't define? Give some other examples of this.

7. Find another example of an absolutely universal metaphysical truth like the principle of causality, but not in this chapter.

(Remember that a truth is not just a concept but a judgment, a proposition.)

8. How does Socrates' example about Plato's concept of justice show that ethics depends on metaphysics? Many philosophers disagree with Socrates' principle that ethics depends on metaphysics, because they are skeptical of metaphysics. How would they avoid Socrates' argument?

9. Try to find an example that refutes Socrates' principle that everything that is, is intelligible. What happens when you try to find such an example?

10. Socrates assumes that if any idea is self-contradictory, it must be false. Try to disprove that. What happens when you do? Try to prove it. What happens when you do?

11. Can an empiricist do metaphysics? Why or why not? Don't automatically agree with Socrates. Imagine you are an empiricist who wants to do metaphysics; how might you try to do it?

12. Do the same with nominalism as you just did with empiricism.

13. If, as Socrates claims, metaphysics is not just platitudes or tautologies or word games, why do most people think it is?

14. Why do logical theory and lived practice often seem to contradict each other? Do they, in fact, or not? Defend your answer.

15. Give at least two or three examples of two ideas that both seem to be true but that contradict each other. How do you negotiate this situation?

16. What is unique about the question, Why is there something rather than nothing?

17. Give an example of something that seems to exist but has no reason why it exists. Explain what is happening there.

18. Does the idea of a self-existing being, or a being that is itself the whole reason for its own existence, make any sense to you? Why or why not? Does this situation (in your thinking) change when you think of the concrete example of God rather than the abstract description of "a being that is its own reason"? Why or why not?

19. Evaluate this argument: Universals, like "humanness", are abstract; and particulars, like "Socrates" or "this man", are concrete. Everything is either an abstract universal or a concrete particular. But God is neither an abstract universal, like "divinity",

nor a concrete particular (this thing, this god, this being, this particular finite entity). Therefore, God does not exist.

20. What is the relation between essence and existence?

21. Creating something means to cause it to exist. If there could be a God who created everything, what could have created God? Is that a good question? Why or why not?

22. What is the relation between philosophy and theology? What is the difference between theology and religion?

23. Can anything be its own cause? Can anything be uncaused?

24. Can "I-ness" be identical with "am-ness" or "is-ness"? If not, how can God be both as one ("I AM")?

25. Are you turned off or on by apparently unanswerable questions like these? Why?

26. The issue of God has come up more than once, and the next dialogue is explicitly about God. If you believe in God, are you surprised and disappointed that neither Nat nor Socrates appeals to faith, only to reason? If you do not believe in God, are your surprised and disappointed that the question is treated as very important, and do you suspect that this book is "spy work" to convert atheists, since it is a Catholic publisher (Ignatius Press) that publishes it?

7

Philosophy of Religion:
Did We Invent God or Did God Invent Us?

The previous chapter was about being, and it naturally led to the question of the being of God: both God's existence and God's essence, or the relation between existence and essence in God. "Being" is a philosophical word, and "God" is a religious word, and though philosophy is not religion, Socrates philosophizes about religion. In the same way, though it is not science or education or politics, a philosopher naturally philosophizes about these important human enterprises. Religious faith is not the starting point or assumption of these arguments, nor is it their end or purpose. Truth—whatever truth can be known by human reason—is both their assumption and their purpose.

SOCRATES: When Aristotle first defined metaphysics (which he called "first philosophy"), he divided it into two main questions: the investigation into being as such and the investigation into the first Being, or the primary Being, which he called "God". He meant by that term neither any one of the Greek gods nor the Judeo-Christian God, which he had not heard of, but simply the ultimate efficient and final cause, the first beginning and the last end of all being.

In our last conversation, about "being", we used the word "God", which, unlike "being", is a religious word. The word "religion" literally designates a relationship between persons, because it comes from *religare*, which means "a binding relationship or task" or "to bind back", suggesting or implying a relationship to one's

Creator or source. There are many religions in the world, and they are very different in many ways, but what seems common to all of them is a human attitude we could call "faith", which goes beyond both sensation and reasoning, both logical and scientific, and which is some kind of relationship with something superhuman or transcendent and absolute, something usually called "God".

NAT: And since our discussion of metaphysics last time naturally moved toward religious language in talking about God, perhaps our exploration of religion will point to and cast some light on our exploration of metaphysics.

SOCRATES: Perhaps. Perhaps not. That is not my main reason for investigating it.

NAT: What is your main reason?

SOCRATES: That this dimension of human life—religion—has always been important and central in most human lives and most cultures, even still today to many people in our modern Western culture, which for the first time in history has about as many people in it who identify as indifferent or unbelieving when it comes to religion as those who believe and practice a religion.

NAT: So if religion is a relationship that has two poles, the human subject and the divine or superhuman object, should we try to shine the light of philosophical reason on both dimensions?

SOCRATES: No, I think we should confine ourselves to the objective pole of that relationship and talk about good reasons for belief or unbelief in a God and leave the other dimension to the psychologists and perhaps also the saints and mystics—I mean the exploration of the human side of religion, and its practice, and religious experience. We are philosophers, not psychologists, and certainly not saints or mystics; and I think the tools of philosophical reason will give us more satisfying results if we confine our investigation to the reasons for and against belief in some sort of God. That's what most of the great philosophers have usually done, and we are not more than great philosophers, but less. We are only beginners.

NAT: So we're not going to mention the psychological plusses and minuses, like comfort versus guilt, or happiness versus unhappiness in individual lives, or the good versus the harm that we observe religion producing in history and society and other aspects of culture, like the arts and the sciences.

SOCRATES: No. I think that would make our topic unmanageably vast. So here, as in our other discussions, let's confine ourselves to the single central question. Here that question is simple and obvious: Does God exist? Is God, or something like God, real or not? Did we invent God or did God invent us?

NAT: Good. And since you love to define your terms first, should we begin by defining what God we are talking about, since as you said, many religions have very different concepts of God? In fact, most ancient religions believed there were many gods, while only one religion, Judaism, believed in only one God. And you were the exception in your culture: a monotheist among polytheists.

SOCRATES: I fear that such a definition would be impossible to agree on, since there are so many important differences between different religions' concepts of God. If we demanded a definition first, we would have to confine ourselves to only one religion. For instance, the supreme God in Hinduism, Brahman, is eternal and necessary, like the God of Western religions, but not usually thought of as a Person with a will and a moral law, and not having created the physical universe out of nothing.

NAT: So let's not define God too narrowly for purposes of this dialogue.

SOCRATES: There is also a second reason for not insisting on a definition of God. It is that every religion claims that God is mysterious and indefinable, at least in the ordinary way.

NAT: That's true, but I think we have to have some kind of answer to the question of what we mean by "God", even if we can't answer that by an ordinary definition. How about a negative one that does not violate what you called your second reason, God's indefinability? Why not say that "God" means simply "that which transcends definition" or "that which is not definable because it has no limits to its perfection"?

SOCRATES: That is essentially what Saint Anselm does in one of the most famous of all arguments for the existence of God, the so-called ontological argument. He first defines God negatively, as that "than which nothing greater can be conceived",[1] which

---

[1] Saint Anselm, *Proslogium, in Proslogium; Monologium; an Appendix in Behalf of the Fool by Gaunilon; and Cur Deus Homo*, trans. Sidney Norton Deane (La Salle, Ill.; Open Court, 1951), 7.

seems to be a very good definition because it allows for mystery and it is broad enough to work for all religions. And then he claims to prove that this God must exist without assuming anything else except that negative definition of God and the one additional premise that it is greater, or more perfect, to exist in objective reality, independent of our minds, than to exist only subjectively, as our invention, dependent on our minds. The conclusion that God must have real existence, just as He has all other conceivable perfections, seems to follow logically from those two premises.

NAT: That argument seems logical, yet intuitively I seem to smell a rat. There's got to be something wrong with it. You can't deduce anything's existence just from its definition, or its essence. Yet while my nose smells a rat, my mind can't see a logical mistake.

SOCRATES: I think you should not ignore either your nose or your mind. Perhaps your mind can follow the scent your nose gives you. I think Kant did this when he showed that the "rat", the erroneous assumption, that is implied in his argument is that existence is one of many perfections—that it is an essence, a "what", a definable perfection or property or attribute. The argument is that God lacks no perfection, and existence is a perfection; therefore, God does not lack existence. But the second premise is false. Existence is not a perfection. It's not a "what" but a "whether".

NAT: I see. That's the metaphysical reason for the logical point that you can't prove the existence of a thing simply by looking at its essence, or nature. So are there any better arguments?

SOCRATES: Before we explore that question, perhaps it would work best if we played two different parts once again as we did before. I think we are both agnostics, in different senses, about God, so we need not suppress any strong specific religious or antireligious convictions that we have in playing the two parts of believer and unbeliever. What do you say to that?

NAT: I agree. How do you see our agnosticisms as different, by the way?

SOCRATES: I think your agnosticism comes from your imbibing the influence of your secular culture, while mine comes from my questioning the influence of my religious culture, the gods that the Athenian state recognized.

NAT: But you believed in some God or other, whoever inspired the Delphic oracle, didn't you? You were not an atheist but an agnostic monotheist, right?

SOCRATES: I suppose those labels are not wholly inaccurate.

NAT: So if we're going to assume roles that fit us, you should play the part of the questioning believer and I should play the part of the questioning unbeliever.

SOCRATES: I agree.

NAT: So what do you think are the best arguments for some sort of God? They may not give you certainty, but which come the closest to it?

SOCRATES: The ones with the most certain premises, since the most usual way to refute an argument is to question its premises. That's why I insisted on defining terms clearly—because if one of the terms in one of the premises of an argument is ambiguous, then the premise may be false in one sense of the term and true in another.

NAT: So what argument do you think has the most certain premises?

SOCRATES: Well, premises may come from either of the two parts or poles of all of our experience, the subjective part or the objective part. I mean, the premises may come from either the world outside us or from the spirit, soul, mind, will, and desire that we sense within us. Which of those two sources do *you* think is more certain and indubitable as the source of our premises?

NAT: The things outside us. I think experience proves that our souls deceive us much more often than our bodies do. I don't think the world deceives us, but I think our minds often do. That's why Anselm's argument is not convincing to me. So let's find premises in the world outside us if we can.

SOCRATES: The most famous of those are five arguments from Saint Thomas Aquinas, all of which get their premises from our sensory observation of features in the physical world that we see and touch.

NAT: What features?

SOCRATES: First, movement, or change. Second, coming into existence. Third, contingency, or mortality, or being able to go out of existence. Fourth, imperfections. And fifth, order, or movement toward natural ends: fire rises, stones fall, acorns grow into oaks, and evolution produces human brains. All things in the universe outside us seem to manifest those five characteristics, don't they?

NAT: Yes, but how does that prove the existence of God?

SOCRATES: Let's take them one at a time. When anything changes, there must be an adequate cause for the change, right?

NAT: Yes. That is a principle of both common sense and science. If things happened without causes and reasons, we could not rely on anything. A donkey might suddenly change into a human being and start to talk. Planets and atoms might remain moving in their orbits without gravity or electromagnetic attraction moving them.

SOCRATES: Now let's apply the principle of causality to that empirical data. Nothing can give to itself what it does not have. An object that lacks energy cannot give itself energy. A stone does not have a mind or a mouth, so it cannot think or speak. Fictional parents, who lack existence, can't cause real children, who exist.

NAT: Of course.

SOCRATES: And these changes that we observe are very complex and long. They happen in multifarious and interacting chains, like dominoes falling.

NAT: Yes.

SOCRATES: And none of these changes, none of these events, none of these links in the chain would happen unless its cause happened, either before the change, like parents having children, or during it, like the foundation holding up a building.

NAT: Right.

SOCRATES: Now, if there were no first cause of change, there could be no second causes, no matter how many those second causes may be. The dominoes do not move themselves, but they move; therefore, there must be something in addition to the chain of dominoes that is not just one more domino—something that moves the whole chain. Events have beginnings, and the universe as a whole is an event, in fact a long chain of events; therefore, it must have a beginning, a first cause. And if it is first, it is not second, not caused. There must be some uncaused cause. And that would be something that needs no beginning and no cause for its activity in causing other things to move.

NAT: I see; so that something is God, or godlike, because it transcends the universe of changing things. But if that God, or godlike thing, does not change, perhaps there is no time gap between that godlike thing and the universe. Perhaps the universe itself as a whole is eternal and timeless, as God is, even though within it things move in time, one after another.

SOCRATES: Even if this is so, even if the universe is coeternal with its cause, there must be a first cause that is like the foundation for all the stories of the building staying up.

NAT: But that something seems pretty far from the God of religion. It is not necessarily a Person, only a force.

SOCRATES: It seems to be a very, very thin slice of the God of religion. But it also seems to be a slice of God, not of the universe, and thus enough to disturb the atheist, does it not? An unchanging cause of all causes may be a very thin slice of God, but it looks like a thin slice of *God*, not anything else.

NAT: I suppose so. And your second argument will take the same form as the first one, I suppose: second causes require a first cause, whether we're talking about a cause of change or a cause of existence, a cause of coming into existence. Something that does not exist cannot cause other things to exist, and therefore there must exist something that causes the whole universe to exist. Not just an unmoved Mover but also an uncreated Creator. A somewhat thicker slice of the God of religion proved by the same logical strategy.

SOCRATES: Yes, I think that's a fair and very brief way of putting it.

NAT: And the third argument?

SOCRATES: Its premise is that all the things in the universe can go out of existence, can die, or can cease to be. They are contingent, not necessary.

NAT: That's true. Even stars die. Even the galaxies are mortal. Everything has entropy.

SOCRATES: But if this is so, then given enough time everything can die eventually.

NAT: Yes.

SOCRATES: And if atheism were true, if there were no Creator, no First Cause, no beginning of the whole universe and all of matter and thus also of time itself (which is not absolute, as Newton thought, but relative to matter, as Einstein showed), then eventually, given sufficient time, everything *would* die.

NAT: Yes. So what?

SOCRATES: But once a thing dies, or ceases to exist, it can no longer make itself exist again. Living things can change to dead things, but dead things can't change to living things.

NAT: True. Again, so what?

SOCRATES: But eventually, everything then will die, and nothing will exist anymore, at all, ever. But things do exist. Therefore, not everything is mortal, or able to die, or contingent, but there must exist something that is necessary, that cannot die or not exist.

NAT: Perhaps there just has not been enough time yet for that to happen. Perhaps past time has been only finite.

SOCRATES: But if the past time of the universe is finite rather than infinite, then it has a beginning. And nothing begins to exist without a cause. Therefore, the universe must have a cause. And that certainly sounds like God, the Creator.

NAT: Hmm, perhaps it is only *possible* that everything together dies, and that possibility has not yet been actualized, has not yet happened.

SOCRATES: But if there is no Creator and thus no act of Creation, no beginning, if the universe is all there is and it is eternal, then its past is infinite, not finite. So there has been plenty of time for it to die. Given infinite time, every possibility eventually will happen. So why has it not yet happened? Why are we here? Why is there anything at all rather than nothing?

NAT: That is a strange and wonderful question. I don't know. Perhaps we cannot know. Perhaps all these proofs have a hidden assumption, the assumption that there can be nothing that is impossible for us to know, and perhaps that assumption is false.

SOCRATES: But nothing in the universe is impossible in principle for us to know, something that makes no sense at all. So if there is something that is impossible for us to know, it must be something like God, something transcendent to the universe.

NAT: Perhaps there is some dimension of the universe that we cannot know.

SOCRATES: What dimension? How is it different from all the other ones?

NAT: Perhaps that, too, is unknowable.

SOCRATES: So the question I just asked is unanswerable.

NAT: Yes.

SOCRATES: Then the difference between the knowable dimensions of the universe and the unknowable dimension of the universe is not itself knowable?

NAT: Yes.

SOCRATES: But in defining that difference, we just did know it. It is definition that defines what is undefinable, as it is reason that defines the irrational, and light that defines darkness. Being defines nonbeing, not vice versa.

NAT: We are getting into metaphysical abstractions that are making my head hurt. Let's move to the fourth argument.

SOCRATES: Fine. Nothing in the universe is absolutely perfect, right? By perfect I don't mean merely complete in its species or its essential nature but having *all* conceivable perfections. That would be God. God cannot be a part of the finite and imperfect universe. For anything finite, we can always conceive something more perfect, just as we can always conceive a higher number than any positive number.

NAT: That is obvious, yes.

SOCRATES: So in the universe we observe that one thing is more perfect than another, both within its species and compared to other species. One human is more intelligent than another, and humans are more intelligent than gorillas.

NAT: Or professional wrestlers.

SOCRATES: But to make such judgments, to know that sages are more perfect than snakes, we must know what perfection is. Actually, snakes are more perfect than sages in their ability to change their body temperature. But sages are more perfect in intelligence. So we must know the standard of perfection in order to judge truly which thing comes closest to that standard.

NAT: All right, but how does that prove that an all-perfect God exists? Perhaps the standard is not God but just an idea that we invented with our minds.

SOCRATES: Then it is not *true*, not corresponding to objective reality. We cannot make judgments of value that are true unless our standard of judging those values is true. If our standard is merely what we think or feel or desire within our own minds or feelings, then our judgment has no validity or authority outside our own minds or feelings.

NAT: So if humans are really more perfect than snakes, an all-perfect Being must be real—is that the argument?

SOCRATES: Yes.

NAT: That sounds like a pretty big leap from the premise to the conclusion.

SOCRATES: Not if you remember your earlier criticism of these arguments: that the conclusion is a very thin slice of the God of religion. The perfect good that this argument proves may be something like a Platonic Form, an eternal essence that is objectively real but not a person with a mind and a will. We have not assumed anything yet about what kinds of things are more perfect.

NAT: Oh. That's probably OK then.

SOCRATES: Is it OK because it keeps a safe enough distance from religion to seem not threatening to you? Or because the logic is consistent?

NAT: The latter, of course.

SOCRATES: I hope that is indeed an "of course". But of course only you and God, if there is a God, can know what your real motives are. Shall we go on to the fifth argument?

NAT: Yes.

SOCRATES: It is usually called the argument from design: nature is full of design, and design requires an intelligent designer; therefore, nature has an intelligent designer, which must be as superior to nature as an artist is to his art. And that gives us a significantly thicker concept of God than the other four arguments because it claims to prove intelligence, and thus personality, in God.

NAT: Didn't evolution refute that argument in explaining the most complex designs in nature, organisms, and especially human brains, by random chance and natural selection?

SOCRATES: No, for three reasons. First, evolution is not data but a theory, although it is by far the best theory to account for the data. Second, because evolution says nothing about minds or souls, only physical brains, because minds leave no fossils. Third, because randomness and intelligent design are not mutually exclusive. Roulette wheels are intelligently designed to be random. God may well have designed natural selection itself to bring about what He designed it to bring about, namely, human brains that could host human minds.

NAT: So what is the argument?

SOCRATES: The data is that things in nature are ordered to ends. In one sense of the word "cause", what Aristotle called "efficient causes", physical causes account for the movement, the energy, in nature, but not the direction. They are like the motor in a car, or the gasoline. But why does the car stay on the road and go to the city at the end of the road rather than off a cliff or into a ditch? That requires another kind of causality, what Aristotle called "final causality" or direction to an end. The efficient cause is like a push from behind, and the final cause is like a pull from ahead, the direction or the specification of where the force will go.

The car itself has no intelligence, yet it acts under an ordering intelligence, or the driver. The arrow has no intelligence, yet it hits the target under the ordering of an intelligence in the archer. And nature acts like a car or an arrow: it moves toward determinate ends. Many scientists have marveled at the order in nature, especially in genetics and in physics. The amount of encoded information in our genes is more complex than all the data in all the libraries in the world. And the mathematical perfection and simplicity of nature is far from random. And the windows of opportunity for the evolution of human life are manifold and very tiny. For instance, if the temperature of the primeval fireball that began 13.7 billion years ago and expanded into the present universe had been the tiniest bit hotter or colder a split second after the Big Bang, carbon molecules that are the basis for all life forms could never have evolved.

NAT: Maybe seeing design in impersonal things is just our projection, our personification.

SOCRATES: Just the opposite! It's because the car or the arrow is *not* a person and does *not* have reason or intelligence that the argument works. It takes an intelligent designer or orderer in addition to energy or force to explain what we see all around us. Nature isn't like a dog making random noise by walking on a piano keyboard but like a pianist playing music. You have to pretend you are as stupid as a dog to call a sonata "just noise".

NAT: I dunno, that just seems suspicious to me, like Anselm's argument. Something in me resists that argument more than the other four. It seems like bad science. How can empirical and mathematical science prove there is a mind there? "Intelligent design" and "intelligence" itself are not scientifically provable things. They are not empirical data, like heat or color or mass, and they are not quantifiable. When we measure IQ, we are not measuring intelligence itself but only how many answers on a test a person gets right.

SOCRATES: I agree. "Intelligent design" is not a scientific category; it's a commonsense category or a philosophical category. But we are doing philosophy today, not science.

NAT: I have other objections to Aquinas' five arguments. They all have assumptions that can be questioned—for instance, that causality, or causal relationships, are objectively real and not just categories we invent and impose on our observations, as Hume and Kant both thought, in different ways.

SOCRATES: All arguments have assumptions, and all assumptions can be questioned, except tautologies. As for that assumption, if it's not true, we can explain almost nothing, because almost all explanations are causal. Denying causality destroys science as well as philosophy and common sense. That's why we were so hard on Hume and Kant when we discussed them.

NAT: What about the assumption that reason in us corresponds to reason in the world? That seems to be a hidden assumption, and one that can't be proved. Maybe that's just projection.

SOCRATES: There is massive evidence that it does correspond, and no proof that it doesn't. Whenever we find something in the world that seems unexplainable, we eventually find things that explain it.

NAT: Not always.

SOCRATES: Can you find any exception to that?

NAT: Evil. Why is there evil?

SOCRATES: Because good is finite and limited.

NAT: Wow. That was short and sweet! The greatest problem in life solved in two seconds! By the guy who keeps saying "It's not that simple"!

SOCRATES: If you ask a two-second question, you get a two-second answer. The point is that there is an answer. There is an answer to every question, even though there are always many more questions and many more aspects of every question that are not answered—*yet*. If we did not believe that was true, we would not do either science or philosophy. We stop seeking a thing if we believe it does not exist.

NAT: I guess that's psychologically true, but it does not prove that God exists.

SOCRATES: I did not say it did.

NAT: Are there other arguments for the existence of God that you want to run by me?

SOCRATES: Yes. The arguments from inner data, or spiritual data: from our intellects and our moral wills and our desires and longings. We all seek "the true, the good, and the beautiful", and theistic philosophers have found arguments in all three of those areas.

NAT: Aquinas again?

SOCRATES: No, the most famous argument about truth is from Augustine, and the most famous argument about goodness is from Newman and Dostoyevsky, and the most famous argument about the longing for beauty is from C. S. Lewis.

NAT: What's the argument about truth?

SOCRATES: That we can know eternal, necessary, indubitable truths like $2 + 3 = 5$. There is nothing in nature that is eternal and necessary and indubitable, and there is nothing in our minds like that either: we are fallible and changeable and to be doubted. Where do we see the truth that $2 + 3 = 5$? Not in matter, which changes, and not in our own minds, or other human minds, which also change. So there must be something above both matter and human minds. That sounds like God, doesn't it?

NAT: So when we do math, we are reading the mind of God?

SOCRATES: Some of it, yes.

NAT: That sounds like the argument from design: reading the mind of the artist from the art.

SOCRATES: There is a similarity there, yes.

NAT: So my objections to the design argument apply to this one too. Also, I have a second objection: it's very abstract.

SOCRATES: That's not an objection. Math is abstract, but true.

NAT: No, I mean this: that truth is not a concrete thing, like a galaxy or a person. It's a relation—the right relation between something subjective and something objective, between a knowing mind and something in objective reality that is known.

SOCRATES: That is true. Truth is not a mind, but an object of the mind. It does not know us; we know it.

NAT: That is true too. But "truth" is much more abstract than "God". I don't see how the existence of truth proves the existence of God.

SOCRATES: It's not truth as such, but the fact that we, temporal and fallible as we are, can know eternal and immutable truths with certainty. That seems to prove we are in contact with an infallible, eternal mind.

NAT: Sounds to me as if it's trying to prove something like our having a mystical, subconscious mental telepathy with the mind of God. I don't think many people would buy that.

SOCRATES: That's irrelevant. They are not here now, only you. Why don't you buy it?

NAT: The sense of smell again. Let's just move on, if you please, to something less ethereal.

SOCRATES: Let's try goodness then, moral goodness. We find ourselves under real moral obligations or duties, don't we?

NAT: I believe so, yes.

SOCRATES: These obligations are moral laws, like "Do unto others what you want them to do to you", or "Love people, don't hate them", or "Don't treat people like things, like property or slaves."

NAT: Yes.

SOCRATES: Laws and commandments come from lawgivers and commanders. So what is the lawgiver?

NAT: Maybe it's just us.

SOCRATES: But if we give the laws to ourselves, we are over the laws, not under them. If we bind ourselves, we are not bound, and even if we are, if we bound ourselves, we can unbind ourselves. If we invented morality, as we invented the rules of a game, we can also uninvent it or change it whenever and however we please.

NAT: What is the conclusion of that argument?

SOCRATES: That there must be a moral lawgiver that is not either matter or man. What else can that be but something like God?

NAT: I dunno. Maybe there are other possibilities. But that argument assumes that moral laws are objective. How can you prove that assumption?

SOCRATES: That's another question, which we will take up when we discuss ethics. Philosophers make many assumptions.

NAT: Catholics would say that proves that the Blessed Virgin Mary was not a philosopher, because she made only one Assumption.

SOCRATES: Aren't you making fun of something holy by that very bad pun?

NAT: Not at all. I'm making fun of philosophers, not of her.

SOCRATES: I refuse to be distracted from the argument. Look, even if morality is only subjective, even if your set of rules is different from mine, even if you reject all ten of the Ten Commandments, at least there is one rule or law that nobody denies, even an ethical subjectivist or relativist.

NAT: What's that?

SOCRATES: That you should never disobey your own conscience. Nobody admires that.

NAT: That's true. But different people's consciences tell them different things.

SOCRATES: That's partly true, but not wholly. Nobody believes we are morally obligated in conscience to hate, rape, enslave, harm, rob, or torture other people, or that we don't have a moral obligation *not* to do those things. But even if you found someone like Nietzsche, who maligned all of traditional morality and called for a new morality, for the new man, the "overman", he would not admire deliberately disobeying his conscience that dictated his new morality to him.

NAT: True. So what?

SOCRATES: So *why*? What gives conscience that rightful authority?

NAT: Maybe it's just society, the desires of other people that we subconsciously internalize, what Freud calls the "superego". Maybe it's just our parents speaking in us.

SOCRATES: Why obey it, then? Why should society be treated as if it were infallible? Why should our equals, other people, have the absolute right to tell us what to do? Even if they're our parents? They're not infallible, and they're not morally perfect. Disobeying them isn't *always* morally wrong, but disobeying our conscience is.

NAT: Maybe conscience is just the way evolution worked.

SOCRATES: Why should evolution, or natural selection, have moral authority? Just because it had the power to make whatever it is in our brains that gives us conscience? Does power make duty? Does might make right?

NAT: No. I see the argument. In other words, we have either to deny the authority of moral conscience or to say it has the authority of God behind it, because no other authority source is absolute, and "obey your conscience" is the one absolute that even a moral relativist admits.

SOCRATES: Exactly. Dostoyevsky says that if God does not exist (in other words, if a perfectly good and moral Being does not exist, a Being who has the authority to tell us to be good, like Him), then everything is permissible. But obviously not everything is permissible. Disobeying whatever your conscience tells you is not permissible. Therefore, God exists.

NAT: That seems like quite a stretch—from my private conscience to a perfect, universal God.

SOCRATES: That is true in a sense: what it proves is still a thin slice of God, not the concrete God of religion. It is agnostic about everything else about God. So to get nearer to the religious God, you would have to add the other arguments. But they seem to converge, like pointing fingers.

NAT: What's the one about beauty? Do you mean the beauty of art?

SOCRATES: Well, I know people who were converted by the music of Bach or Mozart. But that's a kind of immediate intuition, not a logical argument. And I don't know how to make it the premise of a tight logical argument. No, I meant something else, something just as intuitive as beauty but something that also can be the premise of a logical argument.

NAT: What's that?

SOCRATES: The innate desire for something that we cannot attain or even clearly define, something so beautiful that we can barely endure it, something that totally enraptures our souls and gives us a joy that casts out all fear and pain and boredom and anything else that is ugly and evil. We get hints of it in "peak experiences", and we can create a meaningful analogy about it: we can say that it is, in relation to the most beautiful music or love or mystical experience, what those things are in relation to a good drink or a hot bath. We certainly have never had it or experienced it, only the longing for it.

NAT: What if I say I have no idea what you are talking about, that I have never experienced such a desire?

SOCRATES: Then I can only ask you to be totally honest with yourself and to ask your own soul whether this desire is really there, down at its bottom, or not. And if you say "not", I cannot argue further with you. But perhaps there is someone who can argue further with you.

NAT: Who?

SOCRATES: You. In the privacy of yourself and in total openness and honesty. But I have another version of this "argument from desire" that can use a psychologically less interesting but more universal premise: dissatisfaction, disappointments, and pains and sufferings of all kinds. There is always much more in our desires than in our satisfactions. We all have "a lover's quarrel with the world". In other words, this world is not enough.

NAT: Well, that's true enough, but how does that prove the existence of God?

SOCRATES: Let that desire, that "restless heart", be one premise, OK? Either the strong, positive, mysterious one or the weaker but clearer negative one, the dissatisfaction.

NAT: OK.

SOCRATES: Is this desire universal?

NAT: The negative one is. But not the positive one, except perhaps in the depths of the subconscious.

SOCRATES: What makes some desires universal, in everyone, while others are not? Why does everyone want to be loved but not everyone wants to be Superman and fly through the air? Why does everyone want knowledge and pleasure and beauty and friendship and food and peace, and hate ignorance and pain and ugliness and loneliness and starvation and war and death?

NAT: Because everyone is human. These desires come simply from our common human nature.

SOCRATES: Exactly. And why doesn't everyone want to fly like Superman or go to the Land of Oz or own a Tesla or a castle or play football?

NAT: Because those desires come from outside us, from fiction or from advertising or from other people's souls but not ours.

SOCRATES: Right. Now notice something remarkable about these two classes of desires. The universal desires that come from our own nature always correspond to real objects. We may not get them, but they must exist. Hunger always corresponds to food. If there is sexual desire, there must be sex. If there is curiosity, there must be knowledge. If there is dissatisfaction with ugliness, there must be such a thing as beauty, even if we may not see it.

NAT: That seems true.

SOCRATES: But this is not true of the other desires. Some of them correspond to real objects—Teslas and castles and football—but others do not, like Superman or the Land of Oz.

NAT: True.

SOCRATES: So if all universal and natural desires correspond to realities that can satisfy them, and if this mysterious desire for total joy or a perfect world or something unlimitedly satisfying is a universal and natural desire, then the thing desired by that mysterious desire must be real.

NAT: That reality would certainly be beautiful. But is that God?

SOCRATES: It's certainly one property of God. Just as "unmoved mover", "cause of existence", "noncontingent being", "standard of perfection", and "intelligent designer of order" are five other properties, and as "eternal mind containing eternal truths" and "perfectly good moral lawgiver" are two other ones. Can God be anything less than total truth, goodness, and beauty?

NAT: But it says nothing about religion, whether God revealed any kind of relationship with us or not.

SOCRATES: It doesn't aim to do that. It's only philosophy, not religion.

NAT: OK, that's an impressive batch of arguments. But I've got one that's much shorter and simpler and more powerful, I think. The premise of all your arguments is some kind of good. The premise of mine is evil. I think evil is the best argument for atheism.

SOCRATES: How would you formulate the argument logically?

NAT: That's easy: If there were a God, there would be no evil. There is evil; therefore, there is no God.

SOCRATES: Could you justify that first premise?

NAT: Yes. If there is a God, it has to have at least three attributes: unlimited power, unlimited wisdom, and unlimited goodness—omnipotence, omniscience, and omnibenevolence. God can't be weak or stupid or wicked. Such a being would not deserve the name of God. Agreed?

SOCRATES: Agreed.

NAT: But if God is omnibenevolent, He wants only good; and if He is omniscient, He knows what good is and what is good and how to get it; and if He is omnipotent, he has the power to do anything and to get whatever He wants.

SOCRATES: Good argument!

NAT: So how can God create evil?

SOCRATES: He doesn't. His creation is good.

NAT: Then where does evil come from?

SOCRATES: Look in the mirror.

NAT: But why does he let us do evil?

SOCRATES: To preserve our free choice.

NAT: Oh.

SOCRATES: Do you agree that the free choice to love and do good—the free choice that makes love possible, as well as hate—is very valuable?

NAT: Certainly.

SOCRATES: And do you think that if God compelled us to do only good by removing our free will, that good that we did by compulsion rather than by free choice would have much value?

NAT: No.

SOCRATES: So does the good that we freely choose to do outweigh the evil that we choose to do, or vice versa?

NAT: Hard to say. Is there any way to justify either answer to that question? I doubt it.

SOCRATES: Well, if that's not possible for *us*, then it is possible that *God* sees the good of freedom, which is the necessary precondition for love, as greater than the evil that freedom also makes possible, isn't it?

NAT: I find it impossible to answer that question. I'm not God.

SOCRATES: My point precisely.

NAT: OK, free will may explain moral evil, but not physical evil. Why does God allow so much horrible suffering? God miraculously stopping bad choices would take away our free will, but miraculously taking away horrible sufferings and diseases and death wouldn't.

SOCRATES: I'm not sure. Perhaps it would. Did we have free choice in the womb, the only place we ever lived in that had no suffering? But let's assume you are right; if so, physical evil requires a different answer than moral evil. And the usual one is that without suffering we would become lazy, flabby, spoiled little brats. One who has never suffered—how can that be a hero or a saint or a sage or even a fully human being? We need suffering for courage, for moral improvement, and for wisdom.

NAT: That may make sense in general but not in particular. It explains suffering in general but not how it is distributed. Job did not need or deserve the extent of his sufferings.

SOCRATES: True. So the answer is not at all clear with respect to individual cases. Which is at least consistent with the theistic position that God, unlike us, is all-wise and knows what will work out for the greatest good of each unique individual in the end.

NAT: That answer sounds weak to me. We seem to need some suffering, but we don't seem to need as much as we get, and it also seems unjust to let saints suffer so much more than sinners.

SOCRATES: There are only two possible answers. First, we don't know the answer to that question, because we're not God. And second, if God is all-good and all-wise and all-powerful, then it is perfectly logical to believe that His wisdom and power must be such that He can bring a greater good out of the evil that He allows—in the end.

NAT: But we seldom see that happen.

SOCRATES: Do we see everything?

NAT: No, but ...

SOCRATES: And are we at the end yet?

NAT: No, but ...

SOCRATES: Looks like you have a lot of buts. I have a lot too. But isn't it true that both belief and unbelief are at least rationally possible? Neither side is simply stupid, and neither side is so obviously right that there is some argument that refutes the other side conclusively. I don't have to prove my side, just show that it's possible.

NAT: So it's a matter of faith rather than proof in the last analysis.

SOCRATES: Of course. If either choice were either necessary or impossible, there would be no room for faith. Religion would be like math. And I think we can all agree that that, at least, is not the case.

NAT: Wait a moment. The truths of math are certain, and some of the truths of modern science are close to certainty, but the truth claims of religion are much less certain. So if a theory in science conflicts with the relevant math, it must be wrong, and if a belief in religion conflicts with the truths of science, it must be wrong.

So the war of modern science versus ancient religion and the victory of science shows that whatever its value, religion has some fights with science, and science must win every time.

SOCRATES: Can you give me a single specific example of a contradiction between an agreed discovery of modern science and a basic tenet of religion?

NAT: Creation versus evolution. Evolution says species evolved gradually by natural processes. Creation says God created everything out of nothing.

SOCRATES: Some would reply that evolution is not a fact but only a theory. But let's suppose it is a fact. We could define it as the idea that matter, at least on this planet, gradually evolved into higher and higher life forms until man finally appeared. Right?

NAT: Right.

SOCRATES: Does the Bible or the Koran or the dogmas of the Church say that God created each species out of nothing?

NAT: No, I don't think so. But the Bible says that "in the beginning God created the heavens and the earth." So He created matter out of nothing.

SOCRATES: And does it say "from the beginning the earth was fully formed"?

NAT: No, it says that it took six "days" of increasing complexity.

SOCRATES: And what does science say about the origin of matter? Does science say that the very existence of matter was a gradual evolutionary development? No. Matter, once it existed, evolved, but where did the matter come from in the first place?

NAT: The Big Bang.

SOCRATES: Could *that* have been caused by evolution? Evolution presupposes the existence of the matter that evolved. Matter was caused by the Big Bang, so how could the Big Bang have been caused by matter? It was the cause *of* all matter and time and space, so there was no time before the Big Bang, no time before all of time, and no space outside all of space.

NAT: Science says nothing about the cause of the Big Bang.

SOCRATES: So God the Creator may be the Big Banger. Science does not disprove that.

NAT: All right, but even if there are no *contradictions* between science and religion, there is no scientific *need* for God and no scientific justification for believing God exists, because science can explain everything without God and without religion. For everything human is caused by man and everything natural is caused by nature. And nature caused man, by evolution, and man now transforms nature, by technology. That's all there is. Everything is explainable by science, without religion.

SOCRATES: You just admitted that science cannot explain one thing: the very existence and beginning of matter itself.

NAT: That would justify agnosticism, but not theism.

SOCRATES: But that agnosticism would make room for theism as well as for atheism.

NAT: Science does not find supernatural causes, "first causes", ultimate causes.

SOCRATES: That's because science does not seek them.

NAT: Why should it?

SOCRATES: It shouldn't. But *we* should, because we are not only scientists but also philosophers. If you ask only about parts of nature, another part of nature may be the sufficient answer. That's what science does. But if you ask about the whole of nature, no part of it can explain the whole of it. Proximate questions demand proximate answers, but ultimate questions demand ultimate answers.

NAT: Perhaps there are no ultimate answers. That's what agnosticism says.

SOCRATES: But if the other arguments for God, the philosophical arguments, are sound, that is, contain no ambiguous terms, false premises, or logical fallacies—if even any *one* of them is perfectly logically sound—then its conclusion is true, that God exists. Right?

NAT: Yes.

SOCRATES: So we're back to the positive arguments, then. Are any of them sound or not?

NAT: But we can make mistakes about whether they are sound or not, so our certainty cannot be infallible. You always questioned everything apparent because you assumed, rightly, that for us fallible creatures, what is apparently true is not necessarily true. Not only things but also arguments can hide things behind their appearances.

SOCRATES: Yes. And that's why having many sound arguments is closer to certainty than having only one. Even if we do not attain certainty, the likelihood rises with the number of apparently sound arguments.

NAT: And that distinguishes religion from science. Even when there are sound arguments for God's existence, religion appeals to faith, not just to reason, as science does. Science can answer its questions without the need for faith.

SOCRATES: Well, the religious question can't be avoided just because science can answer another set of questions, the scientific questions, with much less uncertainty. So the fact that science apparently does not need God does not count against God. We should not *expect* science to need to assume that God exists. For science seeks, and finds, only natural causes; but the philosophical arguments try to prove that in addition to natural causes there must be a supernatural cause. The fact that science can explain natural causes by other natural causes does not refute the claim that the totality of nature and natural causes still needs to be explained, and that nothing less than God is an adequate philosophical explanation of them.

NAT: Granted. But even if my two objections to God—evil and science—can be answered, as you have done, that does not prove that God exists.

SOCRATES: No indeed. Answering objections cannot substitute for positive arguments any more than positive arguments can substitute for answering objections. One is like defense, and the other is like offense, to use a military analogy.

NAT: So the upshot of it all is agnosticism.

SOCRATES: Only if none of the positive arguments for God are perfectly valid or if not all the objections are sufficiently answered.

NAT: And are you sure that one of them is? That there is no hidden fallacy in it?

SOCRATES: No. I admitted that. Appearance is not necessarily reality, in arguments or in things.

NAT: Then one cannot be absolutely certain that God exists, beyond the shadow of a doubt.

SOCRATES: Of course not. That's why religion is a matter of faith. I did not claim that I could be absolutely certain. Even in science, sound scientific theories like relativity or evolution are not absolutely certain, like mathematical equations. It's just that there are very good and sound reasons for believing that these theories are true, just as there are very good and sound reasons for believing that the "religious theory", if you can call it that, is true.

NAT: Hmm, I'm not sure.... I'm going to have to think a lot more about this.

SOCRATES: An excellent idea—both philosophically and religiously.

NAT: Why do you say "religiously"?

SOCRATES: Because religion, like science, says, in effect, "Seek and you shall find." That is a promise that is testable. But you have to perform the required experiments to do the test, both in thought and in life. That's another way religion is like science, you see.

Questions for Discussion or Personal Essays

1. First summarize, as clearly and logically as you can in your own words, and then evaluate each of the arguments for both sides (theism and atheism). (There were eight arguments for and two against the existence of God.)

2. Go beyond just summarizing the two sides as presented here and add your own reasons and criticisms, either for one side or for both sides, and possibly even for agnosticism, which does not agree with either side but says that neutrality on this most important of all questions is the most reasonable position.

3. You might also add what you think are other persuasive arguments, and other *kinds* of arguments, for both sides—for instance, the historical evidence or the lack of historical evidence for miracles, and the moral behavior and contributions of both great saints (on one side) and great sinners (on the other side). How would you compare such concrete arguments to the abstract, more logical philosophical arguments? Does each class of arguments have a different strength and weakness?

4. Are you as convinced as both Nat and Socrates are that Anselm's ontological argument is invalid?

5. Which kind of argument, the cosmological (from exterior data) or the psychological (from interior data) do you find the strongest? Why?

6. Which of the cosmological arguments did you find the strongest? Why? Which did you find the weakest? Why?

7. Which of the psychological arguments did you find the strongest? Why? Which did you find the weakest? Why?
8. Can you formulate the aesthetic argument ("There is the music of Bach; therefore, there is a God") logically?
9. What do you think is the main value of arguments for and against God? What do you think is their main limitation?
10. If there is an argument for some controversial conclusion, one that many intelligent people believe and many intelligent people do not, an argument that has no ambiguous terms, no false premises, and no logical fallacies, so that the conclusion necessarily follows from the premise or premises, do you see any possible good reason for not believing its conclusion to be true? Can you give an example of a situation where this would be the case?
11. Do you see any relationship between how logically strong an argument is and how important its conclusion is?
12. Evaluate Nat's argument for agnosticism rather than theism at the end. Look up "Pascal's wager" (read Pascal himself rather than abbreviated and edited versions of his argument) and evaluate his argument against agnosticism: "But there is no choice. You must wager. You are already embarked." Evaluate as well his longer and more famous pragmatic or practical argument against atheism. Is it a proof? Is it even an attempted proof? If not, what good is it?
13. Read and evaluate the rest of the imagined dialogue between Pascal and his interlocutor, Pascal's psychological rather than logical analysis and advice, given after the argument is finished. If you believe in God, how do you think an unbeliever would criticize Pascal's analysis and advice? If you are an unbeliever, why do you think a believer would approve his analysis and advice?
14. List and evaluate all the ways Nat and Socrates agree that religion is like science and all the ways it is unlike science. Add some others of your own.
15. Compare the persuasive power of these logical and impersonal arguments with that of the intuitive and personal argument: that great saints who act out their belief in God are morally beautiful while great sinners who act out their unbelief are not. Is this an aesthetic argument from beauty or a moral argument?

8

Ethics: Which Is More Reasonable, Moral Relativism or Absolutism?

Most people find the most interesting and engaging questions in philosophy, and certainly the most practical ones, to be questions in ethics. And the most fundamental question in ethics has to be the status of ethics itself, ethics as such.

Ethics is about good and evil, right and wrong.

The fundamental question is whether this distinction between moral good and evil is objective and therefore discovered by the mind, like the laws of physics and mathematics, or subjective and invented by the mind, like the rules of human arts and games.

If ethics is objective, it can be absolute and authoritative over our will. If it is subjective, it is relative to us and our desires, like the rules of arts and games. If it is objective, it is also universal, that is, essentially the same for all individuals and cultures. And if it is objective, it is also unchanging, that is, essentially the same for all times, as is the essence of human nature itself. Thus, this position is often called "natural law ethics". If it is subjective and invented by us, it is relative, individual, and changeable.

"Moral absolutism" is often the term used for the position, held by most premodern thinkers, that moral values are (1) objective, (2) absolutely authoritative, (3) universal, and (4) unchanging, transcending places and times.

In most premodern times and places, moral absolutism was the majority or default position. The Sophists and skeptics in Greece and Rome were the exceptions. In modern Western culture, moral *relativism* is the majority position, at least among philosophers and educators. This is probably the most striking and consequential philosophical difference in human history. Most moral absolutists see moral relativism as inhuman and disastrous for human happiness; and most moral relativists see moral absolutism as equally disastrous and oppressive to human happiness and progress.

However, even most moral relativists admit that morality as such comes with *some* sort of obligation or duty to "be good"; and even most moral absolutists admit that many, though not all, dimensions of morality are relative to our minds, will, desires, or situations.

NAT: We're going to do some philosophizing about ethics today, right?

SOCRATES: If you agree to that, yes.

NAT: That little answer raises a question for me: We won't do ethics unless we both choose to do it, right?

SOCRATES: Right. Are you implicitly asking whether that implies that we at least both assume and therefore believe that we have free will and free choice? If so, I think the answer is yes. And are you also implicitly asking whether the reality of free will is another implicit assumption behind the very existence of ethics, since we do not praise or blame machines, and all moral language would be rendered meaningless if we did not assume the reality of free choice? If so, I think the answer to that question is also obviously yes—though whether that constitutes a logical proof of the existence of free will is another question.

NAT: No, I didn't mean all those questions about free will, which I think belong in philosophical anthropology. I meant to ask only whether the fact that we have to choose to do ethics implies that the very existence of ethics is something we choose, that we bring it into existence by choosing it. And if so, does that mean that ethics is more like an art than like a science?

SOCRATES: No, because we also have to choose to do math, but that does not mean that we bring mathematical truths into existence by choice.

NAT: All right, but the fundamental question still remains: Do we make the objects of ethics—good and evil—exist, as we make the objects of art exist? Or do we discover those objects, like science, which discovers things about the universe that already exist?

SOCRATES: That is a very basic question indeed, perhaps the single most basic question in all of ethics. But to answer it, I think we must first clarify what it means. It is really two questions and probably has two different answers. In one sense of the question, I think the answer is obvious, but in another sense, it's controversial.

NAT: What two questions do you distinguish?

SOCRATES: I think the clearest way to make that distinction is to look at art and science. Both art and science happen only when we choose to do them, so in that sense science is as subjective, relative, or dependent on us—and as free—as art is. But in another sense, art and science are opposites, for the objects of art are man-made—it's in that sense that art is subjective—while the objects of science are not. They are there already, in nature, objectively real. So the answer to the first question is not controversial: the act of thinking about ethics, like science, is freely chosen and created by our mental efforts. But the second question is highly controversial: What about ethical objects, like justice and rightness and rights and obligations? Do we create those with our minds or wills or desires, or do we discover them as preexisting objective realities?

NAT: That's the difference between moral relativism and moral absolutism, right?

SOCRATES: Yes, we could use those terms if you'd like. They are probably more common than the terms I would think are a little clearer, namely, moral subjectivism and moral objectivism.

NAT: Well, that's the controversial question I want to discuss: whether ethics, or ethical values, or ethical principles, or moral goods—assuming that "ethics" and "morals" mean essentially the same thing—are relative or absolute, subjective or objective. Is this whole dimension relative to man as its maker, or is it absolute and real in itself?

SOCRATES: I see you are still doing metaphysics, as in our last conversation. For you are asking about the *being* of ethics, or rather about its objects, good and evil—about their metaphysical status.

NAT: Yes. I think that's the most important question, at least in our culture today. I think the old view, the traditional view, was that ethics is the discovery, by the mind, of the reality, the real being, of good and evil—what moral goodness and evil are in themselves, both in general and also in particular, that is, which things or actions are morally good and which are evil. And I think the more modern view is that ethics is not about that metaphysical reality of good and evil but simply about our choosing our values, as in art, so that goodness, like beauty, is largely "in the eye of the beholder".

So how do you think we should begin to address that controversial question?

SOCRATES: I think we first need to get a clear definition of our terms. If we don't do that, I think we will find it very difficult or impossible to formulate our question in such a way that we can argue profitably about which answer is the best one. We want to be sure we share the same ground when we contest it, as in war, or that we are playing the same game when we compete.

NAT: That's usually your method, right? Define your terms first.

SOCRATES: Yes. I have this strange habit of wanting to know what I'm talking about.

NAT: So let's do it. Can we call the two sides "moral absolutism" and "moral relativism"?

SOCRATES: If we agree about what those terms mean. How about this? I think we already did define that difference in these three ways: Is the object of ethics—moral good and evil—subjective or objective, is it universal or particular, and is it discovered by our mind or created by our will? I think those three differences naturally go together. For if they are objective and we discover them, as in science, that means we use our reason or our intellect or our mind first of all; and if they are thus objective and do not depend on us, then they are the same for all of us, or universal, like scientific truths. On the other hand, if they are subjective, or relative to our making or choosing them, as in art, then we must do that by our will or our desires or our feelings, and then these values that we make or choose would be different for different people.

NAT: I see the connection among these three things. The first thing, the metaphysical status of moral good and evil, seems to be the most basic. The other two follow from that. For if moral values or principles or laws of good and evil are objective, then they are discovered by the mind, and that's why they are universal, the same for all, as the universe is the same for all scientists. So we could call these values absolute and their defenders moral absolutists.

SOCRATES: Yes.

NAT: So if "thou shalt not murder", that is, deliberately kill innocent human beings, is a moral absolute, then no subjective motive, like compassion for the sufferings of the dying, can justify euthanasia, which by my definition is murder; and no objective situation, like a battlefield in a war, can justify deliberately killing any innocents, as in a bombing raid.

SOCRATES: It seems so, on first glance.

NAT: Why do you imply that it may not be the way it seems?

SOCRATES: Because I don't think it's helpful to look at particular cases first and judge general principles by them. I think we need to do the opposite. I think we need to understand and define our principles first, and only then see how much variety they can allow for as we apply them to particular cases or situations, rather than the other way round. You have to define the rules before you use them.

NAT: But the relativist says that moral values are relative to the person's desires or feelings or motives, or relative to the changing needs of the culture or the world or the situation, or relative to the end they serve, for instance, our happiness. So if relativism is right, then the general principles are relative to the particular situations, not vice versa. The general principles and laws are for the particular cases, not vice versa. They are the means, not the ends. The means are relative to the ends, not vice versa.

SOCRATES: Even if this is so—and that is one of the things in dispute— we must first define our terms, must we not?

NAT: I suppose so.

SOCRATES: So let's finish that first. We mentioned three claims about moral good and evil that the absolutist affirms and the relativist denies: objectivity, rationality, and universality. That would be our definition of moral absolutism.

NAT: And "universality" means the same for all *places*, all cultures and all individuals, and also at all *times*, so that they cannot be changed.

SOCRATES: Yes.

NAT: Well, then, now that we've defined the issue, how do we try to decide it?

SOCRATES: There are two of us here, are there not?

NAT: Yes.

SOCRATES: I've always thought that the best way of deciding any philosophical issue is to hear both sides in a debate. That is, to begin with a kind of methodic doubt, a kind of confession of uncertainty, to have an open mind so that we can fairly and equally look at all the evidence, for both sides. In fact, that method is itself a kind of moral value, a sort of intellectual fairness or justice.

NAT: How shall the two of us split the work, do you think?

SOCRATES: Debate is like dancing. "It takes two to tango", as the song says. And we are two. So let's play the two parts.

NAT: All right. And since you were an ethical absolutist, if Plato's dialogues accurately reported your real views, I think you should argue for that side, moral absolutism; and since I'm a typical modern student and am more familiar and comfortable with the opposite position, I should argue for moral relativism.

SOCRATES: That seems right.

NAT: Well, then, let me begin by saying that we relativists are not necessarily less *moral* than you absolutists. We do not deny that it's good to be good (that would be to deny the law of non-contradiction!). We take ethics seriously. In fact, I think we have strongly *ethical* reasons for preferring relativism to absolutism.

SOCRATES: So let us begin there, with your defense of relativism, and then I will give my critique of it.

NAT: I would like to begin by sharing my instinctive reaction to the issue, and my instinctive preference for relativism, before I begin my logical arguments. Because I think that's the order the two things actually occurred, psychologically, in my psyche.

SOCRATES: You understand, I trust, that your instinctive reactions are subjective and personal, not objective and logical.

NAT: Yes, of course. I will later argue for my reactions by arguments, by logical reasoning. But I want to begin with what I would call my psychological reasons for it, and then, later, give my logical reasons for it.

SOCRATES: Fine. Go ahead.

NAT: I know that in logic, inductive arguments, which move from particular cases to general principles, can be only probable and not certain, while only deductive arguments, which begin with general principles and deduce particular conclusions from them, can prove anything with certainty. But I think sometimes it's useful not to begin with general principles, but with something more concrete and intuited, because that's how our minds usually work in practice. So I begin with a concrete and intuitive look at the difference between old absolutistic societies or regimes in this world and modern relativistic regimes that value tolerance and diversity and inclusion.

SOCRATES: Fair enough. Go ahead.

NAT: I see two very different kinds of cultures or societies or regimes in the world today: free countries, or pluralistic democracies, and monolithic countries that impose on all their citizens their one and only moral system, which is usually also part of a religion, some official orthodoxy, sometimes enforced by a "morality police", as in some Muslim countries. Actually, it's not always religious; it can be antireligious. We find something similar in uniformly Communist countries. They don't value diversity and dissent either.

SOCRATES: Would you say there are also some countries that are pluralistic and tolerant religiously but absolutistic morally, as nearly all premodern regimes in Western civilization were? Cultures that allow religious diversity but not moral diversity?

NAT: Perhaps for a while such regimes existed, between 1648 and 1960, but no more.

SOCRATES: Why do you pick those dates?

NAT: The Peace of Westphalia was signed in 1648, which ended the terrible Thirty Years' War by allowing religious choice for different political segments of Europe, but in which all sides still agreed that morality was uniform and absolute. I think that compromise lasted about three hundred years. I picked 1960, when the invention of the Pill and the sexual revolution that it made possible deconstructed the old uniform and absolute morality, at least about things sexual, in America and Europe. In America today there are still many individuals, mainly traditional Catholics, Eastern Orthodox Christians, Evangelical Christians, and Orthodox Jews, who want to impose a single morality on all, but that narrowness is no longer taught by the public educational establishment—both formal education, at all levels in the schools, and informal education, in popular media and journalism and the arts.

SOCRATES: I think that is partly true, as a matter of empirical fact.

NAT: Why only partly true?

SOCRATES: Because the culture still agrees that murder, theft, rape, slavery, treason, libel, perjury, torture, drug addiction, and many other things are evil. Is that not so?

NAT: Yes.

SOCRATES: And that justice and love and mercy and honesty and courage and wisdom are good.

NAT: Yes.

SOCRATES: In fact, almost the whole of the traditional moral law is still largely agreed upon, except for one area, sexual morality, where it has been almost totally replaced. So I think your two dates are fairly accurate factually. It's true that all cultures and religions throughout the world and through all of time until the sexual revolution were generally in agreement, at least in theory, about the moral evil of lust, masturbation, contraception, abortion, fornication, divorce, adultery, unisexism, sodomy, pornography, prostitution, polyamory, artificial insemination, and transgenderism. That is simply a historical fact that can be discovered by reading the relevant data. Right and Left, business and labor, men and women, educated and uneducated, Democrats and Republicans agreed that all these were evil intrinsically, or by nature, and they thought that was obvious. But in a single generation (or at the most two or three generations), the whole of Western civilization has reversed that judgment. That's why it's called the sexual *revolution*. That seems to be the single most radical and rapid moral revolution in human history. Mind you, I'm not evaluating it, pro or con, just describing it, as a historian.

NAT: But I *am* evaluating it, and I say the revolution was a great piece of progress. Progress in freedom and tolerance. We no longer bend to moral and religious absolutists. Of course, we don't penalize their beliefs or lifestyles or practices—there are no legal penalties or punishments for being a Goody Two-shoes if you want to be. But that's the point: we allow for choice now, as the old morally absolutistic regimes did not. We allow for absolutists, but they did not allow for relativists. We include them, but they do not include us. We tolerate their intolerance, but they are intolerant of our tolerance.

SOCRATES: And now you seem to be implying a logical argument, rather than just an instinctive personal reaction or a historical fact, are you not? You are deducing the goodness of moral relativism from the assumed value premise that tolerance is good and intolerance bad, added to the expressed premise that relativists and relativism are tolerant while absolutists and absolutism are not. And therefore the conclusion is that your regime and its tolerant philosophy is good and theirs is bad. Is that not your argument for relativism?

NAT: Yes.

SOCRATES: Good. Now we have something in place to look at and evaluate logically. Let's call it the argument from tolerance.

NAT: Yes, let's.

SOCRATES: I think everyone, even your opponents, would have to agree with your second premise, the factual premise, since it's simply a fact: the difference between the two cultures in tolerating what previous cultures would call moral evils, at least in the area of sexuality. So the controversial premise is the first one: the value premise or ethical premise or moral premise, that tolerance is good and intolerance is bad.

NAT: Yes. And that premise seems almost self-evidently true to me.

SOCRATES: But would you not agree that "tolerance" is an ambiguous term because it is relative to its object?

NAT: What do you mean?

SOCRATES: I mean simply that the value of tolerance obviously depends on what you are tolerant or intolerant of. Surely you would not defend a culture that tolerates things like murder or rape or theft or slavery.

NAT: No.

SOCRATES: Why not?

NAT: Because those are not just evils but obvious and important evils.

SOCRATES: And you would not defend a culture that is intolerant of deviation from the norm in relatively unimportant things, like colorful clothing or modern music or freedom to express opinions that are not those of the majority.

NAT: Of course I would not.

SOCRATES: And our culture still sees things like murder or rape or theft as serious things that demand strict rules and intolerance for breaking the rules, and it has usually seen things like clothing and music and opinions expressed in speech as not serious enough to make strict rules about.

NAT: Yes.

SOCRATES: So the change in popular opinion about morality has been swift and radical only in one area in the last half century or so, namely, the area of sexual morality. Sexual morality has been transferred from the class of things serious and binding to the class of things optional. That is why we used to have strict rules about sex but it is now seen as something that demands fewer rules and much more tolerance.

NAT: That change seems to be factually true, no matter what value one puts on the change. Why do you think the revolution happened so quickly?

SOCRATES: I think the answer is fairly obvious. The sexual revolution was made possible only by reliable and available contraception. Not only did that change sexual behavior, but it also seems to have changed, in most minds, something even more revolutionary: the essential meaning of sex. Before the revolution, sex meant not merely personal pleasure but also the way a new human life, a new human being, a new person, came into the world. That is certainly a serious thing and much more important than temporary personal pleasure, so sex had to have serious rules around it. But what used to be called the "reproductive system" is now mainly "the entertainment system" because of contraception; and reproduction, which used to be part of its very essence, is now an "accident".

NAT: Is that your argument against the sexual revolution?

SOCRATES: Not at all. It's not an argument; it's just a description. It's my answer to your question about how the change happened. It's simply the observation that every culture puts strict rules around things it deems important but not around things it deems unimportant. And human persons are obviously important. But if sex can be guaranteed not to produce new persons, then it's not seen as such a terribly important thing anymore. I think that is the obvious answer to your question about why we could have such a rapid and radical change in sexual morality.

NAT: That explains the change of attitude toward *contraception*, but how does that explain the change of attitude toward *abortion*? Why did the vast majority assume that abortion was evil and should be outlawed before the sexual revolution, and why do the majority now disagree with that?

SOCRATES: That connection is even more obvious: abortion *is* contraception, backup contraception, so to speak. And contraception is the way to have sex without having babies, just as test tube babies or in vitro fertilization is the way to have babies without having sex. Those two inventions are two halves of the same decoupling. Again, that seems simply the observation of a fact, not a matter of opinion about values.

NAT: I'm still not clear about how the new attitude toward sex changed the old attitude toward unborn human life.

SOCRATES: How that happened is a somewhat more difficult question, a psychological question. *That* it happened is simply a fact. But instead of theorizing about sexual psychology, let's get back from this interesting tangent to the central logical arguments about moral relativism versus absolutism, shall we?

NAT: Yes.

SOCRATES: The divisive and decisive issue philosophically—the issue of moral relativism and tolerance—is not just about sexual morality but about all morality, about morality as such. You were arguing that moral relativism was better because it was more tolerant in general, right?

NAT: Right.

SOCRATES: And I replied that the question is not whether all tolerance, tolerance as such, is good or bad, but where to draw the line between good and bad tolerance. And then we noted that the place where our society thought we should draw the line between good and bad tolerance changed rapidly and radically only about sexual morality.

NAT: Yes.

SOCRATES: So let's get back to the general question of what to tolerate, where to draw the line. Cultures differ about that. For instance, some regimes, especially in Muslim countries, tolerate no alcohol at all, and you would say that is too intolerant, I think; other regimes or subcultures tolerate even very dangerous and destructive drugs, and you would probably say that is too tolerant, right?

NAT: I think so.

SOCRATES: But my logical point is this: in order to *judge* where to draw that line, whether to draw it in a more tolerant way or in a less tolerant way—in order to argue that it is better to be more tolerant rather than less, whether in general or only about one area, be it sex or alcohol or anything else—you must assume the *opposite* of moral relativism.

NAT: What? How? Why?

SOCRATES: You must assume that the principles you use in making that moral judgment of what to tolerate are objective and universal and rational, not subjective and personal and emotional. For if they were only subjective, you would be imposing your subjective and personal and emotional values on others. And that is not tolerant but intolerant.

NAT: I think I see that logical point. So you are saying that my tolerance argument *for* relativism presupposes the opposite of relativism.

SOCRATES: In fact, this goes beyond the tolerance argument alone. If all moral values were subjective, we could not argue about morality at all. We don't argue about things that are merely subjective. If I say I feel happy today, and you say that you feel unhappy, we can't argue about who's right and who's wrong. And we don't. We don't try.

NAT: Not unless we are so intolerant as to make our personal feelings the standard of right and wrong for everyone.

SOCRATES: Which is what we observe more and more people doing today. When have you heard a good, fair philosophical debate about morality?

NAT: I see your point. It is very troubling.

SOCRATES: So if we can and should have rational arguments about moral issues like war and racism and capital punishment and abortion and sexual morality and the rights of the individual versus the rights of the state, we can't do that if we believe that moral values are just subjective feelings.

NAT: I see the logic of your argument. But that argument, too, has a premise that may be questionable: that we can and should have rational arguments about morality. Maybe we can't, and therefore we shouldn't. Maybe all moral argument is a mistake.

SOCRATES: So we *shouldn't* say "shouldn't"? It's *wrong* to argue about what's wrong and what's right?

NAT: Oops.

SOCRATES: That's what some would call a brief act of contrition.

NAT: That position is logically self-contradictory, isn't it?

SOCRATES: Yes. And it's also intolerant. If we don't use our *reason* to determine our behavior, the only alternative is force, either emotional force or physical force.

NAT: I certainly don't want that.

SOCRATES: So if you want to defend tolerance, you will have to say that it's an objective and universal value, not just your subjective and personal feeling. You don't want to be so intolerant as to force your feelings on others, do you?

NAT: No. But I think that's what the moral absolutist's arguments do too. Maybe that's what all moral arguments try to do. Maybe they're all just rationalizations for our wanting to control other people.

SOCRATES: That's a very dark view. If that were true, what alternative do we have?

NAT: Perhaps the best alternative is just to stop arguing about good and evil.

SOCRATES: Do you really think we can do that?

NAT: If we believe that morality is subjective, we can! Just as we can stop arguing about which sports team we love most or which food we prefer. If our values are only our personal preferences, we should stop imposing them on others. And if we *should* do that, then we *can* do it.

SOCRATES: I don't believe you really believe that.

NAT: Why not?

SOCRATES: Can you believe that your condemnation of Hitler and Nazism is merely imposing your preferences on others? Can you believe that a moral value like justice is really only a *feeling*? And that your call for tolerance is also merely your personal feeling and, therefore, when you argue for tolerance, you are trying to impose your personal feeling on others?

NAT: No, I can't honestly say I believe that. I can't tolerate intolerance.

SOCRATES: And do you say to a person who practices and even justifies intolerance simply that you personally wish they were tolerant? Merely that you personally happen to desire that they be tolerant? That the reason *they* should be tolerant is that *you* want it?

NAT: No, of course not. That's intolerance. That's imposing my personal values on them.

SOCRATES: So you have to say, to the defender of intolerance, not "I want you to be tolerant simply because I want it" but "You ought to be tolerant because tolerance is really good, truly good, whether you like it or not; it's the objective truth that we all really, truly ought to be more tolerant." In other words, you must assume that at least some moral values are truths, objective truths, moral facts about how we ought to behave, not facts about how we do behave—that values are one kind of facts.

NAT: Yes. I can't refute your logic. But that proves only that *tolerance* has to be an objective value; it doesn't prove that other moral values are objective. Maybe they're all subjective feelings and that's why we should tolerate them.

SOCRATES: So tolerance is the only objective value? There are no others? Like honesty, and not murdering, and goodwill rather than hate?

NAT: I don't know. Maybe.

SOCRATES: Can you turn that "maybe" into an argument? Why are all moral values except tolerance subjective and relative to your personal feelings, not objective and universal?

NAT: Here's one argument. Let's call it the argument for moral relativism from cultural relativity. We just looked at one great difference between cultures a few minutes ago: the difference between our present Western culture and our own past. There are many other differences about values between different cultures, both in the past and in the present. It's simply an empirical fact of observation that cultures differ about moral values. So it's not a theory but a fact that values are relative to cultures. For example, Nazi culture did not value Jewish life at all, and many ancient cultures believed that the life of small, troublesome, or unwanted children, slaves, or foreigners had little or no value, so there was no penalty for killing these categories of human beings. Even in so-called highly civilized cultures like ancient Rome, a father had the right of life or death over his newborn children.

SOCRATES: So here is your second argument for moral relativism: the fact of radically different cultural opinions about a radically important value, namely, the value of a human life.

NAT: Yes. And you can't argue with a fact.

SOCRATES: Indeed not. And it is indeed a fact that different cultures sometimes have radically different opinions about the value of human life.

NAT: And about other things too. For instance, the culture of the Roma, or the gypsies, did not recognize the value of private property. And modern Western culture after the sexual revolution no longer recognizes masturbation, fornication, cohabitation, contraception, divorce, abortion, sodomy, or transgenderism as morally evil, as it used to do. Most ancient societies had no qualms about cruelty to animals. And many states in America now allow and encourage people not to respect or bury dead human bodies but to use them for compost, like cow dung. That would have shocked Antigone!

SOCRATES: Do you think that *all* opinions are relative to cultures? For instance, opinions about how much two plus three are, or about what causes eclipses, or about whether the earth is round, or about whether a slap in the face causes happiness?

NAT: Of course not. But those are opinions about facts, not values.

SOCRATES: But opinions about things other than values also sometimes differ with cultures.

NAT: Yes. So what?

SOCRATES: Do you not agree that some of those opinions are true and others are false?

NAT: Of course.

SOCRATES: Then there is a distinction between opinion and truth.

NAT: Yes.

SOCRATES: Opinions are subjective, and truth is objective.

NAT: By definition, yes. But whether we can ever reach the truth is another question.

SOCRATES: Remember our discussion in epistemology, where the skepticism that claimed we could not reach the truth was shown to be self-contradictory?

NAT: Yes, I remember that. I do not doubt we can reach objective truth, at least by science.

SOCRATES: And do you remember the other self-contradiction we found, the one in the claim that only by science could we prove objective truth?

NAT: Yes. That idea, too, was shown to be self-contradictory because it could not be proved by science.

SOCRATES: Well, then, we agree that logical analysis shows that in every field, whether science or philosophy or common sense, we must distinguish between subjective opinions and objective truths. The consequence of denying this distinction is logical self-contradiction.

NAT: Yes.

SOCRATES: Why is this true in every field but one, namely, ethics, the division of philosophy that deals with moral good and evil?

NAT: Because good and evil, like beauty and pleasure, are "in the eye of the beholder", that is, are subjective feelings, not objective facts.

SOCRATES: But that is begging the question again, assuming the very thing you are asked to prove.

NAT: I thought "begging the question" meant simply ignoring the question.

SOCRATES: No, that is simply a common misunderstanding of the term. It means smuggling the conclusion into your premise by tricks of language, apparently saying *two* things, the premise and the conclusion, when you are really saying only one and the same thing in different words.

NAT: But language is relative too.

SOCRATES: Of course it is. Language in general is universal and has some universal rules, but languages are plural, and different, and relative to different cultures because it is different cultures that invent different languages. And languages are also relative in the sense that it is different individuals who use or misuse those languages in different ways. But the laws of logic are not relative. We did not invent those; we discovered them. And they are not culturally relative. There is no such thing as Chinese logic versus American logic, or even female logic versus male logic. So a logical fallacy like begging the question, assuming the thing you need to prove, is a fallacy for everybody, always and everywhere.

NAT: All right, I agree with that principle of logic. But I do not agree with your distinction between value *opinions*, which you admit are relative to cultures, and values, which you say are not. For I claim that values *are* nothing but opinions. They are not facts.

SOCRATES: But that is precisely the conclusion you are trying to prove, don't you see? So you are begging the question still.

NAT: Oh, I guess I am. So if I want to prove the conclusion of moral relativism, I need a different premise.

SOCRATES: Yes. And even the other premise in your cultural relativism argument, the factual premise of the cultural relativity of moral opinions, is not wholly true, especially for the most important moral opinions. It is simply not a fact that value opinions are wholly relative to cultures. In fact, the more important and basic the value is, the less difference of opinion there is about it. That's why nearly all societies have some version of the Golden Rule, "Do to others as you would have them do to you." And why nearly all societies have some version of the Ten Commandments, condemning murder, theft, adultery, dishonesty, and greed. Did you ever hear of a society where those things were called good, and respect for life, property, sex, truth, and self-control were called evil? Where people were admired for harming others and condemned for doing to others what they wanted done to them?

NAT: No. But it's conceivable, and thus not self-contradictory, that such a society might exist. Nietzsche did call for a "transvaluation of all values", which is something similar to that. The morality of his "overman" or "superman" saw ordinary morality as "slave morality", saw compassion and love and even justice as weaknesses, and saw cruelty and oppression and arrogance and even arbitrary irrationality on the part of the stronger as virtues.

SOCRATES: And did you ever hear of a whole culture that succeeded in putting that into practice?

NAT: Well, no. Even the Nazis had to accept some traditional values—like honor among thieves.

SOCRATES: And did you never read Dostoyevsky's very realistic stories about characters who tried to act like Nietzsche's "overman"? Men like Raskolnikov in *Crime and Punishment*? We can't simply alter our moral nature like modeling clay. In the end we never succeed in trying to rip up our moral motherboard.

NAT: That may be true psychologically. But it does not prove moral absolutism. It's just a fact about our inner nature, but it doesn't prove there is some moral law out there like the laws of logic or mathematics.

SOCRATES: No, it does not. I agree with that. I do not claim that moral agreement proves moral objectivity. But you claim that the lack of moral agreement proves moral subjectivity. It does not, any more than disagreement about cosmology proves that the cosmos is subjective.

NAT: All right, but the *factual* premise of my cultural relativism argument is not false, as you claim it is. When we do look at the facts "out there", we find evidence for moral relativism. For when it comes to actual practice, there is enormous disagreement between different cultures about values, even very fundamental values like the value of a human person. For example, the culture of the ancient Aztecs believed that their god demanded the sacrifice of perhaps a third of their children. And that was done by the ancient Canaanites too, I think.

SOCRATES: Even that example is evidence for my point, not yours.

NAT: How?

SOCRATES: *Why* did the Aztecs think that was the right thing to do?

NAT: I don't know.

SOCRATES: It was because they believed that if they did not do that, the sun, which was a god, would stop shining and the whole of their culture and the whole of the human race on earth would die. It was a ridiculous belief, of course—their factual premise was terribly wrong, but their assumed value premise was right. That premise was the value of charity, of sacrifice, of martyrdom, of giving up your life for others. The Romans expressed that value by these words, which they made famous: "Dulce et decorum est pro patria mori"—"It is sweet and proper to die for one's country [or one's people, or one's culture]." Every culture accepts the basic value principle that altruistic self-sacrifice is good. There is never basic disagreement about it, except perhaps in your own highly individualistic culture that values autonomy over community, and freedom over responsibility and duty, and creativity and originality and progress over tradition and respect for ancestors, much more than any other culture in history has ever done. When we look at the factual data, we find that there is no disagreement about that principle but only about the application of that principle.

NAT: The application is pretty important: killing a third of all your children!

SOCRATES: Indeed. But the principle is even more important.

NAT: But as you yourself point out, our culture and theirs are very, very different! We are moral relativists; they were not.

SOCRATES: There is also an even more fundamental similarity. For your culture also slaughters about one-third of its innocent children. The only difference is that yours are not yet born, not yet visible, while theirs were.

NAT: There's also a religious difference.

SOCRATES: Yes. You worship different gods, different absolutes. Your god is not an irascible Zeus-like tyrant in the heavens with an unpronounceable name but your own sexual freedom and autonomy.

NAT: Are you trying to provoke me?

SOCRATES: Guilty as charged.

NAT: I will not take that bait. We do not worship any gods. Relativists have no absolute.

SOCRATES: Then they cannot be relativists, for there is nothing for these relativities to be relative to.

NAT: Perhaps relativism itself is our absolute.

SOCRATES: Perhaps. What is not a "perhaps" but a certainty is that logical consistency isn't your absolute. "Absolute relativism"? Isn't that like "certain skepticism" or "false truth"?

NAT: No, it isn't. But I don't want to argue abstract logic; I want to argue concrete morality.

SOCRATES: Good. So let us return to our argument about moral relativism in general.

NAT: Yes, let's. So you claim that moral disagreements about practice, even radical disagreements about whether it's good to kill your own innocent children as the Aztecs and the Canaanites did, always presupposes moral agreement about some principle?

SOCRATES: Precisely. You always find that. For there can be no moral disagreement, no moral argument, about any practice unless there is some basic agreement on some general principle, some premise, and then a disagreement about a more specific thing, about how to apply that principle in practice. In other words, you are partly correct: there is a lot of very serious relativity in value opinions, but always these presuppose some more fundamental moral principle that both sides assume and from which both sides argue.

NAT: Then why do most of our sociology and psychology and anthropology experts deny that? Why are they cultural relativists?

SOCRATES: Either because they are not good philosophers, because they do not know that basic principle of logic; or because they are not good scientists, because they do not look or listen deeply enough to the ordinary people in those different cultures.

NAT: Are you saying that the more educated you are, the more ignorant you are?

SOCRATES: Have you never heard the saying "That idea is so absurd that only a Ph.D. could believe it"? Have you never heard of those who see so many trees that they lose sight of the forest?

NAT: But ... but ...

SOCRATES: You sound like a car puttering and sputtering by trying to start its engine with only fumes for gasoline.

NAT: But moral values *must* be relative to society and culture because it's our society and culture that *enculturates* or inculcates those values in us. If we had been born into and brought up in an Australian Aborigine culture or a Hindu culture or an Inuit culture, we would have had Aborigine values or Hindu values or Inuit values. And what cultures invent and enculturate is culturally relative.

SOCRATES: So this is your third argument for moral relativism, then: that values are relative to societies because we learn them from our society.

NAT: Yes. What's wrong with that argument?

SOCRATES: Well, your factual premise is true: they are *learned* from our society, our culture. But that is not the same thing as their being *invented* by the culture. A thing we did not invent can be taught and learned and passed on, like the multiplication table.

You fail to make a key distinction. As with your first argument from cultural relativity, you fail to distinguish values from value opinions, or opinions *about* values. Society conditions opinions, but that does not prove that society conditions values themselves unless you presuppose that values are nothing but opinions. And that is what you are trying to prove. Once again you are assuming what you need to prove. You are begging the question.

NAT: But we do learn our values from our parents and teachers. In this case, as distinct from the cultural relativity argument, my factual premise is true. Unless you assume the disreputable theory of "innate ideas".

SOCRATES: Indeed. But not everything we learn from our teachers is relative and subjective and invented. Some things are, like our language, and the civil laws of our country, and proper dress codes. But other things are not, like the laws of logic and mathematics and physics. So the mere fact that we learn moral values from our teachers does not by itself decide whether those values are objective or subjective. Perhaps they are like the laws of logic. Perhaps there is a moral logic. Perhaps "do good and not evil" is to morality what the law of non-contradiction is to logic.

NAT: But because different people teach them, the values we learn in our culture are different from the values learned in other cultures.

SOCRATES: We went through that argument before. First of all, they are not totally different, not in fundamental principles. And even if they were, that would not prove that they are not objective. One side might be simply wrong about them. Some people believed the earth was flat, and some believed it was round; yet it's an objective fact, not just an opinion, that it's round.

NAT: But science has a method of proving its opinions and theories so that eventually everyone agrees. Ethics does not.

SOCRATES: That's true. That's why ethical disagreements will always remain, while at least most scientific disagreements will eventually be settled. But that does not prove that the things we disagree about in ethics are not objective, unless we assume that everything that we keep disagreeing about and can't resolve by the scientific method is only subjective.

NAT: Well, isn't that premise true?

SOCRATES: Certainly not. Some people believe that there is a God and a life after death, and some do not, isn't that so?

NAT: Yes.

SOCRATES: And there will probably always be believers and unbelievers, right? No matter how strong the arguments are on either side or both sides, there is no way to settle that question to everybody's satisfaction by anything like the scientific method.

NAT: Right.

SOCRATES: But either God exists or He doesn't. We won't be able to be absolutely certain and convince everyone else of either answer before we die, yet either God exists or not. That's just the logical law of excluded middle. A proposition is either true or false, whether or not we can know or prove it. Do you deny that?

NAT: No, that's true.

SOCRATES: And you admitted that the claim that only propositions provable by the scientific method could be known to be true was self-contradictory since that claim cannot be proved by the scientific method. Do you want to retract that admission?

NAT: Socrates, your logic is consistent. You have the abstract rules of logic on your side. But I have common sense on my side. How can moral values be objectively "there", like rocks or trees? They are not *things, beings, entities,* historical events, or facts about how the universe behaves or even how persons behave. How can they be objective if we can't see them or bump into them?

SOCRATES: Can you see my mind?

NAT: No.

SOCRATES: Do you believe that my mind is therefore only your subjective dream, that it's not objective to your mind, independent of your mind?

NAT: No. But it's not outside my mind in the same way as rocks or trees are.

SOCRATES: Not in that way, but in another, more fundamental and general way. You discover my mind; you do not invent it. I am not your fiction, nor are you mine. So "outside" is only an analogy, a metaphor. Minds are not material objects in space. But my mind is "outside" your mind ontologically, or metaphysically, or in its very existence, even though not materially outside.

NAT: That's true. So what does that prove?

SOCRATES: It proves that it's not true that everything you can't see with your eyes is subjective. There are things we can "see" only with our minds, not our eyes. Numbers, for instance, and equations, which are truths about numbers.

NAT: So if values are objective instead of subjective, if we discover them rather than create them or invent them, as you say, then where are they and how do we find them?

SOCRATES: As to where they are, they are nowhere in space and they are everywhere where there are things of value. They are not bound by any space or place because they are not made of matter. And as to how we find them, we discover them with the inner eye of moral conscience.

NAT: But conscience is a feeling. It's subjective.

SOCRATES: First of all, even if that were true, it would not prove that its values are subjective and generated by conscience itself, any more than the fact that our sense experience is subjective and dependent on us proves that the material world we see is generated by us and not out there, independent of us.

And secondly, it isn't true that conscience is a feeling. It's a seeing. If I feel like killing you and my conscience says I shouldn't, my feelings are *contradicted* by my conscience. How I feel is judged by what I know. I *know* I shouldn't do wrong, even when I *feel* like doing it.

NAT: But everybody says conscience is a feeling.

SOCRATES: Not everybody. Only moral relativists. And they're wrong.

NAT: But you can't prove it.

SOCRATES: And therefore it's not an objective truth?

NAT: Yes.

SOCRATES: We went over that argument before too, remember? There are many objective truths we can't prove.

NAT: But my conscience isn't yours, and it tells me different things than yours tells you.

SOCRATES: And my mind isn't yours either, and it tells me different things than yours tells you. But that does not prove there is no objective truth. One of us can still be right and the other wrong in what our minds believe.

NAT: About values as well as facts?

SOCRATES: I think the word "values" confuses us. It sort of *sounds* subjective, unlike "good" and "evil" and "laws". You know, no one used that term ("values") in morality until recently. People spoke of moral "laws", not moral "values". "Values" was used in economics, not ethics. God did not give Moses ten "values". You can't have subjective laws, but you can have subjective values.

NAT: But the fact that "values" can be either objective or subjective means that that word doesn't beg the question the other way, as the word "laws" does. So maybe that ambiguity is good. It's more generic.

SOCRATES: All right, let's keep using the word "values" then, to keep the question open, so we can argue about whether moral values are objective or subjective without begging the question either way.

NAT: So you're saying that moral values and facts are both equally objective?

SOCRATES: Yes.

NAT: As objective as the facts about the material universe or the laws of mathematics?

SOCRATES: Yes. In both cases, the *act* of knowing is subjective—it's my act or your act—but the truth known is not. It's our object.

NAT: It doesn't feel that way, in my experience. It feels like it's all coming from me.

SOCRATES: Well, that proves nothing, because we all know that feelings may be deceptive, even when they are common. More than that, I think your feelings or experiences tell you the opposite. For I think you must admit, if you are honest with your own moral experience, that whenever your conscience speaks, it speaks *to* you; it *corrects* your feelings or opinions. It imposes a *duty* or an obligation on you; it does not feel like just a *desire*, like hunger, or an ideal that you invent, like Utopia, or the rules of a game that you invented and chose to play even though you were under no obligation to play it. Your conscience is judgmental. It judges your desires as well as your actions. It says you ought to desire good, not evil, and other people's good, not just your own.

NAT: That doesn't mean it comes from outside me. Maybe it comes from my superego instead of my id or my ego.

SOCRATES: If it's only from what Freud called your superego, which is only an echo of other people's desires for you to behave in ways that they like, why is it authoritative? Why do even relativists say we should always obey whatever our individual conscience says? If it's only other's people's desires, why treat them as if they were the will of God? Why not just trash conscience, as Raskolnikov in Dostoyevsky's novel *Crime and Punishment* tries to do?

NAT: I can't answer that question. I can't admire Raskolnikov, or Nietzsche's "master morality" versus "slave morality". But I don't see that fact about what I admire as a proof that moral values in general are objective. I don't see the force of the argument.

SOCRATES: The force of the argument is that conscience *commands* you.

NAT: So what?

SOCRATES: The relation between being commanded and commanding is a relation between two different wills, or two different persons, or two different forces, is it not? The thing that obeys or disobeys the command is one thing, and the thing that commands is something else, isn't it?

NAT: Yes, of course.

SOCRATES: Then the relation between conscience and the "you" that obeys or disobeys conscience is a relation between two different things.

NAT: You mean it's from God?

SOCRATES: I don't know whether it is or not.

NAT: So you're not claiming that the existence of this "external" or "objective" conscience proves the existence of God?

SOCRATES: No. I don't know whether it does or not.

NAT: What does it prove, then? Maybe it's just my deeper self commanding my shallow self, not just Freud's "superego", which I admit is a kind of feeble explanation for the force of conscience.

SOCRATES: Are you two persons or one?

NAT: One.

SOCRATES: And you directly experience being commanded, being under moral obligation to do good and not evil.

NAT: Yes.

SOCRATES: And you do not experience the act of commanding, as you experience yourself acting in commanding another person. You are not sure where the command that your conscience delivers to you comes from: from society, from your superego, from your "deeper self", from God, or from something else.

NAT: That's right.

SOCRATES: Well, let's look at what it might be. In order to issue a command, you must be a person, with a will, right? Rocks and trees cannot command, any more than they can know.

NAT: That's true. So are you arguing now that conscience proves the existence of God, as you said you were not?

SOCRATES: Not at all. That's another question, the question of what is proved by this datum of experience that we call conscience. I want only to accept the datum and get it right. Some other day we will argue about God, but today we are arguing only about our own experience. I'm not trying to refute atheism, but I am trying to refute moral relativism, from your own moral experience.

NAT: Let me try one more argument for moral relativism. Two, actually. First, morality is about motives: goodwill versus badwill, love versus hate. And motives are subjective and personal. Therefore, morality is subjective and personal. And here's a second argument: Morality is about concrete human situations, which are changing and relative. Therefore, morality has to be changing and relative. For instance, lying to the Nazis about where the Jews are hiding isn't wrong, but right. And killing in self-defense or to protect the innocent is not murder. Situations change values.

SOCRATES: They do, but only somewhat: the applications are changing and relative, but not the principles. And as to the motives, they are indeed subjective, but that does not mean they are not absolute. Perhaps goodwill is an absolutely good motive, and selfish pride and competition is an absolutely bad one. Once again, I think you fail to make necessary distinctions, so that you are right in what you affirm and wrong in what you deny. You see that morality has a subjective dimension: personal motives. But that does not mean that good and evil in motives are not absolute. Hating persons is absolutely wrong. You also see that morality has relative and changing dimensions: applying principles differently to different situations. But that dimension is not subjective but objective, even though it is changing. But morality also has a third dimension, a list of things that are always right and things that are always wrong, and those are not subjective or relative. Moral virtues like charity and justice and honesty and courage are always and everywhere good. Can you deny any of those three dimensions? Do you deny that we must always do the right thing, for the right motives, and in the right way? The right thing is objective and absolute, the right motives are subjective and absolute, and the right way is objective and relative.

NAT: Perhaps we are both right, then. I got two of the dimensions right, and you got the third one.

SOCRATES: That is all I want to prove: that there is a dimension of morality that is neither subjective nor relative. We must do the right thing as well as have the right motive and do it in the right way or the right situation. No one of those three dimensions excludes any of the other two. Traditional commonsense morality always includes all three of those dimensions: the act itself, the motive, and the circumstances, or the situation.

NAT: I shall be completely honest with you, Socrates. I must admit that at the beginning of our dialogue, I thought your absolutism was narrow and oppressive and inhuman and also unintelligent and irrational. That's why I wanted you to defend it, since I never thought of you as that kind of person. Now I can see that your position is very different from what I thought it was, and much closer to moral common sense. I'm not wholly convinced I was wrong, even though I couldn't refute most of your arguments. But I thank you for taking me and my relativism seriously and arguing rather than preaching. As I said at the beginning of our discussion, I was a moral relativist only because I saw it as more moral than moral absolutism. This was not an argument between a moralist and an immoralist.

SOCRATES: I admired your moral motive for your moral relativism, though not your arguments.

NAT: What did you think was my motive?

SOCRATES: Two things: the good and the true, the human and the intelligent. I doubted only whether your relativism served as the best means to that purpose.

NAT: What moved me the most in the direction of your moral absolutism was your appeal to moral experience. I have to admit that when I see something as my moral duty, or my obligation, or what I ought to do, it feels as if something else or someone else is commanding me or correcting me, something with moral authority and superiority. I don't mean you, Socrates. But it feels almost as if an angel is whispering in my ear. I thought that was only childish superstition, or perhaps only my weak, infantile self afraid to grow into a self-reliant adult self, as Fraud seems to think.

SOCRATES: Freud, you mean.

NAT: Did I say "Fraud"? I guess that was a Freudian slip.

SOCRATES: So you are now becoming skeptical of your moral skepticism.

NAT: Yes. And I'm wondering about the next step.

SOCRATES: What do you mean by the next step?

NAT: I mean the identity of whatever is at the other end of the moral rope. I feel commanded, but I don't know the identity of the commander. Do you think it's God?

SOCRATES: I don't know. But I do not think that conscience proves the existence of God, at least not immediately.

NAT: Why not?

SOCRATES: Because if moral absolutism is true and conscience is not just a subjective feeling but an understanding of objective truths about good and evil, and subject to that objective standard, then my conscience, like my theoretical reason, can make mistakes. It can tell me that my duty is one thing when it is in fact something else, and it can be too strict or too lax. But God makes no mistakes. A fallible God would be hardly worth the name. So even if conscience is God's prophet, it is a fallible prophet, not an infallible one.

NAT: So how do you explain conscience?

SOCRATES: It's part of human reason. And that's why we have moral arguments like this one.

Questions for Discussion or Personal Essays

1. Did Socrates and Nat prove the existence of free will or free choice by freely choosing to assume it? If not, why not? If so, how can one *prove* anything by *assuming* it? Aren't proving and assuming mutually exclusive opposites?
2. Why does Socrates say that the question of this dialogue is "the single most basic question in all of ethics"?
3. What are the two different questions Socrates distinguishes? What is the basis for the distinction?
4. Socrates and Nat use the terms "ethics" and "morality" as synonyms. How and why do many people distinguish between these two terms?
5. Why does Socrates always want to begin with definitions?
6. Why does Socrates think that ethics depends on metaphysics?
7. What are the three differences Socrates points out at the beginning between traditional moral absolutism and typically modern moral relativism? Why do they naturally belong together? Can you imagine a philosophy that accepts just one or two but not all three of the claims of absolutism? Explain.
8. Do you think Socrates would agree or disagree with Nat's claim that Nat's relativism is no less moral, or no less ethical, than absolutism? How might Socrates use his later distinction between the three aspects of the act, the motives, and the circumstances or situation to answer that question?
9. Why might "absolutism" and "relativism" not be the best words to describe the difference between the two most basic answers to this most basic ethical question?
10. Are most of Nat's arguments for relativism deductive or inductive? What about Socrates' arguments?
11. List and summarize, in short logical form, each of Nat's arguments for relativism and Socrates' answers to them. Keep in mind the three ways it is possible to answer a logical argument. Which of these three answers does Socrates use the most?
12. Can you think of any other arguments for moral relativism than Nat's? If so, how do you think Socrates might answer them?
13. Which argument for moral relativism (whether one of Nat's or another one) do you think is the most popular and effective

in contemporary culture? Which do you see as the logically strongest? How are those two questions related?

14. Why does Nat pick 1648 as the date that marks the beginning of a new answer to a difficult question? What question is this?

15. Do you agree that the change from absolutism to relativism has been confined to sexual morality? How *total* do you think that change in sexual morality has been? What do you think was its main reason or motive? (This is not a logical but a psychological and historical question.)

16. Do you see the sexual revolution as having given more or less value to sex than traditional sexual morality? Why?

17. Why do you think tolerance has become the most popular virtue in our time?

18. Does Socrates offer any arguments for absolutism other than his critiques of Nat's relativism? If so, where? If not, what do you think they would be if you asked him for some?

19. Should intolerance be tolerated? How can you avoid self-contradiction in answering that question? How might a relativist answer Socrates' argument that mere tolerance would tolerate even intolerance and that the value of tolerance thus contradicts moral relativism?

20. How are facts and values similar? How are they different? In what way or ways are they proved differently? In what way or ways are they proved in the same ways?

21. How might the relativist answer Socrates' argument that if morality is subjective, it would be impossible to argue rationally about it?

22. If you think that some moral values are absolute (objective, universal, and discovered by reason and rational conscience) and others are relative (subjective, personal, and willed into existence), where would the dividing line be between these two kinds of values? Why would it be there and not elsewhere?

23. Can a value be a *moral* value if it is only subjective and willed into existence by us? How can we be duty bound by it if we have bound ourselves?

24. Compare the consequences of Socrates' rejection of scientism as distinct from science, that is, of the claim that there is no certainty outside of science, with scientism's consequences.

25. How do you see the relation between religion and philosophy in ethics? If your first answer to that question is vague and noncontroversial, make it more specific and argumentative.

26. Socrates says something very controversial, even outrageous in some circles, about our educational establishment in the social sciences, namely, about why most sociologists, psychologists, and anthropologists are relativists and most less educated people are not. Evaluate this.

27. What is the most frequent logical device, technique, or method that Socrates uses in answering Nat's arguments? Is there a stronger one?

28. Evaluate Socrates' "either-or" logic, for example, "Either God exists or He doesn't."

29. Does Socrates presuppose a kind of Platonic metaphysics that grants reality not only to (1) objective matter and (2) subjective minds or spirits but also to (3) the immaterial objects of those minds, like objective truths and values? If so, evaluate this metaphysics. If not, why is Socrates not presupposing this? If you do not believe this metaphysics, why is it so popular? If you agree with this metaphysics, why do you think the alternative of either materialism (only the first of these three kinds of being) or dualism (only the first two) is so popular?

30. If conscience is a seeing, knowing, or understanding, why do most people see it as a feeling? Do you think the answer is the ambiguity of "intuition", which can mean either immediate *knowledge* or immediate *feeling*? Or is there a stronger answer to that first question? If conscience is intellectual rather than emotional, is it immediate and intuitive mental "seeing" or is it rational, that is, logical, a process from premise to conclusion? How are these two things related in our experience?

31. Socrates frequently insists on distinctions because he thinks we are often half-right and half-wrong: right in what we affirm and wrong in what we ignore or deny. If so, how do we find out which things are affirmations and which are denials? How far can we rely on the linguistic structures? Can we construct linguistically negative ways to express metaphysical affirmations and linguistically positive ways to express metaphysical denials? Examine some examples.

32. Evaluate Socrates' reconciliation between absolutism and relativism by distinguishing the three dimensions of morality. Who would disagree with this and why?

33. What do you think is the relation between the voice of conscience and the voice of God?

34. If our conscience, unlike God, is fallible, why should we always obey it? Is authority the same as infallibility? If not, what is the difference?

35. Which is morally worse: to do the wrong thing because you obey a mistaken conscience or to do the right thing because you disobey a mistaken conscience? Why?

9

Ethics: What Is the Greatest Good?

The meaning and importance of this topic is self-evident and also made plain in the dialogue itself, so it should need no introduction.

NAT: Socrates, before we begin today, I want to ask you something about yourself. I'm not complaining, and I appreciate the structure for the curriculum of this "Socrates University", this log with you and me on it. But you seem more like Plato than Socrates. You teach not only by questioning but also by answering, expressing your own opinions and judgments as well as logically judging those of others. You have compromised your Socratic method.

SOCRATES: This is true in one way—I have compromised, or at least added to, my teaching style—but it is not true in another way: I have not assumed the truth of any of Plato's distinctive answers to the great questions, nor anyone else's.

NAT: Why have you changed your method?

SOCRATES: To fit your needs. I designed this simple "university", and these questions as its curriculum in philosophy, by your needs. You are not a fourth-century B.C. Athenian but a twenty-first-century American, so I have altered even my speaking style for purposes of communication and clarity. For instance, you Americans have less tolerance than we did for long, abstract, and multi-step logical arguments, so I have simplified and summarized most of the arguments to fit your more modern, impatient attention span. But I have tried to be unprejudiced and fair to both sides of each controversial question. And I think that is especially important when we consider today's question, which has to be the single most important ethical question of all: What is the greatest good, or ultimate end, or meaning of life, assuming it has one?

NAT: Well, I hope we can be without prejudices or assumptions, especially for today's question, if it is as important as you say. But I think you are assuming three things in your very posing of the question: first, that it is a question of ethics; second, that it is the most important one; and third, that there *is* such a thing as the greatest good.

SOCRATES: Congratulations, Nat, for catching one of the symptoms of my good infection of Socratic philosophizing: the habit of bringing to light hidden assumptions.

NAT: As to the first assumption, whether this is a question of ethics, why do most contemporary ethical philosophers not deal with it? And why do you?

SOCRATES: Because most modern philosophers take ethics to be something narrower in scope than I do. They think of ethics as about interpersonal relationships, or right individual actions and right social systems and policies, or social justice—which is not wrong, just incomplete and ignorant of its foundations. And thus they take ethics' fundamental category to be justice, or right and wrong, or rights and duties. They also sometimes include a second dimension: individual virtues and vices, or moral character. And there, too, rights and duties seem central terms. But they don't usually ask about a third dimension, which seems to be the most important one of all, namely, what is the greatest good, the absolute good to which all other goods are relative, the end to which they are means, the standard by which they are all judged.

NAT: I am surprised to hear you call the question of the greatest good a question of ethics. Ethics sounds very concrete and personal, either communal or individual, while the "greatest good" sounds very abstract and metaphysical. What you called the first two dimensions of ethics, namely, social ethics and individual ethics, seem to cover everything: the good for individuals and the good for society. It sounds very abstract to say that everything in ethics is relative to the greatest good.

SOCRATES: Then think of this concrete analogy. Think of human beings as a fleet of ships, and ethics as their sailing orders. The orders tell the ships three things: how to cooperate (that's social

ethics), how to stay afloat and shipshape (that's personal virtue ethics), and above all why they are at sea at all, both individually and
collectively. Are they ferrying passengers, or fighting battles in a
war, or transporting freight, or on a pleasure cruise?

NAT: I see. And I also see the reason for your second assumption, that
this is the most important question. Because it's about the end, or
goal, or purpose of everything else in life.

SOCRATES: Yes.

NAT: But to play devil's advocate for a moment, are you assuming,
then, that the end justifies the means? Isn't that questionable?

SOCRATES: No, because that's what a "means" *means*: a means to an
end. You wouldn't want money if you didn't want to buy anything, and you wouldn't want a pen if you didn't want to write
anything.

NAT: That's true. Why, then, do you think people say that "the end
does not justify the means"?

SOCRATES: I think they mean that a morally good end does not morally justify a morally bad means. Feeding the starving poor is a
good end, but it does not justify murdering the rich and cannibal-
izing their bodies.

NAT: I think that's reasonable. What about the third assumption,
then, that there is such a thing as the greatest good or final end?
Not everyone would agree with that, probably because it sounds
too metaphysical. What's a good reason for assuming there must
be one?

I suspect the very questionableness of your third assumption—
that there is such a thing—is the reason most philosophers don't
address the question of the greatest good. They think it's too metaphysical, and they are skeptical of metaphysics. And if they do
metaphysics, they are probably nominalists and deny the reality
of universals. Or perhaps their epistemology is too skeptical or
empirical and they think that our reason is incapable of knowing
whether and what such a thing is. And if we cannot know *whether*
it is, we should not waste time on the question of *what* it is.

SOCRATES: But surely people do live as if they knew the answer, and
their lives are very different depending on what their answer is.
Surely it is not a waste of time to discuss whether someone who
lives as if the greatest good is selfish pleasure or power is wiser or

more foolish than one who lives as if the greatest good is justice
or charity.

NAT: Surely.

SOCRATES: So we must be able to discuss, with at least some degree of
certainty or probability, this great question. That logically follows,
doesn't it?

NAT: Yes. It is a waste of time to discuss unanswerable questions, and
it is not a waste of time to discuss this question; therefore, this is
not an unanswerable question.

SOCRATES: Good syllogism, Nat.

NAT: Why is it, do you think, that so many people agree with those
two premises yet so few agree with the conclusion that follows
from it?

SOCRATES: I don't know. They are not here now to ask, are they?
But you are.

NAT: So prove to me first that there is such a thing, a final end to
which everything else is a means, a greatest good to which all
other goods are relative. Because if there is not, then the fleet of
ships is in pretty desperate straits. How can they work together if
they have fundamentally different ends? How can they cooperate
if there is no "co" in their "operating"?

SOCRATES: That's easy. Everyone agrees that there are some good
things, because everyone argues about what they are. And everyone
agrees that some goods are greater than others, because we give up
some goods, like money, for the sake of other goods, like health.
We value things, and we value them differently, not equally.

NAT: But if we invent values rather than discover them, then that
can be only an argument from what nearly everyone thinks, or
opines, subjectively. Nearly everyone may be wrong. Give me an
argument from the nature of things, objectively.

SOCRATES: Gladly. Goods are either means or ends, either desired for
their own sakes, like pleasure, or for the sake of other things, like
tools or money. And if there are many ends, some are means to
further ends, as exercise may be pleasant but also a means to the
end of health, and health is a means to the end of work, and work
is a means to the end of whatever product we work at, and so
forth. Isn't that right?

NAT: Yes.

SOCRATES: And if we do not desire an end, we do not desire a means to that end, isn't that right? If money can't buy anything, we don't desire those dirty pieces of paper.

NAT: Right.

SOCRATES: So if there were no end that we desire for its own sake, we would not desire the means to it. But we do desire those things.

NAT: I see. It is like the cosmological argument for the existence of God: Just as if there is no first cause, no uncaused cause, there could be no second causes, no caused causes, in the order of efficient causality. So also in the order of final causality, or purposive desire, if there is no greatest good or last end that is desirable for itself, there could be no desirable means to that end. But there are desirable means. Therefore, there must be some last end.

SOCRATES: Exactly.

NAT: Well, not exactly. The efficient cause argument is an argument for the existence of a First Cause, and its basis is the causal structure of the cosmos, or the universe. But this argument is only about things we desire, not about the universe that was there before we were, so it's only human. So it can't prove the existence of God.

SOCRATES: I did not say that it did.

NAT: But the fact that it naturally raises the God question may explain why contemporary philosophers avoid the whole question of the greatest good. They want to keep religion and philosophy, faith and reason, distinct.

SOCRATES: That may or may not be their motive. My business is to philosophize, not psychologize. Also, as I said before, these other people, with their own motives, are not here now, but you are.

NAT: All right. So let's look at the question of the "greatest good", or "end of ends". If it must be, it must be something, and if it must be something, what is it? Unlike most of the other questions we explored, this one does not have just two answers, a yes and a no. There are many candidates for the position. So we should explore the pros and cons of each one, I think, as we explore each of the many candidates who stand for election.

SOCRATES: Good. Do you think we should take them in a random order or a logical order?

NAT: A logical order, of course. But since we do not know yet which ones are the best ones objectively, we cannot arrange them by that standard. So let's use the subjective standard of popularity, observing what people do in fact desire most often.

SOCRATES: Fine. With what shall we begin?

NAT: Well, if we get what we desire, we are happy. So let's ask what makes the most people happy. If I saw a big smile suddenly appear on my friend's face, I'd probably ask him, "What happened to you? You look as if you just won a million dollars in the lottery." In other words, money is the first thing we think of to answer our question. But that's probably the stupidest of all answers, as well as the most popular, because money is, by definition, only a means, and not an end—a "means of exchange" of goods.

SOCRATES: That's a short and sweet "con", but what do you think is the "pro" that attracts so many people to this good as if it were their greatest good?

NAT: That's easy. Money can buy "all the things that money can buy", and that's a very large set of things. It can get us not just one good, like food or cars or entertainment, but many.

SOCRATES: So even though people are stupid in pursuing this means as if it were an end, they are not totally stupid. Money is like a large tent, which can contain many good things.

NAT: But I think money is not only a stupid answer but also a dangerous one, a dangerous thing to set your heart on, because it has a kind of fake infinity. You can always want more of it and get more of it. You can't do that with food or entertainment, because there is a natural limit to them, in fact to all the things money can buy. After three or four good meals in one day, you don't want any more. But you can always want more money. Money does not contain its own inner limits, as everything in nature does. So money is a more dangerous false answer than any of the things money can buy.

SOCRATES: So what have we learned from this false candidate for our election besides the fact that it is false?

NAT: Why do you ask that?

SOCRATES: We can learn something from everything, including errors, can we not?

NAT: Yes. And what we have learned, I think, is that since this candidate, though most popular, is also unusually dangerous, popularity has no necessary correlation with real goodness.

SOCRATES: I see no fault in your logic.

NAT: Well, we've eliminated two candidates: money and the things money can buy. How many more do you think we will have to do the same with?

SOCRATES: That depends not on what I think but what you think. What other goods do you see people treating as their greatest good?

NAT: Well, I think most people crave approval from others.

SOCRATES: In previous societies that was usually called "honor".

NAT: That word is not used much anymore, but the desire is certainly still alive. I think the word isn't used much anymore because it used to mean being thought well of because you were superior in some way. People thought hierarchically. Today people are more often accepted for *not* being superior, for being one of the crowd, for being egalitarian.

SOCRATES: That is a fascinating sociological and psychological phenomenon, but the essential nature of both kinds of honor is the same, isn't it? It comes from others' good opinions of you.

NAT: Yes, and that's why this can't be the greatest good—because if you desire honor, or acceptance by others, you are externalizing your own good. Honor, or acceptance, is in the other person—in the honoring, not in the honored. But we're looking for what is the greatest good, and thus the greatest happiness, in you, in each person. My good cannot possibly consist in how many likes I get on Facebook.

SOCRATES: And yet that seems to be the most popular answer today's teenagers give to the most important question in the world. It seems as if they have returned to polytheism, for they are putting their happiness and their identity and their meaning into the hands and smartphones of many gods by virtually worshipping their friends' opinions. One psychologist said that America is the most polytheistic nation in history: the Greeks named a few thousand gods, Hindus and Buddhists many more, but Americans name 330 million.

NAT: But it surely *is* very good to be accepted and loved and esteemed by others. However silly this answer is, it is not totally ridiculous. The candidate has some plus features, otherwise not so many would vote for it. If I honor you, that is almost a kind of loving you. And that is certainly a thing we all want and need.

SOCRATES: Yes.

NAT: And the same could be said of fame or glory, which is something like honor magnified.

SOCRATES: And again this seems to attract the young more than the old. Their ambition is often to be a very famous entertainer, especially a singer or an actor or actress. So what refutes that answer? Why can't we elect fame to the office of the greatest good?

NAT: That's obvious. For one thing, the life expectancy of famous people, especially in entertainment, is quite low, mainly because their drug consumption is usually high. Whatever the cause of that, it's a fact, statistically.

For another thing, the life expectancy of fame itself, like fashion, is short and fleeting. It rarely leaps the "generation gap".

And for still another thing, no matter how extensive other people's knowledge of you may be, it can't create or change what you are or have in yourself. It's another externalization, like honor.

And other people's knowledge of you is not the true you; it's just a knowledge of the mask you wear in public to attain that fame. If you identify your greatest good with fame, you disappear into your mask.

And the more you worry about your external fame and your image, the weaker you are inside. The more your ego needs flattery, the weaker and unhappier it is. If you were truly happy and good, you would not need millions of people to flatter you.

SOCRATES: Yet we do quite naturally and rightly praise and glorify our heroes.

NAT: Yes. But we praise them because they really are heroes, because of what they are or do; they are not heroes because we praise them.

SOCRATES: Indeed. I see that the candidates for this election are going to have to give a better account of themselves if they are to get your vote. Which one shall we look at next?

NAT: Power. We seem to fear loss of power more than anything else: slavery, imprisonment, blindness, lameness. Even poverty is a loss of power. Even pleasure has to take second place to power, because if I had the power and control, I could give myself pleasure and anything else I wanted whenever I wanted it. Power even seems godlike: it seems we make it God's other name when we call him "Almighty God".

SOCRATES: So why isn't power the greatest good?

NAT: Because it's almost as obviously only a means as money is. Power for what? Power to do or get what?

Also, when we get it, we worry. "Uneasy lies the head that wears the crown." It gives us more fears and more responsibilities.

And of course power is easily misused. And even if it isn't, it can be. It's open to evil just as much as to good. It's not good in itself; it's neutral. In fact, it inclines or tempts us more to evil. As the English historian Lord Acton said, "Power tends to corrupt and absolute power corrupts absolutely."

It's also external, like all the previous candidates. When you love power, you mean you love power over other persons or other minds or things, not power over yourself.

SOCRATES: Do you see any one feature that doomed each of these candidates to failure?

NAT: Yes. They were all external. I think we should change our direction, then, and look within instead of without.

SOCRATES: That is probably why bodily health is a popular candidate, especially for those who have either a very lot of it or a very little of it: either strong athletes or those who lack it or are in danger of losing it.

What evidence or argument do you see against that very obvious and reasonable candidate?

NAT: Well, it is obviously a good, and a natural good, and a very important good, because people will give up all their money to get their health back. But when I look carefully at human bodily goods and compare them with those of other animals, I see, literally, with my body's eyes, that there is always some animal that exceeds man in some excellence of the body. Elephants live longer, eagles have better sight, birds can fly, fish swim better, lions are more powerful, and cheetahs run faster. But man exceeds all animals in happiness, and also in unhappiness, because he has reason and understanding. Animals can be content, but they cannot experience joy. So if man is not superior to all animals in bodily goods and is superior to them in happiness, then it logically follows that bodily goods cannot constitute man's happiness.

SOCRATES: That was admirably logical—a single valid syllogism—and admirably empirical: a trip to the zoo refutes a whole quite popular materialistic philosophy!

NAT: So now we move one step further inward, to pleasure. This seems much more promising as an answer, for it seems to be, by definition, that which pleases us, and to be pleased seems to be pretty much the same as to be happy.

SOCRATES: Yes, and that is why hedonism, which identifies happiness with pleasure, is probably the single most popular ethic, not only among ordinary people but also among philosophers. Utilitarianism, for instance, claims that the "greatest good" is simply "the greatest happiness for the greatest number" and that happiness means simply pleasure.

NAT: Many people mean by "pleasure" simply physical pleasure, the opposite of physical pain. But most people, I think, are wise enough to realize that inner pleasures are more satisfying, more reliable, more long-lasting, and more under our control than external, merely physical pleasures, however intense the latter may be for a short time.

SOCRATES: But we should not go too fast. The most intense pleasures are short, like sexual orgasm, yet many deem these the highest.

NAT: We all understand that, and I think we also understand that that answer is a crude one and does not stand the test of time.

SOCRATES: Why, then, do so many otherwise sensible people value such fleeting moments over anything else?

NAT: Because they do not listen to reason but to their passions.

SOCRATES: I wonder whether that is as obvious as you think. Let me play devil's advocate for them for a moment. Perhaps we will find a partial truth, or a half truth, or a distorted truth there, even if their answer proves to be inadequate—some truth that will be profitable or even precious to us.

NAT: Let's try. Where do you want to begin?

SOCRATES: With a simple question: Time is a quantity, is it not?

NAT: Yes.

SOCRATES: And intensity can be a quality as well as a quantity, can it not?

NAT: I don't see that. How?

SOCRATES: We can measure the physical intensity of things like heat on an external instrument, like a thermometer, which has a sliding scale of numerical quantity; but the intensity of a felt pleasure cannot be measured by quantitative numbers, except by analogy. When we move up the stairway of pleasure, we discover discrete steps of differences in quality when we move from temporary satisfaction to contentment to happiness to joy. Joy is different in kind, not just quantity, from happiness, and happiness is different in kind from contentment, don't you agree?

NAT: That is true.

SOCRATES: So does it not follow, then, that it is not wholly irrational to rank more lasting but milder pleasures inferior to a quantitatively brief but more intense pleasure, like sexual orgasm or mystical experience (to take two things on opposite ends of the spectrum of matter and spirit)? The qualitatively more intense pleasure, though it is short-lived, seems to be a better image of the highest happiness, and perhaps even of eternal happiness, because it is not boring but fascinating. Don't you agree?

NAT: Yes.

SOCRATES: And we do not need to confine ourselves to mystical experiences, which are rare, but we can speak simply of ordinary religious experiences of the presence of God, or being loved by God, or doing God's will, in Western religions, or moments of attaining "enlightenment", as in Eastern religions.

NAT: I see. Perhaps that is the subconscious rationalization for wild hedonism. A longing for mystical experience.

SOCRATES: But wait. I think we are confusing two things here. There are two different ways one pleasure may be "higher" than another. The first is the objective nature of the thing we are pleased about, and the second is the subjective feeling we have of desiring it when it is absent or enjoying it when it is present. The objective thing that causes the subjective pleasure is one thing, and the power it has to appear subjectively fascinating to us personally is another thing. The first is a good reason for ranking pleasure closer to the supreme good, because that reason lies in the thing itself, not in our subjective response to it. But the second thing cannot judge the worth of the thing we take pleasure in, only our reaction to it or our desire for it, which may be foolish and mistaken. For instance, compare the pleasure of someone who appreciates a great symphony with the pleasure of a baby in tasting sweet candy. And it's not just that the very same thing, pleasure as such, can come from two different objects, but also that the nature of the pleasure, the subjective feeling, is different. Higher pleasures take us out of ourselves and make us self-forgetful, sometimes even to the point of ecstasy, which means literally "standing outside yourself". Lower pleasures do not do that.

NAT: If I understand your distinction, and the value judgment implied in it, and if you are right, then that would be the reason why the joy of mystical and religious experience is not a weak substitute for the pleasure of sexual orgasm, as Freudians claim, but rather the reverse.

SOCRATES: Exactly.

NAT: Well, then, since we have some control over experiencing sexual orgasm, as we do not over mystical experience, we could test the Freudian theory by supplying mistresses to all romantic adolescents and see whether we observe the consequence that all mystical and religious experiences disappear in them.

SOCRATES: Your society has been performing exactly that experiment ever since the sexual revolution of the sixties. So what has the result been?

NAT: It's inconclusive. Religious belief has declined, but not, I think, religious aspiration and interest. In fact, I think it has become more mystical and personal, and less institutional and creedal.

SOCRATES: Do you think that has any bearing on the value or validity of either religion or the sexual revolution?

NAT: No. My reference to the experiment of the sexual revolution was simply to test the hypothesis (the Freudian one). And it seems to have refuted it.

SOCRATES: Then what is your verdict on these different kinds of pleasure—the intense but brief versus the controllable—as candidates for the greatest good?

NAT: Both fail.

SOCRATES: Why?

NAT: To put it crudely and quickly, orgasms don't last and contentment gets boring.

SOCRATES: So does that mean that no kind of pleasure is the greatest good? Or that pleasure has nothing to do with the supreme good?

NAT: Well, now, let me think about that for a minute.

SOCRATES: I am very pleased when you say that! It is a rarity.

NAT: That's a pity. The alternative is to rush in where angels fear to tread.

(*Nat is silent for a few moments.*)

NAT: Well, now, I think that whether pleasure is a part of the greatest good or not depends on its object, that is, what the pleasure is *about*, or what we take pleasure in, or the real reason why we are pleased. I don't think that the subjective state of being pleased, as such, can be the greatest good because being pleased is always being pleased with something, or about something, and when that something is the greatest good, our subjective pleasure follows from it, caused by it. So I think pleasure is like the smell of delicious food. It seems to accompany the good but not to be its essence.

The point is simple. We are pleased *because* some good is present, but what is that good and what makes it present? Pleasure itself does not answer either of those two questions. You might say that pleasure is the effect of the supreme good, but not its cause.

SOCRATES: I think that is very reasonable and checks out with our experience. Well, if the greatest good is not pleasure itself, what is it? We seem to be moving higher and higher, as on a ladder, or closer and closer, as on a journey. What is the next step? What is closer to the answer?

NAT: I'm not sure. But it must be a good of the soul, not just of the body. And when I think of the soul, the first thing I think of is the mind, the reason, the understanding.

SOCRATES: And what is the end of the mind? What does the mind seek?

NAT: Truth.

SOCRATES: And why do we seek the truth? For what end?

NAT: All sorts of ends: for instance, to calculate pleasures, to make money, to survive disasters, to solve problems ...

SOCRATES: Do we also love the truth for its own sake, just to understand it and contemplate it, even if nothing else comes from it?

NAT: Yes, if we are wise.

SOCRATES: Then perhaps that is the greatest good. The knowledge, or understanding, or contemplation of truth.

NAT: I don't see the knowledge of the truth about how many gallons of water there are in the ocean as part of the greatest good.

SOCRATES: No, because that's not wisdom; it's just knowledge.

NAT: I see. I guess that's it, then. Wisdom is the greatest good.

SOCRATES: Are you sure?

NAT: I think so. For wisdom is not just knowledge but understanding, and not just understanding of *anything*, but of the supreme good. So wisdom must be the supreme good.

No, wait a minute. The knowledge or understanding of a thing is not the same as the thing itself. So knowledge itself, or contemplation itself, or understanding itself is not yet the supreme good even if it is knowledge of the supreme good. But what is *that*? What is the thing itself?

(*Nat thinks silently again for a few minutes.*)

Perhaps it's beauty, or the contemplation of beauty. We want that not for any other end but as an end in itself. So perhaps beauty itself is the supreme good.

SOCRATES: I suspect that the supreme good and the supreme beauty may be two different words for the same thing, so perhaps we have indeed reached the end of our road. But perhaps not. Do you want me to play devil's advocate and try to refute this promising answer?

NAT: Yes. Because I want to be certain. I don't just want something that feels right today and might not feel right tomorrow.

SOCRATES: Well, then, look at these data of experience. Datum number one: Did you know that many of the Nazis who ran the concentration camps were deeply in love with beauty, especially the beauty of music?

NAT: Yes, I knew that.

SOCRATES: But they were very wicked, were they not?

NAT: Of course.

SOCRATES: Let that be datum number two. Put those two premises together, and what conclusion follows?

NAT: That the supreme good cannot be simply the appreciation of beauty. Oh, that was short and unsweet. But what else might it be?

SOCRATES: What do you think?

NAT: Let's see. It's got to be in the soul, not the body. And the soul has three powers that the animals don't have. One of them is the reason, or mind, or understanding. That produces both science and philosophy. But we already considered that. Then there is also the creative imagination, the power to create and appreciate beauty. But we already considered that. So the other power is the will, the moral will, the power to choose between good and evil. Well, then, I suppose the supreme good must be there; it must be moral virtue itself, moral good.

SOCRATES: Do you mean obeying the moral law, doing your duty?

NAT: Not just that, because that can be dour and sour. I mean having a good character, being a good person. That seems to be at least a part of the supreme good, or a prerequisite for it, because if you're not morally good, your soul is sort of broken or diseased. I used to think it was only a preachy platitude when my parents told me that you can't be happy unless you're good, but now I see that's obviously true. It's confirmed by experience. By everybody's experience. When we're good, when we have all the moral virtues—honesty and charity and justice and wisdom and courage and unselfishness—it makes a real difference. It seems to make us more *real*. Especially genuine love, honest love, unselfish love. I think that's the single most important of the virtues. And when we're selfish, unloving, unfair, dishonest, foolish, or cowardly, we know the difference that makes too. We feel it, deep down and in the long run. We feel somehow unreal, or fake. We punish ourselves when we're bad, and we reward ourselves when we're good. Didn't some philosopher say that virtue is its own reward and vice is its own punishment?

SOCRATES: I think many philosophers have said that. But does that mean that we have found our answer, that virtue is the greatest good?

NAT: Why not? Do you see a problem with that?

SOCRATES: Let's see whether *you* do. Love is in the soul, or begins in the soul, right?

NAT: Yes.

SOCRATES: And our love is imperfect, is it not?

NAT: I guess so. Why is that?

SOCRATES: Because love is in time, just as our knowledge is in time. Our body is in both time and space, and our soul is not in space or made of matter, but it *is* in time, and it changes; it grows or shrinks, and it gets better or worse. So it's not perfect; it's only on the way toward perfection, hopefully.

NAT: I see. So even a virtuous and loving soul can't be in itself the supreme good. It's just the part of us, or the power in us, that pursues the supreme good or loves it, and the part or power in us that receives it, or experiences it, or attains it.

SOCRATES: To put it in logical form, our virtue is imperfect and the supreme good is not imperfect; therefore, even our virtue is not the supreme good. The supreme good is what we are striving for, so it can't be the striving itself.

NAT: But I'm not sure where else to go to find the supreme good. What is higher than love? Nothing, I think.

SOCRATES: What about perfect love?

NAT: But we are not perfect love.

SOCRATES: And we are not the supreme good either.

NAT: Oh! So ... perfect love is the supreme good! But do you mean the Platonic Form of love? The abstract ideal? Or do you mean a real being, a God who is love itself? And since love comes only from a person, a God who is love itself would have to be a Person.

SOCRATES: I fear that question is beyond my pay grade. Someone else will have to help you finish that journey.

NAT: But both answers—Plato's philosophical answer and Christianity's religious answer—seem beyond our capacity.

SOCRATES: What capacity? Our capacity to conceive?

NAT: I suppose not, since we have just conceived them. But they are beyond our capacity to comprehend adequately. We have the concept, but we don't understand it very well at all.

SOCRATES: Are they beyond our capacity to desire?

NAT: No. Because we are not perfectly satisfied with limited goods. We want to move beyond that limit. So we can desire the supreme good even though we cannot comprehend or understand it. But how can we desire what we cannot understand?

SOCRATES: That is a great question, and I don't think I know the answer to it. But if it is a fact that we desire it and if it is a fact that we cannot understand it, then we can desire something we cannot understand. And therefore there must be some way we do that, since we do that, even if we do not know, or perhaps even cannot know, *how* we do it.

NAT: You surprise me, Socrates. You sound like a mystic.

SOCRATES: That was two syllogisms, not a mystical experience! This is something we know not by some special mystical experience but by the ordinary experience of loving and being loved, insofar as we do it, even on a human level. Can we fully understand what love is? It may not be mystical, but it is certainly a mystery. It is a paradox, an apparent contradiction. How can we find our true selves only when we lose ourselves? How can we come to know ourselves only when we *forget* ourselves? How can the overcoming of our deepest natural instinct, self-fulfillment and self-contentment, be the supreme happiness of the self?

NAT: Are you asking *me*?

SOCRATES: No, I am asking myself.

NAT: And are you being answered?

SOCRATES: No.

NAT: Does that not bother you?

SOCRATES: Bother me? It fascinates me.

NAT: Me too.

Questions for Discussion or Personal Essays

1. Why does Socrates call the question of the greatest good "the greatest of all questions"?

2. What is the significance of the fact that in our culture this question is no longer seen as the primary question in ethics, or even as a question about ethics at all?

3. What is the difference between the question of "what good is" and the question of "what is good"? Why is the first question so hard and the second one so easy?

4. What do you see as the advantage of centering on the concept of "good" in ethics rather than "right" or "ought"? What is the advantage of centering on "right"? On "ought"?

5. In what sense is it true that the end justifies the means? *Why* is it true? In what sense is it false? *Why* is it false?

6. What good reason is there for assuming that there is one supreme good for everyone? How far can "different strokes for different folks" be true? Why?

7. How much of this dialogue would a moral subjectivist and relativist find meaningful? Why?

8. Are there limitations of the means-end categories Socrates uses? Why or why not?

9. Compare the argument for one supreme final end with the argument for one supreme First Cause. How are they similar? How different? Which is stronger? Why?

10. In what order do Socrates and Nat examine the various candidates for the greatest good? Do they keep to this order or not?

11. List each of the candidates Socrates and Nat review and then summarize the basic argument or motivation *for* each one and the argument *against* each one.

12. What practical conclusions follow from each examination regarding how to live out these arguments?

13. Which of the rejected candidates are not simply rejected but play some part in the final answer? How?

14. Which of the candidates do you see as the most popular today? Which do you see as the most dangerous? Which do you see as the closest to the best answer?

15. Do Socrates' frequent religious references, terminologies, and analogies presuppose the truth or validity of religion? Why or why not? Why would some people give the opposite answer?

16. Do you see any of the arguments as invalid or weak? Which? Why? How would you correct it?

17. Why are we surprised to see a trip to the zoo seem to refute a whole philosophy?

18. How do you think pleasures can best be ranked or classified?

19. What, exactly, is the relation between pleasure and the supreme good?

20. How would you distinguish pleasure, satisfaction, contentment, happiness, and joy?

21. If money is only a means to the end of natural goods, and natural goods give us more pleasure than money, why is the thirst for money greater?

22. Evaluate Socrates' take on the sexual revolution.

23. Test each of the candidates by the "boring" criterion. Not being bored is certainly not the *sufficient* criterion for the supreme good, but it is certainly a *necessary* criterion, isn't it? Why?

24. Why isn't the idea of seeking the truth simply for its own sake impractical and otherworldly?

25. When considering "the true, the good, and the beautiful", why do you think Socrates led Nat through these three values in the order that he did?

26. Which of the rejected candidates, do you think, received the least just and adequate treatment? How would you improve this candidate's positive argument?

27. What kind of love does Socrates mean when calling it the highest virtue? Evaluate this implied definition of love and his claim for it.

28. What do you see as the relation between Plato's and Christianity's answers to the question of the greatest good?

29. Is there an easy answer to the final paradox about human love? If so, what is it? If not, why not?

Applied Ethics: War and Pacifism

Since the rest of the dialogues are about more specific and focused issues, they are considerably shorter than the more fundamental issues in the first nine dialogues. For the same reason, they also need less introduction.

SOCRATES: Next we're going to begin to explore some of the specific ethical issues that, to most people, are the most interesting questions in philosophy. I've picked three of them, war, abortion, and sex, as some of the most controversial.

NAT: When you say that most people find these specific ethical issues the most interesting, are you implying that you don't?

SOCRATES: Not necessarily. I don't deny that most people are quite right to find them interesting.

NAT: Why are they right?

SOCRATES: For one reason, because they're about ethics, about good and evil.

NAT: That emphasis on ethics implies moral absolutism, doesn't it?

SOCRATES: How?

NAT: Well, if moral relativism is true, and if it's not true that good and evil are objectively real and that what's *really* good trumps what *feels* good or what seems nice or popular or comfortable or successful, or anything else we subjectively value, then ethics isn't *really* that important, is it?

SOCRATES: I think that consequence logically follows, as you say, yes. And I also think it's natural for most people to focus on specific ethical issues, because they are concrete and practical and they directly and immediately affect their lives.

NAT: But since you are not "most people" but a philosopher, what do you find more interesting than those questions, if anything?

SOCRATES: Actually, all nine of the issues we have discussed already, since they are the foundations for these more specific issues. Especially, in ethics, the issue of the metaphysical status of the moral principles behind specific issues, particularly whether those moral principles or values are objective or subjective, whether the good is real or only mental, and whether we make it or it makes us. I find that the most important for the same reason a foundation is the most important part of a building. The foundation does not depend on the building, but the building depends on it.

NAT: That's true. But it's also true that the building is not there for the sake of the foundation; the foundation is there for the sake of the building. It's the means to the end of the building. And the end is more important than the means because that's what motivates or justifies the means. Therefore ...

SOCRATES: Oh, good for you! You're not only arguing back to me, but you're arguing in my favorite way, by a syllogism.

NAT: Why is that your favorite way, by the way?

SOCRATES: Because it's the most natural and commonsensical way of arguing. The major premise is a general principle, the minor premise is a particular case, and the conclusion is the application of the principle to the case. But I also understand that to most people abstract general principles are less interesting, and less exciting, than concrete specific issues, especially issues that are literally matters of life or death, like war and abortion and sex.

NAT: Why do you see sex as a matter of life or death?

SOCRATES: Don't you?

NAT: No. Why do you?

SOCRATES: Are you alive right now?

NAT: If I'm not, I'm making a very big mistake in thinking that I am! "Cogito ergo sum."

SOCRATES: And why are you alive? Why do you have life? Did a stork bring you? Were you assembled on an assembly line? Were you "decanted" in a test tube, as in Brave New World? Or was it sex?

NAT: Oh, I see. Sex, of course.

SOCRATES: Why were you surprised at your own answer? Why the "oh"?

NAT: Because I don't usually think of sex that way, as a matter of life or death.

SOCRATES: Why not?

NAT: I don't think most people do.

SOCRATES: But most people did, until quite recently. I suspect we'll get into that issue when we focus on sexual morality later. For now, I just want to justify my choice of these three ethical issues, and my justification is two things. First, they're important intrinsically, in themselves, because they're about human life itself. And second, they're exciting to us because they're hot-button issues.

NAT: I don't think war is very controversial. I never met anyone who loved war. Did you ever hear the slogan "Give war a chance"?

SOCRATES: What starts wars? Do they start in the same way that natural disasters like hurricanes start?

NAT: Of course not. People start them. I see your point. So there must be some such people, the people who want wars and start wars, the warmongers, the few wicked and tyrannical people.

SOCRATES: Have you ever met any of those people, the people who are responsible for creating wars?

NAT: No, not personally.

SOCRATES: If the people who start wars are so rare that you've never met any of them, why are wars so common, do you think?

NAT: I suppose it's because the few, the warmongers, have the power.

SOCRATES: If that's true, then how do you think the few get that power over the many, and stay in power—especially in democracies? And how do they so often get the support of the people?

NAT: I don't know.

SOCRATES: Do you know how Hitler came to power?

NAT: It was in a democracy. He was elected. So it was by the people's free choice. But once he had the power, he used it to increase it and to stay there.

SOCRATES: That's true. But it's also true that once he was in power, most of his people loved him until he started losing the war. That is simply a fact. Even tyrants who are not freely elected are often very popular. Why do you think that is?

NAT: It's a puzzle, all right.

SOCRATES: Do you have any solution to the puzzle? Why do we love dictators?

NAT: I know dictators are often very popular. And they tend to start wars. I think it's hate, not love, that motivates wars, and I think it's hate that dictators appeal to. So I think the puzzle is why hate is so strong and love is so weak, not only in the warmongers but also in the people who support them.

SOCRATES: I think that's a good analysis so far. Let's do a little more amateur psychologizing about these people. Tyrants and nontyrants share human nature, do they not?

NAT: Yes.

SOCRATES: And the common essence, or the essential nature, of anything is more fundamental than its different accidents, isn't that so? All humans differ from dogs more fundamentally than any humans differ from each other, right?

NAT: Right.

SOCRATES: So what dictators have in common with us, who are not tyrants, is more fundamental than how they differ from us.

NAT: Right. So what does that have to do with the origin of war?

SOCRATES: I think we might be able to see the big thing, war, if we look at the smallest and closest and commonest versions of it first, don't you agree?

NAT: Yes.

SOCRATES: Have you observed the ordinary little wars among the ordinary little people, for instance, between close friends or people in the same family?

NAT: Of course. Especially in a family.

SOCRATES: Let's look at a typical "war" in a family. For instance, one family member, usually a younger one, wants more freedom to live a hedonistic lifestyle, unconstrained by traditional virtues, while the parents want to stop that and control the bad behavior of their "black sheep", especially during the teenage years. Does that sound typical?

NAT: Yes.

SOCRATES: Now let's look into the motivations on both sides of the conflict. I think on both sides what is hated depends on what is loved. Do you see why?

NAT: No. Please explain.

SOCRATES: Isn't it usually true that the parents hate their child's life-style and think it has too much freedom because they love order and virtue more than their child does? And isn't it usually true that the young person hates his parents' authority and rules and order and old-fashioned virtues because he loves the freedom he got when he became a teenager, the apparent freedom of the hedo-nistic lifestyle?

NAT: Yes. That's pretty universal and obvious.

SOCRATES: So even if these little wars are motivated by the hates, the hates, in turn, are motivated by the loves. And thus these little wars are in the last analysis motivated by the loves, by the differences between the loves, by the loves for different things.

NAT: That seems to be right.

SOCRATES: And, human nature being the same in the small and in the large, it seems likely that the same law holds true regarding large wars between nations. It is not just a hate but first of all a love that motivates wars; and the different hates depend on the different loves, the love of different things. How can you hate anything unless you see it as threatening something you love?

NAT: That's true.

SOCRATES: So it's love that causes wars.

NAT: But bad loves.

SOCRATES: Yes. Especially irrational and disordered loves. Love of lesser goods like personal lifestyle freedom more than greater goods like personal moral virtue. Love of lesser goods like territories and power more than greater goods like freedom and peace.

NAT: So if love is the cause of wars, how do we abolish wars?

SOCRATES: Certainly not by abolishing love. That's like spiritual euthanasia: killing the patient to cure the disease. It's also impos-sible: we are all driven by our loves. As Augustine said, "Pondus meum amor meus": "My weight is my love."[1] Our loves *pull* us.

NAT: How, then, do we abolish war without abolishing the love that causes war?

SOCRATES: By wisdom and virtue, of course. By first knowing the right things to love and then by actually loving the right things in the right order and in the right way.

---

[1] Saint Augustine, *The Confessions*, trans. Maria Boulding, O.S.B., ed. David Vincent Meconi, S.J., Ignatius Critical Editions (San Francisco: Ignatius Press, 2012), bk. 13, chap. 9.

NAT: And how do we distinguish wrong things from right things and wrong ways from right ways?

SOCRATES: By good philosophy. By wisdom.

NAT: Are you saying, then, that if only we practiced true philosophy, we would not have any wars, either among ourselves in the little battlefield of the family or on the larger global battlefields?

SOCRATES: I would not insert the word "any" into that sentence, but otherwise, I would say yes. If we all became philosophers, there would be far fewer wars.

NAT: But that's not ever gonna happen.

SOCRATES: That is not absolutely certain. But it is certain that it won't happen if you believe it won't.

NAT: And it also won't happen just because you believe it will.

SOCRATES: That is almost equally certain.

NAT: So what have we discovered that we did not know before? Nothing.

SOCRATES: I disagree. We have discovered that wisdom is a necessary but not sufficient cause of choosing the good. And that at least heads us off from two easy mistakes: to think that wisdom is not necessary and to think that it's sufficient by itself.

Actually, my disciple Plato seemed to think that it *was* sufficient, and he put that idea into my mouth in his so-called Socratic dialogues. But it's obvious, from universal human experience, that we need moral virtues like courage and self-control as well as intellectual virtues like wisdom. Even philosophy, the love of wisdom, is a love, and love is a moral virtue, so we need moral virtues in order to acquire intellectual virtues.

NAT: OK, so let's do some wisdom-loving, some philosophizing. And let's move to the concrete controversial question, the question of war.

SOCRATES: How would you formulate the question?

NAT: I think the question is whether war is sometimes ethical or moral or good or just. Whether there are any "just wars".

SOCRATES: And which answer do you believe? Yes or no?

NAT: Obviously war is not good or moral or just. It's stupid. It's trying to resolve disagreements by killing one another. That's insane.

SOCRATES: Does that mean it's always wrong to enter a war, even in defense? Do you want to defend pacifism?

NAT: No, I don't.

SOCRATES: Why not?

NAT: Because in a world full of potential tyrants, the result of pacifism will be the death of pacifists.

SOCRATES: Why?

NAT: Because pacifists don't kill tyrants, but tyrants kill pacifists.

SOCRATES: Well said. But that's the *practical* problem with pacifism, not the solution to the problem in *principle*, in philosophy, unless we assume two things: first, that successful practice justifies any principle, that we have to judge the morality of an action by its expected consequences; and second, that the death of pacifists is always the worst possible consequence.

NAT: I don't think I want to accept either of those two assumptions.

SOCRATES: So what is the ethical argument and justification for either pacifism or for a just war, in principle?

NAT: I don't know. How do we find out?

SOCRATES: Let's begin by accepting the view of the great majority, and not merely of pacifists, that violent and life-threatening aggression, that is, *starting* a war, is the wrong way to solve disagreements. Even the Koran, which defends the "jihad", or "holy war", says that "Allah hates the aggressor." I don't think that's very controversial. The controversial question, then, is whether *defensive* war, or responding to lethal force by lethal force, is also wrong, as pacifists claim. Or are there some situations where there is just cause for meeting violent force with violent force? You see, there are two questions here that are easy to confuse. Even if war is in itself evil, is *waging* war or *going to* war also always evil, even in defense? Even if there is no just war, is there a just warring? And if so, is the difference between a just and an unjust warring simply the difference between aggression and defense? How would you answer that question?

NAT: I think it's too simple to say that's the only difference. What do you think?

SOCRATES: We're not here to discuss what I think but what you think. What do you think of the classical answer to that question, namely, the traditional "just war theory" that adds a few more principles besides justifying defense but not aggression?

NAT: Summarize the just war theory for me, please.

SOCRATES: It says that going to war is just only if, first, it is in defense; and second, it is for a just rather than an unjust cause; and third, it is a last resort after all other ways of settling the dispute have been tried, such as diplomacy; and fourth, the force is proportionate so that it does not do more harm than good; and fifth, innocent noncombatants are not to be deliberately killed. That makes the window of opportunity for a just war pretty narrow. For instance, that last principle would make all weapons of mass destruction, such as nuclear bombs, clearly unjust.

NAT: That seems reasonable. But I want to begin with my instinctive feelings, rather than examining that detailed and specific list of reasons, OK?

SOCRATES: OK, but why?

NAT: Because I know my own instincts better than I know international diplomacy or politics, and because that response is already there, in me, and I think it's naïve to ignore it, and I want to critique it by reason, as you do, since instinctive feelings are not infallibly right.

SOCRATES: Fine! Then let's look at your instinctive feelings first. What are they?

NAT: On the one hand, I admire pacifists like Buddha and Ghandi, even though I don't agree with pacifism in principle. But I do not admire a nation that refuses to protect its own people militarily when it is attacked, any more than I admire a parent who refuses to protect his children when they are threatened.

SOCRATES: Do you think those two instinctive ideas contradict each other?

NAT: In a sense, yes, because it seems to mean that there is a double standard in my instinctive reaction: one moral standard for individuals and a different one for nations or families. So my feelings seem to contradict each other. I admire individual pacifists but not collective pacifists.

SOCRATES: Why do you see that as a moral contradiction?

NAT: Hmm, now that I think about it, perhaps it's not a simple contradiction at all, just a difference. Let's see now. I need to take a minute off from speaking to do some thinking.

SOCRATES: I think that is an excellent idea, and one that is rarely practiced.

(*Nat is silent for a few moments.*)

NAT: When I ask whether an action is good or evil, I see not just two but three possible moral judgments about it: it may be a duty to do it, or a duty to avoid it, or an option and not a duty either to do or avoid. So I think pacifism, the refusal ever to use lethal force, may be a legitimate moral *option* for individuals, and not either a duty to practice or a duty to avoid. In other words, individual refusal to use lethal force even in self-defense is neither commanded nor forbidden. That's what my moral instincts say, anyway. So even though it seems to me that individuals have the *right* to self-defense, even by violence and lethal force if necessary, it also seems to me that individuals may freely choose to give up their right to self-defense and sacrifice their own lives rather than kill the aggressor. So that option is morally *permissible* even though it's not morally *obligatory*, for an individual.

But that total pacifism can't be morally right or permissible for nations because, unlike individuals, they have the responsibility for many lives, the lives of their innocent citizens. I think the rulers of a nation are like the parents of a large family. Their responsibility for their children gives them not just the right but even the duty to fight and even kill, if necessary, to protect those innocent children who are under their care. What virtuous father or mother would not try to save the lives of their innocent children even by killing the crazy person who is in the act of murdering them, if that was the only way to save their lives?

SOCRATES: I think most people, and moral common sense, would agree with you about families. But many might disagree with your assumption that nations are in the same moral position as families, that its citizens are like its children. And that might allow a bit of a wedge to justify political pacifism. Or, again, maybe not.

NAT: Frankly, I don't know enough about politics and political morality to feel certain about that.

SOCRATES: But at least you have reconciled your instinctive feelings and your moral reasoning.

NAT: Yes. But still, it troubles me because it seems to entail a double standard of morality, one for individuals and a different one for nations.

SOCRATES: I see no intrinsic contradiction in a double moral standard as such. We often rightly hold some to a higher standard than others. We do not expect the same virtues in our politicians as we expect in our parents. A politically competent and useful sinner

may do more good to a nation than an incompetent and harm-
ful saint.

NAT: But here the two standards are so different that they are morally
contradictory: what is good for one is evil for the other. How can
the very same thing—pacifism, the refusal to use lethal force—be
admired in individuals and condemned in nations and families?
Can you help me think through this puzzle?

SOCRATES: Let's try. Do you agree that we each have the right to self-
defense as individuals against an aggressor who threatens our lives?

NAT: Yes.

SOCRATES: Do you agree, then, with the principle that Jefferson put
at the beginning of your American Declaration of Independence,
that life is a natural right, that all persons have a right to live, a right
not to be killed by another, just as they all have a right to liberty, a
right not to be enslaved by another, and a right to private property,
a right not to be robbed? (The original version of that document
said "property" instead of "the pursuit of happiness".)

NAT: Yes.

SOCRATES: And do you agree that this right is "inalienable", that is,
inherent and not to be taken away by anyone else or by the state
because it was not given to each one of us by anyone else or by the
state but by nature, our human nature, or by God, or both?

NAT: Yes.

SOCRATES: Then if an individual has a right to life and a nation
does as well, there is no double standard. Both have the right to
self-defense.

NAT: So the right to life is a natural right, and natural rights inhere
in human nature, and we all have human nature; therefore, we all
have that right. So then what justifies using my right to life to kill
another human being who also has that right?

SOCRATES: I suppose it must be the fact that the aggressor has given up
his right to life in threatening the life of another. Imagine you are
hiding Jews from the Nazis during World War II, and the Nazis
demand that you tell them the truth and show them where the
Jews are hiding. It's obviously right for you to lie to the Nazis even
though we have a natural right to truth just as we have a natural
right to life, because the Nazis who want to kill the Jews have given
up their right to truth. Or if you legally own a gun and try to use it

to kill people, it's right for me to take your property away forcibly even though you have a right to private property, because you've given up that right by threatening the rights of others. I think that's the answer most people would call moral common sense, right?

NAT: Right.

SOCRATES: And do you agree with it?

NAT: I think so. In terms of rights, then, the individual pacifist has the right to go beyond the morality of defending his own rights and to practice pacifism. He has the right to choose to give up his own right to life and right to self-defense by accepting martyrdom from the aggressor. But the nation does not have that right, because the individual alone is responsible only for himself, while the rulers of a nation are responsible for its citizens, just as parents are responsible for their children. That seems reasonable to me.

But then pacifists are wrong to universalize their pacifism, either by making it a duty rather than a choice even for individuals or by extending the goodness of individual pacifism to states and families. I guess that is why pacifists are always a very small minority. Most of us instinctively see that universal pacifism is wrong.

SOCRATES: Of course you recognize that the fact that pacifists are in the minority does not prove they are wrong or prove your case for a just war. As they say, "you don't find truth by counting noses" or taking polls.

NAT: Indeed. But do you think there is any defense of pacifism against those arguments against it?

SOCRATES: Let's see. We did not take the time to enter very deeply into their side, did we? We were quite hasty. So let me try to defend pacifism as well as I can, to see whether this position is as defensible as the other.

NAT: OK.

SOCRATES: I think the most popular defense of pacifism is a religious one. Most people in our culture are still basically religious, and the most popular religion in the West is some form of Christianity, and the most popular religion in the East is some form of Buddhism. If Jesus and Buddha are models for ideal human behavior, the religious argument for pacifism is something like this: Can you imagine either Jesus or Buddha with a machine gun on a battlefield trying to kill another nation's soldiers?

NAT: No. But that's not an argument.

SOCRATES: Why? Just because it's religious? Religion is full of arguments.

NAT: No, because it's not a principled reason; it's a concrete example, a saint. Reasons are universal; saints are individual.

SOCRATES: That's true. But the example of the saint as a pacifist, coupled with the general principle that we all ought to behave like the saint, logically entails the conclusion that we all should behave like a pacifist. That's an argument, a syllogism. What's the mistake in that argument?

NAT: I deny both premises. First of all, not all saints are pacifists. Even Jesus used force at least once, when he whipped the money changers out of the temple. And I also deny the other premise, that we should all live like saints. Religious believers might believe that, but unbelievers don't.

SOCRATES: I think you are confusing faith with behavior. Even unbelievers would say it would be better if we all did behave like saints, wouldn't they, no matter whether they were believers or unbelievers? Saints are universally admired in principle for their moral behavior, even if their theology isn't.

NAT: But they're not imitated much in practice. They're the exception, not the rule.

SOCRATES: True. But ethics is not about how we do in fact act but about how we ought to act. It's philosophy, not psychology. Isn't it true that the more saintly you are in your behavior, the better you are and the better it would be for everybody?

NAT: But it's impossible. We can't all be Jesus or Buddha. And what's impossible is not a moral duty. Didn't someone argue that "ought implies can"?

SOCRATES: Yes, and ironically, his name was Kant, not Can. But Jesus and Buddha both said that we all ought to become saints, and they also said that we all can, even though we won't. But whether we can or not, ethics isn't about what we can do but about what we ought to do. Even if we can't reach the ideal, isn't it our moral duty to get as close to it as we can? So shouldn't we all at least try to be saints and therefore pacifists like Jesus and Buddha?

NAT: No, because, as we agreed just a few minutes ago, it's our moral duty to protect the innocent who are under our care. That's why the most popular answer to the moral issue of war has been neither warmongering nor pacifism but the just war theory, which is a kind of mean between the two extremes of pacifism and militarism.

SOCRATES: The pacifist might respond that in practice, down through history, Christians, like Muslims, have disobeyed even their own just war theories very badly.

NAT: But that doesn't mean the theories are wrong. In fact, it assumes that they're right! For it's not wrong to disobey wrong theories, only right ones. If we are wicked because we disobey our theory, that presupposes that the theory is good. If the principles were bad, disobeying them would be good.

SOCRATES: You are becoming a formidable logician, Nat! And now, since we're just sampling issues, like appetizers, rather than finishing them, like main meals, let's settle provisionally on our commonsense compromise for now on the issue of war, even though both sides will have many more objections to it, and go on to our next issue, which is also about human life, namely, abortion.

NAT: I look forward to that.

Questions for Discussion or Personal Essays

1. Do you think it better to begin with the particular questions of applied ethics, which have the most immediate life-changing consequences, and then work our way back to the general principles, reasons, or premises in general ethics and anthropology and metaphysics, or vice versa? Why?

2. Do you think logical reasoning is more powerful and effective and successful when it deals with particular questions in applied ethics or when it deals with more abstract and general questions in other areas of philosophy? Why?

3. Do you see any problems in distinguishing war as such and warring, or the decision to go to war?

4. Do you see any problems with Socrates' assertion that hate always depends on love? Do you see any practical consequences of that principle?

5. If most people hate war, why do you think war is so common?

6. Evaluate Plato's principle that if we only knew the good, with total clarity and certainty, we would always do it, because we

would know that it is in our best self-interest and gives us the most happiness, which all of us desire.

7. How important for ethics is the fact that pacifism tends to be self-destructive because "pacifists don't kill tyrants but tyrants kill pacifists"? Is personal survival an ethical obligation? If so, when?

8. Do you admire individual pacifists like Ghandi? Do you admire fighting just wars? Which of these two admirations is stronger in you? Why?

9. Evaluate the five traditional criteria for a just war. Apply them to different wars in history.

10. Is there a better argument for pacifism than is presented here?

11. Socrates assumes the Jeffersonian theory of natural rights. Are there objections to this? If rights (like the right to life itself) are given to us by others or by the state, does it follow that they can be taken away from us by others or by the state? Why or why not?

12. If Jesus was a practicing pacifist and Muhammad was a warrior, why do you think that both the Christian and Muslim traditions in history came up with a similar just war theory?

13. Do you agree with the principle that "ought implies can"? If so, does this prove the reality of free will, or free choice? If not, why not?

14. Evaluate the truth of "ought implies can." Does "can" have two different possible meanings? If so, how does that affect the truth of that principle?

Applied Ethics: Abortion

NAT: We reached a reasonable compromise about the issue of just war, but I don't see any commonsense compromise about abortion. I don't see any "just abortion theory" parallel to a just war theory. Why should some abortions be morally right and some wrong? What factor is present in just abortions and not in unjust abortions, or vice versa?

SOCRATES: What factor do you think that could be?

NAT: I don't see any. I see no clear dividing line, but only a matter of degree, a gradualism, either metaphysically or ethically, both between the embryo (or even the zygote) and the fully formed fetus or the infant in process of being born, and between the rightness or wrongness of abortion at each stage. It seems obvious that the wrongness or rightness of killing anything depends on what that thing is. And that can't be just a gradually changing accident like age. Whether it's OK to kill a person or a cow or a bug can't depend on how old or young it is.

SOCRATES: So what do you conclude from that analysis?

NAT: Logically, the only two consistent positions seem to be total pro-life or total pro-choice—either saying that even a zygote has a right to life or saying that the infant doesn't get one until it's born.

SOCRATES: And which of those do you choose?

NAT: Instinctively, both seem absurd. How can a single cell, the zygote, be a person with a right to life? And how can you suddenly get a right to life at the moment when you begin to emerge from the womb? What moment? How much of the body has to emerge? Or is it the moment when the two blades of the obstetrician's scissors meet to cut the umbilical cord so that you now get your oxygen not from your mother's blood but from breathing air? Why should that scissors event change a bunch of cells that is not a human person into a human person?

So if the pro-life side is right, all abortion is murder. But if the pro-choice side is right, all prohibitions of abortion are a tyrannical oppression of a woman's own body.

Of course, if the thing that's being killed is somebody else's body, that makes everything different. But how can we prove that?

SOCRATES: Perhaps we can. Let's see. If A is one of the parts of B, and B is one of the parts of C, does that mean that A is one of the parts of C? For instance, if the walls of a room are a part of the room, and the room is a part of the house, are the walls a part of the house? Or if atoms are parts of molecules, and molecules are parts of cells, then are atoms parts of cells? Or if fingernails are parts of fingers, and fingers are parts of hands, are fingernails parts of hands?

NAT: Yes, of course.

SOCRATES: Now, the eyes are a part of a person, right?

NAT: Yes.

SOCRATES: What about sex organs? Is a penis a part of a man or a boy?

NAT: Yes.

SOCRATES: Then if her fetus is a part of a woman's body, pregnant women have four eyes and half of them have penises.

NAT: That's silly. Are you saying that proves that abortion is wrong?

SOCRATES: No, just that the premise of one of the arguments for it is false. The argument is that a woman has a right over her own body and that her fetus is a part of her body.

NAT: That doesn't apply before the eyes and the penises and the other organs grow.

SOCRATES: But even before the organs grow, there are two different DNAs from the very beginning, hers and her fetus'. How can a single human body have two different DNAs?

NAT: Well, if the rightness or wrongness of abortion depends on the thing that is aborted, and the thing gradually grows and changes, so does the morality of abortion, and so does its right to life, its right not to be aborted. Both are a matter of degree, then.

SOCRATES: But the thing or the person, or whatever it is, keeps gradually growing outside the womb too, so by that principle it would be less wrong to kill a one-year-old than to kill a ten-year-old.

NAT: What about using viability as a criterion?

SOCRATES: That seems no better, because viability is also gradual and depends on the medical equipment that's around to keep premature babies alive.

NAT: What about dependence on the mother? The fetus is totally dependent on the mother.

SOCRATES: That, too, is also gradual, not sudden. As growth gradually increases, dependence on the mother gradually decreases, both before and after birth. I see no clear dividing line.

NAT: Birth is a clear dividing line. After birth we breathe on our own and live outside our mothers' bodies. That seems pretty strong and clear.

SOCRATES: If you are on a ventilator, you do not breathe on your own; does that mean you are a different entity and you don't have a right to life? And if you move from one place to another, even from the earth to a space station, does that change your right to life?

NAT: So what is your conclusion from this analysis? That the issue is settled and absolute?

SOCRATES: Is that necessarily unthinkable, from either side?

NAT: No, but there seem to be gradual factors in this issue too, not just black-or-white either-ors. Don't you see any grays?

SOCRATES: I do indeed.

NAT: Where?

SOCRATES: Let's derive the answer to that from our most basic principles of morality. What makes an act morally right or wrong?

NAT: The act itself. What you choose to do: to kill or to heal, to love or to hate, to help or to harm, to do the right thing or to do the wrong thing.

SOCRATES: So it is the essential nature of the act itself.

NAT: Of course. That's obvious.

SOCRATES: What about the actor's motive?

NAT: That counts too, of course. Goodwill or badwill.

SOCRATES: And what about the situation that surrounds the act and the choice? What about the circumstances?

NAT: That too, of course, especially the consequences.

SOCRATES: And those two factors are complex and gray, so to speak, even if the nature of the act itself is simple and clear.

NAT: Yes.

SOCRATES: So even if the goodness or badness of the act itself is a very clear and simple thing, these other two factors are often very complex and very different in degree—degree of goodness and badness, are they not? For instance, to have an abortion for a trivial motive, such as so that you don't get a flabby midsection for a while, is obviously morally different from having one because you're extremely poor and can't feed your existing children, or because you've been raped.

NAT: Of course. Because the motive would change the moral quality of the actor, personally, subjectively. But not of the act itself, objectively.

SOCRATES: And the circumstances count too, don't they? And they are not clear and absolute.

NAT: That's true.

SOCRATES: And isn't it true that those three aspects or dimensions of a moral choice—the act itself, the motives, and the circumstances—are different and have to be judged differently and separately?

NAT: I think so, yes. Because they are so different. The act is objective, but the motives are subjective; and the essential nature of the act may be always the same, but the circumstances are relative and ever-changing.

SOCRATES: And that is indeed a range of grays.

NAT: I agree. But the act itself is neither subjective nor relative and ever-changing. It has its own essential nature. So *that* moral dimension, at least, remains an either-or. And the motive and the circumstances can't determine the nature of the act itself any more than the nature of the act itself can determine the motive or the circumstances. So a bad act can't lose all of its badness just by better motives or circumstances, though it may lose some of it.

SOCRATES: I think this is true.

NAT: Then when we judge the act itself, rather than its motives or its circumstances, no matter how various and complex the motives and the circumstances are, the act itself is either morally good or evil by its nature, by the kind of act it is.

SOCRATES: I agree. But you must mean the *ethical* kind of act it is, not necessarily the *physical* kind. For instance, a bribe is bad by its ethical nature and paying your debts is good by its ethical nature, but both can take the same physical form of putting money into another person's hands or wallet or bank account. And the physical nature of the act can also be different and can change when the moral nature of the act is not different or changing. The money for an unjust bribe can be physically cash or a check or a promissory note or an online deposit. And the same is true for a just repayment.

NAT: That seems clear. So how does that apply to abortion?

SOCRATES: Let's see. It seems that the act of abortion, in itself, by its own essential nature, is either morally bad or not, right?

NAT: Yes, at least to some degree.

SOCRATES: And if it's not bad, then it's either morally neutral or morally good, right?

NAT: Right.

SOCRATES: Now, no one claims that it's morally good by nature— that all abortions are morally good—so the alternative to it being morally bad is that it's morally neutral.

NAT: Yes, and that is the pro-choice position.

SOCRATES: So it's either bad by its essential nature (that's the pro-life position) or it's not (and that's the pro-choice position). There's no compromise possible on that either-or because of the laws of logic. It's an "is or isn't".

NAT: Yes.

SOCRATES: But the other two factors have a moral nature too. And they matter morally too, especially the motive. In fact, Kant seemed to say that the motive was the only thing that mattered morally: a morally good will or bad will. Even if Kant is wrong, motives matter much.

NAT: I agree that both motives and circumstances matter and change the goodness or badness of an act, whether completely or only to a degree. But what we're trying to do here, now, as philosophers, is simply to judge the act itself. We're not psychologists judging motivations or sociologists judging social situations and circumstances right now. That comes in too, of course, but so does the act itself. And that seems to be the first and most important thing.

SOCRATES: Why do you think so?

NAT: Because the other two dimensions can't change something that's essentially evil to something that's not, but they can change it from good to evil. All three factors or dimensions have to be right. The rightness of any one of the three factors can't excuse the wrongness of another one, any more than they can in a work of art, as in a novel, where excellent characters can't excuse a stupid plot, or as in a symphony orchestra, where beautiful strings can't excuse ugly horns.

SOCRATES: That analogy seems apt, and that principle seems true. But it's also true that the ethician has to judge the other two factors. And there is also a fourth factor, or perhaps a part of the third one, the circumstances, namely, the attitudes of society and of the two sides of this controversy. That has to be judged morally, especially because each side often labels the other with terrible names, like "religious bigot", "fundamentalist hypocrite", and "narrow-minded, judgmental Nazi" on the one side or "in league with the Devil" and "cold-blooded murderer" on the other side.

NAT: That's obviously not ethically good. But that's a red herring, a distraction from the issue. What we are supposed to be doing now is ethical philosophy, and that's supposed to be judgmental not of social attitudes but of deeds, of acts. Like abortion.

SOCRATES: But the issue is necessarily controversial in society, because either abortion is every woman's right over her own body and autonomy—a right that should not be taken away from any women—or else it is the taking of a right to life from an unborn human being, an individual of our species, and the ethical name for that act is murder, whether society defines it thus or not.

NAT: So what does the morality of abortion depend on?

SOCRATES: It has to depend partly, or even mainly, or at least first of all, on the nature of what is aborted: Is it a human being or is it something less? If it is a human being, then aborting an unborn human being is like killing a partially grown human being, an infant or a teenager. And if it is not a human being, then abortion is like removing unwanted growths, like cancer cells.

NAT: And what do you think philosophy can say about that question?

SOCRATES: What do *you* think?

NAT: I'm not sure. I know that it can't ignore facts and that science tells us some facts, at least. Physical dependence and viability, for instance, have to count somehow, and so does the fetus' independent DNA. What defines an individual human being? How can good philosophy do that?

SOCRATES: I think philosophy can at least try to define "human being" in an honest and objective way rather than in a way that begs the question by using slanted and emotional and rhetorical language, or ideological language, or religious language, if we are doing philosophy rather than either psychology or religion. Philosophy used to be called a science, you know, and even though it doesn't use the modern scientific method and limit itself to empirical and quantifiable data, it is like science in that it tries to begin without unproved assumptions and it proceeds by logical reasoning. And modern science is certainly relevant here, because we know much more about embryology and genetics than we did in the past.

NAT: OK, let's listen to the scientific data. What does modern science tell us?

SOCRATES: Well, until quite recently—the 1970s, I think—there was a universal consensus about the answer to that question. I think every science textbook in the world defined an individual member of a biological species in one of two ways: either as being a member of a species that has the potentiality to reproduce itself (that was the usual definition before modern genetics) or as something that has the complete set of chromosomes that genetically identify it as a new, individual member of the species that produced it. (That is the more exact genetic definition.) That was before the abortion controversy clicked in.

NAT: But by that definition, even the one cell of the zygote is already an actual new human being. Its DNA is human, not ape, or even Neanderthal, and it is different from that of its parents. That feels like an extreme position.

SOCRATES: Does science judge what things are by subjective feeling or by objective data?

NAT: By data. But the differences in development are data too, and those differences are so great that we have different scientific words for those different stages: zygote, embryo, fetus, infant, toddler, child, teenager, and adult.

SOCRATES: Some comedian joked that the solution to the abortion problem is that human life begins when the fetus gets a college degree and a good job. That was meant to be a joke, and it's significant that everyone recognizes it as a joke, not a serious answer. No one suggests we kill teenagers when they are unwanted because they don't have a good job.

NAT: Was that an answer to our question?

SOCRATES: No, of course not. Let's see what those different words mean about human life. Are toddlers human beings?

NAT: Of course.

SOCRATES: Are infants?

NAT: Yes.

SOCRATES: And fetuses?

NAT: They are human fetuses, of course. And human zygotes are human. But there's no consciousness there at all, in a zygote, and no brain and organs, and no pain. How can that be a human being?

SOCRATES: When you are in a coma and there is no consciousness going on at all, are you still a human being?

NAT: Yes, because when I wake up out of the coma, I have the brain and nervous system that it takes to have a human future, with reason and free choice.

SOCRATES: Can any other animal besides a human being have a human future, with reason and free choice? Can a monkey in a coma wake up to a human future?

NAT: No, of course not.

SOCRATES: So no animal has either the history, in the past, or the actuality, in the present, or the potentiality, in the future, for rational consciousness, as we do. But we do have that. And that "we" includes even a human zygote, except that it has no individual past, just as a person who dies has no individual future in this body. That's just a biological fact. Even a human zygote already has the distinctively human potentiality for a distinctively human future. So there is something already there in even the zygote—the power or potentiality for eventual future rational thought and choice— that mere animals do not have. Let's call it human reason.

NAT: But it's not acting in any human way yet. Its reason is not actual, only potential.

SOCRATES: It's not yet *acting* in a distinctively human way, no. But it's already got a distinctively human potential. That potential is actually there. The potential for human activity is already actually present.

NAT: To say that "potential is actual" sounds confusing, to say the least.

SOCRATES: But it's also actually acting in a distinctively human way. It's doing something nothing nonhuman can do: it's growing a human brain and nervous system. And even though that product (the human brain and nervous system) is not yet actualized, the process of making it is actually there, from the beginning. As soon as the zygote exists, it begins to replicate in a distinctively human way.

NAT: But it doesn't even have a brain yet.

SOCRATES: No, but it's starting to grow a brain.

NAT: Yes. What logically follows from that?

SOCRATES: If it's starting to grow a human brain, a distinctively human brain, not a merely animal brain, it's already doing something only a human being can do. So it must already be a human being. Only human beings can grow human brains, just as only human beings can become scientists or philosophers, even if they're only infants now. They're already actually human, but not yet actually scientists or philosophers. But their potentiality is already there. In that sense, that potentiality is actual, although it's not yet actualized. It's like potential energy. That's a scientific category. For instance, the potentiality to ignite. A match has it, but a drop of water does not.

NAT: But this idea of real potentialities isn't scientific. You can't see or measure potentialities.

SOCRATES: Actually, you can. You can measure potential energy. You can scientifically verify different potentialities in different elements. A sufficient quantity of water has the potentiality to float a large boat; and water, by its chemical nature and structure, has the potentiality to put out fire, which neither hydrogen alone nor oxygen alone can do. Is it unscientific to take account of these facts?

NAT: Are you saying that outlawing all abortions logically follows from the scientific data?

SOCRATES: No. You need a legal premise to justify a legal conclusion, and you need a moral premise to justify a moral conclusion, and we don't have that yet. I'm simply saying that the scientific data show that a human fetus and even a human embryo is a human being.

NAT: Do you say, then, that it must have an inherent right to life?

SOCRATES: If all members of the human species do, yes; if not, then no.

NAT: I think there are reasons to say no. One is that a human being gets a right to life only when it reaches a certain stage of development.

SOCRATES: But there's no sudden change in its development, except birth.

NAT: Then maybe the dividing line is birth.

SOCRATES: But the thing that's born is the same thing as the thing that's not quite born yet. It's just in a different place—outside the womb—and getting its oxygen in a different way—through the air and its breathing instead of through the mother's bloodstream.

NAT: So there's no sharp break. So perhaps the right to life is as gradual as the development.

SOCRATES: But that would mean that teenagers have more of a right to life than preteens and that it's worse to kill a kid in tenth grade than to kill a kid in ninth grade.

NAT: No. That doesn't seem reasonable either. So maybe the right to life is not inherent at all but exists only when human society agrees to give it that right.

SOCRATES: But "society" doesn't mean anything superior to human beings; it simply means other human beings. And if it's other human beings who give you a right to life, then they can remove it too, because whoever gives you something can also refuse it. In fact, that was the view of some ancient societies that gave fathers the right to kill their children and masters the right to kill their slaves. In fact, that's the Nazi philosophy, that those in power have the right to kill those without power. That's not civilized morality; that's tyranny. I have no authority over your life.

NAT: So the problem is where to draw the line in the process of growth. Is it the quantity of intelligence, the IQ, or what?

SOCRATES: No, the problem is not *where* to draw the line but *who* is to draw the line. And the whole point is that it is not God or nature but some human being who draws it, that some other person or persons give you the right to life. That's tyranny.

NAT: No, we are too civilized to say that people with high IQs have a right to give life to or take life from people with low IQs.

SOCRATES: Then why is it OK if we, who don't have Down syndrome, kill our unborn children who do?

NAT: I don't know. I do know that we both have neglected to try to understand and evaluate the reasoning of a woman who wants to abort.

SOCRATES: Well, we have at least learned Lesson One. Perhaps some other time we can move to Lesson Two, whatever reason says that is.

Questions for Discussion or Personal Essays

1. At the beginning of the conversation, Nat says he has no hope of finding a compromise position on abortion similar to the

one on war. Does the end of the dialogue offer such a compromise or not? Why?

2. From the beginning, both Nat and Socrates assume that the
   first and most fundamental question about abortion is what it
   is, its essential nature: Is it the killing of a human being or of
   something less? Evaluate this assumption logically.

3. If this is indeed the necessary and first question, and if we are
   to be both honest and logical, why is it so seldom dealt with in
   most of the literature on the subject? Or is it dealt with by one
   side but not the other? If so, why?

4. Why does it seem, instinctively, absurd to call a one-celled
   zygote a human being? Evaluate this instinct.

5. Is there any difference between what we all mean by a human
   being and what we all mean by a human *person*? If so, what
   makes some human beings nonpersons? In our history, who
   has believed that some human beings were not persons?

6. Evaluate Socrates' argument about parts of parts at the beginning of the chapter. Is he serious or joking about women having penises? If it's "my body", why isn't it "my penis"?

7. Socrates repeatedly says to Nat that an argument that proves that
   the fetus is a human being is not necessarily an argument that
   proves that abortion is always immoral. What other premises
   need to be added in order for that conclusion to follow necessarily? How might the pro-choice side challenge one of those
   premises? How might the pro-life side challenge that challenge?

8. Formulate the basic pro-life argument as a syllogism. Of the
   three possible faults or weaknesses in a syllogism, namely, using
   a term ambiguously, assuming a false premise, or committing a
   logical fallacy, which would a pro-choice person use to answer
   that argument?

9. Do the same thing you did in the previous question with the
   basic pro-choice syllogism.

10. Do you see any reason to question the assumption that there
    are three ethical determinants (the act itself, the motive, and the
    situation or circumstances) or that each of these dimensions or
    factors must be evaluated separately and independently? Can
    changing circumstances change the essential nature of the act
    itself? Why or why not? Give examples.

11. What moral role do you think social attitudes or the social consensus plays in evaluating the morality of an act?

12. Why do you think the *political* context or situation was not mentioned? Should it have been?

13. What do you think is, or should be, the role of DNA in establishing the identity of a human being?

14. The pro-choice side often attacks the assumption that all biological members of the human race are persons with inherent rights as "species-ism", since very few thinkers would give such rights to subhuman animals. It also often attacks the notion that DNA establishes identity as "biologism" or "materialism". Evaluate these two arguments logically. Why do you think the author did not include them in his dialogue?

15. Can you find and justify any clear line in the process of human growth and development between conception and death that would define the beginning of the possession of rights?

16. What is the relation between one person's rights and another person's duties? How does this principle affect the abortion debate?

17. Is potentiality a scientific notion or not? If not, why does it seem to be? If so, why does it seem not to be? What difference does this make to the debate?

18. What are the necessary premises or assumptions and what are the necessary consequences of the view that rights are not inherent but given (or not given) by others or by the state?

19. Is there any argument to justify abortion that would not also justify infanticide? If so, what? If not, what follows logically from that?

20. Why does the dialogue end so unsuccessfully?

21. What reasons might justify a woman, but not a man, in being pro-choice? If none, why? If some, how?

12

Applied Ethics: Sexual Morality

NAT: The third specific issue that you mentioned as a controversial application of ethical principles is sexual morality, which is just as hot an issue as abortion.

SOCRATES: Which should not be surprising, since abortion is about sex.

NAT: No, it isn't. A fetus can't have sex.

SOCRATES: But sex can make a fetus.

NAT: That's true.

SOCRATES: And sex is the reason for abortion.

NAT: What do you mean by that?

SOCRATES: Why does anyone want an abortion? Because contraception failed. Abortion is backup contraception. And why does anyone want contraception? To have sex without having babies.

NAT: I thought we were supposed to be talking about the ethics of the sexual revolution. There are a lot of issues there. Contraception is only one of them.

SOCRATES: But contraception is the foundation of the whole sexual revolution. Only the Pill made it possible.

NAT: Yes, but contraception isn't abortion. It doesn't kill anybody.

SOCRATES: I didn't say it did.

NAT: So it's OK then.

SOCRATES: I didn't say it was.

NAT: But ...

SOCRATES: Or that it wasn't.

NAT: But everyone accepts contraception now, except the Catholic Church. And even most Catholics don't listen to the Church. So it's only a tiny few who think it's a controversial ethical issue at all, much less that it's morally wrong.

SOCRATES: Actually, the facts are exactly the opposite: the vast majority say it *is* morally wrong.

NAT: Socrates, your polls must have come from a very selective and small sample size.

SOCRATES: Actually, my polls have a far larger sample size than yours. They include what Chesterton calls "the democracy of the dead",[1] extending the franchise not only to those persons whom some would disqualify "by accident of birth", but also to those whom some would want to disqualify by accident of death. Why deny them a vote?

NAT: What's your point, Socrates?

SOCRATES: Simply the fact that all premodern cultures, throughout all of history, saw contraception as immoral and unnatural, and so did all religions, until one Protestant denomination, the Church of England, allowed it with very strict restrictions in 1930. And that opened the way for the sexual revolution, by separating sex from reproduction. Only after the Pill did the whole of Western civilization change its mind, including all the churches except one. Before the Pill, even many atheists, like Freud, agreed with the majority, that is, with all other cultures except yours. Those are simply facts.

NAT: But as you admitted, you don't find the truth by counting noses.

SOCRATES: Of course you don't. What I said is not an argument, just a fact. I don't think the popularity or unpopularity of an opinion proves anything. But *you* seem to think it does, since you quote the majority of your contemporaries as some kind of authority. I prefer to agree with the medieval platitude that the argument from human authority is the weakest of all arguments.

NAT: That's not medieval, that's modern. You are turning things upside down, Socrates.

SOCRATES: No, it's a medieval platitude.

NAT: You seem to be standing on your head and upside down.

SOCRATES: Which is exactly how you would see me and my old world if in fact it was you and your brave new world that is standing on its head.

---

[1] G.K. Chesterton, *Orthodoxy* (London: John Lane Company, 1908; San Francisco: Ignatius Press, 1995), 53. Citation refers to the Ignatius edition.

NAT: If the change is as radical and revolutionary as you say, and we are on opposite sides of it, I suppose that everything we say about the sexual revolution will be influenced by those two opposite perspectives. How can we argue profitably unless we know which of us is really upside down?

SOCRATES: That is exactly my point. That is why I do not want to argue about many different specific sexual issues but go to the root of all of them.

NAT: I see.

SOCRATES: At the beginning of this discussion I mentioned three ethical issues that were all very important because they were all literally matters of life and death and also because there was great and passionate disagreement about them. They were war, abortion, and sexuality. And when I listed those three, you probably thought we could discuss the first two profitably because they were single, specific, concrete issues. But you thought we could not possibly discuss all of sexual morality in a few minutes, as we did with the other two issues, because sexual morality is not a single specific issue but a whole complex set of issues, right?

NAT: Right.

SOCRATES: But now I hope you see that they all seem to depend on one question: what sex *is*, what it *means*, what its purpose is, and whether that purpose includes procreation, new people, baby humans.

NAT: But that question assumes that its purpose is not simply whatever we want it to be, that it is not simply *our* purpose, what we want from it with our will rather than what we understand it is with our mind. If its purpose is whatever we want it to be, that end might not be procreation but pleasure and usually also intimacy and expression of love. But it wouldn't *always* be that either if it was only what we willed it to be, since our will, unlike the essential nature of a thing, is changeable.

SOCRATES: You are thinking very logically, Nat. You cut to the single heart of this third issue, what sex *is*. And the answer to that question, in turn, depends on the issue we discussed in metaphysics, namely, nominalism: whether things really have natural, inherent, essential universal "natures". And if they do, whether that nature includes what Aristotle called final causality, an objective goal or end or purpose, inherent in its nature.

NAT: So perhaps nominalism is true and there are no universal natures. Or perhaps there are universal natures but not universal goods and ends and purposes.

SOCRATES: But as we saw when we discussed metaphysics and cosmology, that makes very little sense: all eyes have the nature of eyes, and that nature includes the natural end or purpose of eyes, namely, seeing. After all, the sex organs have always been called "the reproductive system", not "the entertainment system".

NAT: Well, then, perhaps we made a mistake when we discussed metaphysics and cosmology.

SOCRATES: Just because they lead to a practical conclusion you don't like?

NAT: No, I admit that's not reasonable. But I have to agree with your point that we will not make much progress in discussing all the many controversies about sexual behavior—contraception, homosexuality, transgenderism, divorce, adultery, and the like—if we ignore the unifying principle behind the whole sexual revolution, which is philosophical and even metaphysical.

SOCRATES: I think experience confirms your opinion there. People argue vociferously about these issues, but they rarely make any progress in understanding one another, or even themselves, if they ignore the premise and foundation for the opposite opinion. If they do trace their disagreements back to premises, their premises are usually either ideological and political or religious, and those premises are usually accepted on faith or desire or instinct rather than reason.

NAT: I think you are right there. And I don't think we usually deal with those arguments, because most people don't want to think logically, especially philosophically, and most especially metaphysically. So I don't think there is much chance that our philosophical reasons for accepting or rejecting metaphysical nominalism or moral relativism will change anyone's mind, no matter how strong our reasons are.

SOCRATES: I'm not sure I agree with your pessimism about most people and about changing minds, but let's say I do. What, then, should we do about that?

NAT: I think we have already done it: we have identified the most basic premise of both sides. We have unearthed the foundation of the building.

SOCRATES: What, then, should we do next?

NAT: We should explore and argue about that foundation.

SOCRATES: But we have already done that, on another occasion, when we discussed metaphysics.

NAT: So perhaps we should just leave it at that for today. We have made progress and helped both sides see their ideas more clearly— which is more than most philosophical arguments achieve, I think. And we have avoided rhetoric and slanted language, and we have avoided ideological premises and faith premises, and we have explored only those that are open to rational exploration by everyone. So I am satisfied. Even though we have not settled the issue, we have clarified it.

SOCRATES: If we have indeed done that, I agree that we deserve a compliment. But of course, as you suspected, I am far from satisfied. I have hope for more progress, but not for universal agreement. For philosophy is not mathematics; its arguments cannot be done by computers, and its conclusions are not equations.

NAT: Perhaps instead of philosophical arguments we could try to settle it by a kind of laboratory experiment in life. Which philosophy works best, in the long run? Which most deeply satisfies us? Which one makes us better persons and helps others and our society the most? It's a fair question, I think. And an important one.

SOCRATES: I agree with you. But that lived experiment is something we cannot do simply in words. So I think our words are finished for today.

Questions for Discussion or Personal Essays

1. The issue of sexual morality is very wide and very controversial. Why do you suppose the conversation about it here is so short? Could it be explained by anything other than personal laziness or fear on the part of the characters or the author?

2. Evaluate Socrates' claim that abortion is a sexual issue. Do not let vague feelings replace clear definitions.

3. In what sense is contraception the foundation of the sexual revolution? Is it the sufficient cause? Is it a necessary cause? Are there any other necessary causes of the sexual revolution?

4. Evaluate Chesterton's principle of "the democracy of the dead".
5. If the medievals believed and practiced the principle that the argument from merely human authority is the weakest of all arguments, as Socrates reports, why do you think they have the reputation of believing the exact opposite and being "authoritarian"?
6. What other connections do you see among the three issues of war, abortion, and sex?
7. Evaluate Socrates' assumption that the first and most necessary question about anything is *what it is*. Why do you think that assumption is ignored or denied more regarding sex than regarding most other areas of human life?
8. Why do you think the word "sex" has changed its meaning, from the older meaning of something we have to the newer meaning of something we do? Why do you think "gender" used to mean something nouns have and now means something people have? (I do not think you will find an answer to these questions in the dialogue.)
9. Do you find more value in this short dialogue about a single question, which ignores the many specific, controversial issues of sexual morality, or in a longer dialogue that addresses many specific issues but ignores the single most fundamental question? As with all these questions, give not just your answer but also reasons for your answer.
10. If you want to attack a specific controversial issue, read Pope Paul VI's anticontraception encyclical *Humanae Vitae* (1968) and argue about it philosophically rather than theologically. (What is the difference between arguing philosophically and arguing theologically, by the way?)
11. If you want to enter the realm of theological and religious arguments, summarize and evaluate the arguments about that controversial encyclical, including Pope John Paul II's defense of it in his *Theology of the Body*.

13

Philosophy of History: Conserving the Old versus Progressing to the New

SOCRATES: I had planned to discuss political philosophy today, because it seemed to follow naturally from our two discussions about ethics, since political philosophy is about the public good, or the collective good, while ethics is about the private good, or the individual good.

NAT: You said you "had planned" to do that. So why did you change your mind?

SOCRATES: Because I think it would be a more logical progression to move to the philosophy of history today and discuss the role of the past and the future and whether we should prioritize conserving old, traditional things or progressing to new things. That's the issue we ended up discussing when we looked at the sexual revolution, which is probably the most interesting and radical specific change and which raises the issue of the controversy between traditionalism, or conservatism, and progressivism in general. That issue would also be a good foundation for our look at political philosophy next, because if history shows moral progress, that would be a strong reason for being a political progressive and if not, not.

NAT: Fine.

SOCRATES: Ambrose Bierce, in *The Devil's Dictionary*, defines a conservative as one "who is enamored of existing evils, as distinguished from the Liberal, who wishes to replace them with others".[1]

NAT: But the reason for progressivism, or liberalism, seems pretty clear. No one admires the morality of Neanderthals, or even primitive cultures, over modern cultures.

[1] Ambrose Bierce, *The Unabridged Devil's Dictionary*, ed. David E. Schultz and S. T. Joshi (Athens: University of Georgia Press, 2000), 41.

SOCRATES: What do you mean by primitive cultures?

NAT: Cultures that lived before the invention of writing.

SOCRATES: How do we know the morality of those primitive cultures if they are so primitive that they left no writings?

NAT: By science.

SOCRATES: What science?

NAT: Archeology.

SOCRATES: And what archeological discoveries tell us anything about primitive cultures?

NAT: Well, for one thing cavemen seemed to live in caves instead of houses.

SOCRATES: And is that morally inferior to living in houses?

NAT: No, I suppose not.

SOCRATES: And what archeological discoveries have told us what the cavemen did in their caves?

NAT: Nothing, I guess.

SOCRATES: Wrong. They painted very good pictures of animals. At Lascaux, for instance.

NAT: Oh. I guess that's not evidence for bad morals.

SOCRATES: If anything, it seems the opposite. And they also left funerary works: burial sites and markers.

NAT: What does that tell us about their morals?

SOCRATES: That they respected and honored their dead.

NAT: But science doesn't tell us how they respected and honored one another.

SOCRATES: Actually, it does. For instance, there are skeletons of middle-aged people with serious handicaps that begin at birth, like being born with legs that could not walk, or dwarfism, or eye sockets that were missing.

NAT: What does that prove about their morals?

SOCRATES: That they took care of their handicapped people for many years, until they died, even though they were not socially and practically "productive".

NAT: Oh.

SOCRATES: And among modern cultures, is it true that the more primitive they are in other ways, especially technology and education, the more immoral they are? Are the Aborigines morally inferior to moderns? Are Native American tribes inferior to the Americans

who wiped most of them out? Was Germany the most morally
advanced nation in the twentieth century, as well as the most edu-
cationally and scientifically and technologically advanced?

NAT: Uh, no. But ...

SOCRATES: I'm listening.

NAT: Well, what most of us know of our own extended families back
a few generations, and what we know of recorded history, seems
to confirm progressivism. Previous generations were much crueler
and more insensitive than we are. They lacked compassion and
tolerance and sympathy for the suffering.

SOCRATES: By these "cruel" generations do you mean the ancient
ones that produced Moses and Jesus and Buddha and Confucius
or the more recent ones that produced Lincoln and Ghandi and
Mother Teresa and Martin Luther King, Jr.?

NAT: Both. I mean both the ancient ones that produced Attila the
Hun and Judas Iscariot and Vlad the Impaler and the more recent
ones that produced Hitler and Stalin and the Marquis de Sade.

SOCRATES: Good for you! You see, then, that our two arguments
from highly selected examples are equally worthless.

NAT: But surely we are less cruel and more tolerant, sympathetic,
compassionate, and forgiving than previous generations.

SOCRATES: Probably so. And those are all "soft" virtues. What about
the "hard" virtues like honesty and humility and self-control and
courage and honor and chastity? Are we better than our ancestors
there?

NAT: No. Our relativism seems to work against those hard virtues
and in favor of the soft virtues.

SOCRATES: Which are the easy ones.

NAT: We could go on arguing like this forever. The bottom line,
it seems, is that neither the ancients nor the moderns are more
saintly or more sinful than the other. They are just saintly or sinful
in different ways.

SOCRATES: Right! So how, then, can we choose between traditionalism and progressivism?

NAT: We can prove the superiority of progressivism by the premise
of the superiority of addition to subtraction. Progressives add to
the past. Traditionalists subtract from the future.

SOCRATES: How can you subtract from something that doesn't yet
exist?

NAT: Traditionalists subtract from the present, then. Progressives look through the windshield; traditionalists look at the rearview mirror. Which is the wiser way to drive?

SOCRATES: By this analogy do you mean to say that traditionalists ignore the future and progressives ignore the past?

NAT: Yes.

SOCRATES: So which is worse? Surely that depends on whether there is more of value for us in the past, in tradition, or in the present or future.

NAT: So both sides beg the question.

SOCRATES: Yes. I could equally use the analogy of our material possessions that give us pleasure, such as houses, cars, pets, or music. We have many of these, and we also desire more of them. Which is prior, to conserve and enjoy what you already have or to try to get more?

NAT: Whatever makes us happier.

SOCRATES: By that definition conservatives are happy, because they don't want to change what they have, and progressives are unhappy, because they are not satisfied with it, so conservativism is wiser.

We could also use the analogy of the train versus the snowball. A train must leave past stations behind in order to progress to future stations along its way, and all the passengers want that. Is that how we move through our history, simply forgetting the past? Should we forget the lessons of Hitler's Holocaust? Are we not more like snowballs, which roll down a long hill? The snow they pick up in the beginning of their trip down the hill remains at their heart, and their shape shapes the larger snowball as snow accumulates around its outside. Is it not better to have both the early snow and the later snow?

NAT: I see. It's a kind of Freudian analysis applied to the whole human race. The importance of early childhood. But I could also use an analogy to prove progressivism. Say you have a house painted white, and you want to keep it white—you want to conserve the whiteness. The only way you can do that is to keep repainting it every few years. So to be a conservative, you have to be a progressive, to move forward and progress from grayish white to pure white.

SOCRATES: All our various analogies seem apt, but none of them settle the issue.

NAT: We have gotten nowhere.

SOCRATES: That is because the arguments from analogies are a fallacy. They are question-begging. They are chosen on the basis of the conclusion they seek to prove. Analogies are useful in that they help us see things in new ways and see some of the many connections between things, but they are not arguments. They do not prove anything.

NAT: So how do we evaluate the two philosophies of conservatism and progressivism? Do you think that that very question is what we should question?

SOCRATES: Yes!

NAT: Why?

SOCRATES: Because you can find analogies and examples to support both. Because the only two answers to that simple question are both oversimplifications. And because there is no necessary relationship between newer and better in morality, as there is in science and technology, where newer is almost always better. In fact, we ourselves have just admitted that when we both agreed that older generations were better at some virtues (the hard ones) and that you moderns are better at others, the soft ones.

NAT: So perhaps we should abandon the question.

SOCRATES: That would be a revolution indeed. For most people today seem to judge things by simply classifying them as conservative or progressive. You choose your ideological fishnet instead of choosing each fish.

NAT: Perhaps you are right. To abandon that easy way of thinking, in which we try to tell the truth with a clock, may be the most truly progressive thing we could do.

SOCRATES: That would make this dialogue by far the shortest one we have had, and probably the most disappointing.

NAT: So is there no other philosophical question about history that we could address?

SOCRATES: Well, yes, but it is even more speculative, and most answers to it are probably vastly oversimplified.

NAT: What question is that?

SOCRATES: It is about the meaning and end of history. History seems to be a story—our story—and a story has a plot, with an end, and a theme, a meaning. Philosophers like Hegel and Marx thought they could discern the storyline, or the theme, of history. Hegel thought it was the self-discovery of universal spirit, and Marx thought it was the liberation from oppression and from class divisions. And theologians like Augustine believed that the meaning of history could be seen in the Bible, which they took for divine revelation, and which is also a story, a narrative.

NAT: But that's faith and theology rather than natural reason and philosophy.

SOCRATES: Yes.

NAT: But the first question, logically, has to be whether history in fact has any such preset plot or theme or point. If not, we can't have anything like a philosophical science of history.

SOCRATES: Yes, and that is the point of view of many thinkers.

NAT: I suppose that skepticism of the philosophy of history is more common for secular than for religious thinkers, who think they have a kind of God's eye point of view of history, right?

SOCRATES: Not really. In fact, philosophies of history flourish more among rationalists like Hegel and Marx, while orthodox believers like C.S. Lewis are often more skeptical of any strictly rational philosophy of history. In fact, I happen to have here his verdict on this division of philosophy, which I was going to bring up today anyway. Here it is:

> About everything that could be called "the philosophy of history" I am a desperate sceptic. I know nothing of the future, not even whether there will be any future.... I don't know whether the human tragi-comedy is now in Act I or Act V; whether our present disorders are those of infancy or of old age....[2]
>
> Some think it is the historian's business to penetrate beyond this apparent confusion and heterogeneity, and to grasp in a simple intuition the "spirit" or "meaning" of his period. With some hesitation, and with much respect for the great men who have thought otherwise, I submit that this is exactly what we must refrain from doing. I cannot convince myself that such "spirits" or "meanings" have much more reality than the pictures we see in the fire.[3]

[2] C.S. Lewis, "De Descriptione Temporum" (lecture, Cambridge University, Cambridge, England, November 29, 1954).

[3] C.S. Lewis, English Literature in the Sixteenth Century Excluding Drama (London: Oxford University Press, 1954), 65.

And here is his reason for that skepticism:

> Between different ages there is no impartial judge on earth, for no
> one stands outside the historical process; and of course no one is so
> completely enslaved to it as those who take our own age to be, not
> one more period, but a final and permanent platform from which
> we can see all other ages objectively.[4]

NAT: But if he's right, then we should just turn around and abandon
this will-o'-the-wisp and get on with areas of philosophy where
we can give good logical reasons for our opinions.
SOCRATES: And that might be the most valuable thing we could do.
NAT: Well, you said at the beginning of this conversation that you
were planning to discuss political philosophy, but we decided to
look at the philosophy of history first. Can we turn to political
philosophy now?
SOCRATES: We can indeed.

Questions for Discussion or Personal Essays

1. Why do we label oral rather than writing cultures "primitive"?
   What can we learn from them? See Huston Smith's chapter on
   "The Primal Religions" in The World's Religions.
2. Is there any natural connection between primitivism in science
   and technology and primitivism in morality? Why or why not?
   If not, why do we use the word "primitive" to designate both
   at once?
3. How much do we know about primitive cultures? How do we
   know that?
4. Do you see moral progress or regress or both in the history of
   the last two centuries? Of the last two millennia? Give better
   arguments than Socrates or Nat does for your answer.
5. If it is true that there has been moral progress in the soft virtues
   and moral regress in the hard ones, which of these two changes
   do you think has been the most important? Why?

---

[4] C. S. Lewis, Reflections on the Psalms, in The Inspirational Writings of C. S. Lewis (New York:
Inspirational Press, 1991), 194.

6. What makes the hard virtues hard is that they require suffering and sacrifice, while the soft virtues do not. How do you deal with the paradox that suffering is needed to develop the hard virtues, yet it is virtuous to *lessen* others' sufferings?

7. Do any of the analogies used by Nat and Socrates persuade you? Why, if analogies are not arguments?

8. Is our tendency to classify ideas as "conservative" or "progressive" helpful? Is it only recent, or does it characterize all ages?

9. Do you see any overall theme or storyline in history?

10. If skeptics of the philosophy of history like C.S. Lewis are right, why is the above question so popular and interesting?

11. What do you think is the logical relationship between the philosophy of history and political philosophy?

14

Political Philosophy: The Relation between the State and the Citizen

SOCRATES: In each of the many different general, large, and complex divisions in philosophy, we have been trying to identify and attack a single central issue that is crucially important, that makes the biggest difference, and that is the most controversial. What do you think that issue would be in the field of political philosophy?

NAT: Well, it's probably what we have been talking about in the last two dialogues, namely, traditional or conservative versus modern or progressive views. That seems to be a major theme in ethics, both in general (absolutism versus relativism) and regarding sexual morality, and also in the philosophy of history. Of course, that also divides political philosophy, which today seems to be ever more starkly divided between Left and Right.

SOCRATES: And what seems to be the single specific issue that divides these two sides most fundamentally?

NAT: I think it used to be the Left's focus on freedom, or liberty—thus the term "liberals"—and the Right's focus on authority; but those terms—"Left" and "Right"—seem to change their meaning when you change the time (early modern versus contemporary) or the place (Europe or America). Today a liberal tends to socialism or even Communism, or at least globalism and internationalism, while a conservative tends to both individualism (or libertarianism) and to nationalism, or patriotism. So I am confused about the terms today.

SOCRATES: So am I. For instance, if we use the categories we found central to ethics, namely, relativism versus absolutism, we find that

the Left tends to relativism on issues of individual morality, especially sexual morality, while the Right tends to relativism regarding war, poverty, and sometimes even racism. The Left seems to
see human life as valuable among the poor, in regard to the immi-
grant, and on the battlefield (they tend more to pacifism) but not
in the abortion clinic or when discussing euthanasia (there, it is
they who are the "libertarians"), while the Right is the opposite: pragmatic or compromising regarding war and poverty but
not regarding individual ethical issues. So I think we should use
more perennial categories than these currently popular but ever-
changing ones of Left and Right.

NAT: So what do you think the perennial central issue of political
philosophy is?

SOCRATES: The standard answer to that question is, What is the best
form of government? And the three main forms are rule by one,
that is, monarchy; rule by the few, that is, oligarchy or aristocracy;
and rule by many or by all, that is, democracy. But I think that
controversy is largely over, because nearly everyone rates democracy as best, though with some secondary, modifying ingredients
of oligarchy (such as Congress and the Supreme Court) and monarchy (a single president).

NAT: Wow! You just solved the fundamental problem of the most
argued about division of philosophy in one paragraph. Are there
any other issues to solve? Let's get at them before the inspiration
leaves you.

SOCRATES: I appreciate your sarcasm. Of course it's not that easy. But
if you want an even more fundamental problem, here it is: When
we speak of politics, we speak of a relationship between the citizens and the state, a kind of polarity. The fundamental question is,
Which is primary? Are individuals more important than the state
or vice versa? Which is the means, and which is the end? Is it as
JFK famously said, that we should "ask not what your country can
do for you; ask what you can do for your country"? Or is a country to be judged by what it can do for each individual?

NAT: Perhaps it's both: "All for one, and one for all", as the Three
Musketeers said.

SOCRATES: Well, what you have in America seems to aim at that, if
possible.

NAT: But how can it be both? If A is a means to B as the end, how can B also be the means to A as the end? The end is more important than the means. How can A be less important than B and B less important than A?

SOCRATES: Shall we explore that puzzle?

NAT: Not if you think there is an even more fundamental issue in political philosophy. Can you think of any other issue more fundamental than that?

SOCRATES: I can think of two: What *is* the individual, and what *is* the state? The first is dealt with in philosophical anthropology, or philosophical psychology, or philosophy of the human person. But the second is the heart of political philosophy: What is the polis? What is its essence?

NAT: I see. As in sexual morality, where the fundamental issue is what *is* sex?

SOCRATES: Yes. You see, I have this strange habit of preferring to know what in the world I am talking about when I use a word.

NAT: And how would you formulate the controversy? What are the two opposite answers?

SOCRATES: I think it is whether the state is a natural or an artificial thing—an organism, like the family, or an invention, like technology.

NAT: Why is that so central?

SOCRATES: Because if the state is like an organism, each individual can be like a cell or an organ, and in an organism the whole works for each part *and* each part works for and serves the whole. So that would explain how it could be both "all for one and one for all".

NAT: I see. But *is* the state an organism? Isn't it an artifice, something more like a building, or even a machine? Didn't we invent it by a "social contract"?

SOCRATES: I think we have to distinguish two different but related questions here. One is whether the state is natural or artificial. The second is whether it is an organism or a contract.

NAT: I see only two views here, not four. "Natural" and "organic" go together, and so do "artificial" and "contractual". Not all of nature is organic, but all organisms are. And not all artifices are contracts, but all contracts are artifices.

SOCRATES: Yes, those two features usually go together, although it is logically possible that the state is natural but not an organism, or that the state is an organism but artificial rather than natural. Those views are historically rare, and historically the controversy is almost always between the natural and organic view, which is more typically ancient, and the artificial and contractual view, which is more typically modern.

NAT: And isn't democracy part of the modern package too? If the state is a man-made artifice, and a social contract, doesn't that mean it is made by the people?

SOCRATES: Usually, but not necessarily. Your American Founding Fathers seemed to think that democracy was natural, in speaking of universal "natural rights".

NAT: But they were in process of inventing a new state, by contract.

SOCRATES: Yes, so they believed both that the existence of the state *as such*, the political dimension of human life, was natural and also that the particular *kind* of state—democracy or republic or aristocracy or monarchy or a blend of them—was a matter of free choice and contract, thus a human artifice that they were in process of constructing. So they, like Locke, the philosopher they were most influenced by, were a synthesis of the traditional view and the modern view. In fact, even Saint Thomas Aquinas, back in the thirteenth century, and even Aristotle, whom he was influenced by, said that the best state included elements of both democracy and aristocracy and monarchy.

NAT: I see. The two questions are logically independent of each other. The kind of state we have depends on its human designers, who design something like a legal contract, whether only among themselves or also with all the citizens, who ratify it; but the state as such, the fact that we always do make states and need them, seems to be natural and given and universal.

SOCRATES: Yes, and the reason usually given is that human life demands for its perfecting and flourishing three or four layers—individuals, families, tribes, and nations—and then perhaps also amalgams of nations. Life becomes richer the more resources and the more relationships it can contain.

NAT: And positions in political philosophy also seem largely to depend on positions in the other divisions of philosophy. For instance, nominalists in metaphysics would tend toward individualism in politics, and Platonists in metaphysics would tend toward benevolent monarchies, like Plato's "philosopher kings", and moderate Aristotelians in metaphysics would tend toward a blend or a compromise or a range of best regimes. And politics has to depend on ethics too, if ethics follows metaphysics and anthropology and if it deals with the question of the greatest good, which has to be for both the individual and the whole human race.

SOCRATES: Yes. Classical political philosophers saw politics as simply political ethics, not as a kind of extrinsic check on politicians' behavior but as a logical deduction from general principles in ethics and in anthropology and even, implicitly, in metaphysics.

NAT: That makes sense. Because the good for the individual and the good for the state, which is made by, of, and for man, must be essentially the same.

SOCRATES: But when Plato tried to deduce the one from the other, he ran into problems. I think he showed very clearly that the just individual soul must be an aristocracy, not a democracy, for not all desires and thoughts should be given equal rights. But to extend that to politics and to identify the role of the lawmakers with the role of the mind, the role of the guardians with the role of the will, and the role of the producers, or the masses, with the role of the desires, is not nearly as clear; and his system of classes in politics has never been as popular as the psychology of the three powers of the soul. Even Freud fit into Plato's tripartite psychology, although he changed the meaning and content of each to superego, ego, and id instead of intellect, will, and appetites. But social and political class systems like Plato's have provoked revolutions against them, as in France and Russia. So I think his sharp division of the soul into three different powers—the intellect, the will, and the passions—does not logically or necessarily entail a sharp division in the three different classes of the state—the philosopher-kings, the guardians, and the producers.

NAT: So there has to be something of a double standard for individuals and states, just as we discovered when we discussed just war theory. So you can't just deduce politics from the rest of philosophy. Perhaps the rules of deduction change in politics.

SOCRATES: No, I think that is not logically possible. Just the content. Certainly some deductions work in political philosophy. For instance, take this deduction from anthropology. If each individual soul is immortal, as some philosophical arguments try to prove, and if no state is immortal, as history empirically shows, then the individual is more valuable than the state. But if the individual soul is not immortal, then it seems to follow that the state is more valuable because it is made up of many individuals, and many is greater than one.

NAT: Does that mean that the denial of individual immortality opens the door to state totalitarianism?

SOCRATES: It seems to at least make it possible, and more likely.

NAT: But did we not agree when we were discussing pacifism that there had to be a double standard regarding the use of lethal force, that it was at least possible or even honorable for an individual to renounce its use even if it meant being martyred, but that it was dishonorable for a state to refuse to defend its citizens against an invader, or for parents not to defend their innocent children against a guilty aggressor?

SOCRATES: Yes, we did. So what conclusion do you logically derive from that?

NAT: That political philosophy is much more relative and uncertain than any of the other divisions, and less amenable to being clarified or settled by logical reasoning.

SOCRATES: I think Plato would disagree with that, but I suspect that is indeed the correct conclusion. That is one of the reasons I never entered politics. I would have been a great incompetent.

NAT: So when Plato used you as a model for his so-called ideal state in the *Republic*, he did you a disservice.

SOCRATES: In suggesting that his ideas were my ideas, yes indeed. I think there is good reason why his psychology has lasted for centuries but his politics have never been successfully implemented, even though he saw those two things as implying each other and as a perfect parallel.

NAT: Socrates, I am surprised and disappointed with this conversation.

SOCRATES: Why?

NAT: Because we have not done what we did in most of the other ones, namely, to keep a logical argument focused on a single fundamental question, at least for a while.

SOCRATES: Look on the bright side: any student who uses this as a textbook will have two very short and easy chapters to read.

Questions for Discussion or Personal Essays

1. Do you think there is more agreement or more disagreement about political philosophy today than in the past? What evidence is there that this is the correct answer? What do you think is the cause for that change?

2. How do you account for the fact that the political Left is called liberal yet tends more to socialism while the Right tends toward libertarianism?

3. How have the terms "liberal" and "conservative" changed their meaning in the last century or two? How can it be that contemporary American conservatives are similar to nineteenth-century European liberals? Or are they?

4. Why are "progressive" and "traditional" more definable terms than "Right" and "Left"?

5. A number of different answers are given in this dialogue to the question of what the central issue of political philosophy is. What are they? Which do you see as most central? Why?

6. One of these most central questions is whether the individual or the state is primary, or the end, or the greater good. One answer to that question is *both*: "All for one, and one for all." Why is that not a contradiction?

7. Why is it easier to understand and give that answer if the state is an organism? How are the parts and the whole related in an organism such as the human body? How are they related in a machine? In a work of art?

8. Hobbes and Rousseau were two political philosophers who seemed in radical disagreement. To oversimplify, Hobbes saw human nature as innately selfish and competitive and moved by fear, and he saw a powerful monarchy as the best answer to that; conversely, Rousseau saw human nature as innately happy, free, and innocent, and he saw states (civil society) as the origin of artifice, evil, and suffering. Yet both agreed that the state originated in a social contract and that Aristotle was wrong when he defined man as a naturally political animal. Which of those two differences seems greater to you: between Hobbes and Rousseau or between both and Aristotle? Why?

9. Can the state be both organic and artificial? Can it be both natural and contractual? Why or why not?

10. Does rejection of Plato's close parallel between individuals and states, with each requiring a three-part system of powers or classes, necessarily mean that the good of the individual and the good of the state are not the same? Why or why not?
11. Why is political philosophy more uncertain and confusing than most other divisions?
12. In what ways were you surprised by this dialogue? In what ways were you disappointed?
13. Did it help you figure out whom to vote for?

15

Philosophy of Education:
What Is Education's Purpose?

The division of applied philosophy that inquires about education is called, unsurprisingly, the philosophy of education. The question that seems to be the primary philosophical question about education involves its purpose, or end: What good is it? What is it for?

SOCRATES: I think this log we are sitting on has been functioning not merely as a log but as a university, as "Socrates University". And what enterprise have we been engaged in, here on this log, our Socrates University? What have we been doing throughout the last fourteen conversations we have had? And what are most of the readers of these dialogues doing right now in reading them, do you think?

NAT: Philosophizing, I hope.

SOCRATES: And of what larger enterprise is philosophy an important part?

NAT: Thinking. Living. Existing. I don't know what you mean by that question.

SOCRATES: In what visible institution do we find philosophers and historians and linguists and theologians and physicists and chemists and astronomers and psychologists and sociologists and economists and computer scientists?

NAT: In universities. The institution your most famous student, Plato, invented.

SOCRATES: And we are here now in the simplest of universities, this log, with only two people on it. So if the log is a university and we are its two simplest parts, what are those two parts?

NAT: The teacher and the student.

SOCRATES: And what is the relation between those two parts?

NAT: The teacher teaches and the student learns.

SOCRATES: And what do we call that two-part relationship, in a single word?

NAT: Education. But that's much older than university education. Farmers and shoemakers and warriors and doctors and carpenters and horsemen learned their work from their fathers or apprenticed themselves to teachers for a very necessary and practical reason, in every culture in history, long before universities were invented. And the purpose of each one is well known.

SOCRATES: So what is the purpose of *university* education? Why does it exist? Why did we design it?

NAT: Oh, now, that is a different kind of question.

SOCRATES: How is it different?

NAT: The answer is not simply a fact discoverable by experience, and therefore not everyone agrees about the answer.

SOCRATES: Correct. So what do you suppose we ought to do now, in discussing the philosophy of education?

NAT: We ought to discuss this question, since it is a philosophical question, a question we need wisdom to answer, not just factual information and empirical experience.

SOCRATES: As we have already begun to do, I think.

NAT: But that very question assumes something—something that is as controversial as the answer to it: that there *is* a purpose to education that is objective and universal rather than just subjective and personal. It's similar to the fundamental question we asked about ethics, or morality.

In fact, my first answer to the question is that there seems to be no one objective answer since people freely choose to enter this thing called education, and they enter it for many very different reasons or purposes or motives or ends. Some seek education for profit, to train for a profession that will make them a desired amount of money. Some seek it for pleasure, simply because they enjoy doing it. Some seek it for prestige, fame, or honor. Some seek it to advance certain skills they have. Some seek it to learn how to be of service to society. They enter universities for different purposes, so there is no such thing as *the* purpose of education in general.

SOCRATES: What you say is obviously true, factually. But it does not follow that there is no universal purpose to education itself.

NAT: Why not?

SOCRATES: Is it not possible that some of these individual purposes are wiser and better than others?

NAT: From the viewpoint of moral values, yes. One student may study economics to get rich himself, another to learn how to help the poor out of their poverty.

SOCRATES: I mean something a little different: not the judgment of an individual's motives by moral standards but the judgment of different answers to our question of the purpose of education itself by the standards of the thing itself, this thing we call education.

NAT: I don't understand.

SOCRATES: Let me give an example. Some answers to the question of the purpose of education may be not only less moral but also less logical. For instance, take the person who enters a university in order to get rich. He invests a lot of money in this thing called education for the same reason a farmer sows a lot of seeds in a field: he wants to make more of the thing he gives up. In the one case that is beans or corn or wheat, and in the other case it is money. "To get a good job" is in fact the most common of all answers in your society today to the question of why to invest in a university education. Now, if I met such a person, I would ask him a series of questions about his motive. In fact, why don't we play those roles now for a moment so that I can illustrate this thing called philosophizing about education. Will you answer as such an ordinary person would answer?

NAT: All right.

SOCRATES: So you are paying large amounts of money to the university, which pays large amounts of money to its teachers. What do these teachers give you in return?

NAT: Education, of course, in many subjects.

SOCRATES: And what will this education profit you? In what will you be better off when you leave the university than you were before you entered it?

NAT: Knowledge. I will know many more things and have many more skills.

SOCRATES: And in order to profit the most, you want to learn the most?

NAT: Yes.

SOCRATES: And how do you or the university test how much you have learned?

NAT: With tests and exams and assignments such as writing papers.

SOCRATES: And you get high or low grades on them, right?

NAT: Yes.

SOCRATES: So that your final grade point average, when you graduate, is one of the reasons a prospective employer might employ you.

NAT: Yes, together with how prestigious the university is from which I graduate.

SOCRATES: And that is why you study hard.

NAT: Yes.

SOCRATES: So it is to get a good job that you seek this education.

NAT: Yes.

SOCRATES: What makes one job better and more attractive to you?

NAT: The obvious answer is how well it pays. But there are others. I want to be able to enjoy my work too.

SOCRATES: Would you choose to work at a job you enjoyed more but got paid much less for, such as a job in entertainment or the arts, or would you choose instead a job you enjoyed less but got paid much more for, such as a job as a stockbroker or lawyer or CEO of a large business?

NAT: The latter.

SOCRATES: Why? Why do you want more money rather than less, so much so that you are willing to give up a job that pays much less even though you would enjoy it more?

NAT: Because of the cost of living, of course. Things are expensive nowadays. Especially if you want a family. A house, a car, possibly two cars.

SOCRATES: And you want to give your children good things too, right?

NAT: Of course.

SOCRATES: Such as a good education at a good university.

NAT: Yes.

SOCRATES: And that's expensive.

NAT: Very expensive indeed.

SOCRATES: So that is why you are studying so hard: so that you get high grades and a high GPA, so that you can impress employers, so that you can get a good job, so that you can make a large salary, so that you can send your children to good universities so that they, too, can study hard so that they can get good grades and ... Do you see a logical structure here?

NAT: I see an endless loop.

SOCRATES: Or what logicians call "reasoning in a circle". You are like a man who put a lantern on a large rock in the middle of a busy highway so that the lantern would warn the cars away from the rock and so that the rock could keep holding up the lantern. Each step of your reasoning is justified by the next step, its end and motive and purpose; but the question of the purpose of the whole thing is not yet answered.

Think of a university as something like a large and expensive bridge built over a large river so that daily commuters can get to and from work more efficiently. Let's say one is a surgeon, one a steelworker, one an engineer, one a mathematician, one a financier, one a farmer, and one a car salesman. The surgeon repairs bodies that were injured in car accidents on that bridge. The steelworker supplied the material for the bridge. The engineer designed it. The mathematician taught the engineer. The financier financed the building of the bridge. The farmer grew food to keep alive and healthy the people who built the bridge. The car salesman sold cars to the commuters who used the bridge. You see? It's like the lantern and the rock, only more complex.

NAT: So "to get a good job" is a bad answer to "why go to university" only because it's illogical. Suppose you don't care that much about logic.

SOCRATES: No, it's not just illogical, not just reasoning in a circle. It's living in a circle.

NAT: Oh, I see. There has to be some lived end, some greatest good.

SOCRATES: Ultimately, yes. But even proximately, there must be something that is not just a part of that circle, but something for which the circle itself exists, some reason for the whole thing.

NAT: Well, I suppose that is truth, or knowing the truth, learning the truth.

SOCRATES: But each of the many different kinds of education that existed before universities were invented, which you mentioned at the beginning—farmers and warriors and shoemakers and so forth—also taught truth: the truth about farming and fighting and making shoes, and how to do it successfully. My question is about the university: What does it seek truth about?

NAT: About everything. Isn't that the distinctive feature of "liberal education"? To seek the truth for its own sake, not merely as a means to some other end?

SOCRATES: So why do we need universities to do that?

NAT: Not just to help us get a good job, if we are to learn from your critique of that answer. And I suspect that most of the other answers would fare no better. So what is *your* answer? What stands somewhere between the ultimate answer, the greatest good, on the one hand and, on the other hand, all the specific and practical answers supplied by preuniversity education or vocational education or practical education? We don't need universities in order for us to know the greatest good. If we did, then no one before Plato ever knew it. And we don't need universities to teach farming or shoemaking. If we did, then no one would have done that before Plato either. Individuals can choose to seek the truth for its own sake too. So why do we need universities? Why aren't little two-person logs like this one enough?

SOCRATES: You formulate the question well.

NAT: But I fear I cannot formulate the answer well, or even know the answer. I fear our society may have no good answer to that question. How absurd—so much money and effort and time put into an enterprise whose purpose we cannot know! I have this vision of the whole system being simply a larger version of your image of the bridge, an enormous system in which each part is needed for each other part but the purpose of the whole machine is unknown.

SOCRATES: At least you know one thing: the inadequacy of the answers usually given to the question of the purpose of university education.

NAT: Perhaps the answer is not personal and individual but social. Perhaps it is the betterment of others, of society.

SOCRATES: In other words, getting is for the sake of giving.

NAT: That sounds right.

SOCRATES: But if you don't know what is worth getting for yourself, how can you know what is worth giving to others, who are just as confused as you are? It is like giving away pointless junk or, at the best, mere toys. Or like the blind leading the blind.

NAT: To read most of what our pundits say about this, I'd call it the bland leading the bland.

SOCRATES: You are beginning to see why philosophers make trouble, I think. Other subjects seek to make life easier and to make thinking easier, but philosophy makes life and thinking harder.

NAT: Perhaps that is one reason universities today are drastically cutting back on philosophy, and all the humanities, and putting almost all their growth and money into the STEM courses, which are more lucrative, more practical, and more like parts of that endless loop, that gigantic circle, that enormous machine. I learned that fewer than 4 percent of universities today require any philosophy courses at all.

SOCRATES: That's because philosophy is not any kind of technology. Technology makes things easier; philosophy makes them harder. Technology is an ever more elaborate means to our ends, while philosophy questions our ends.

NAT: Are you a Luddite, Socrates? Are you antitechnology?

SOCRATES: Of course not. Ignoring the means is almost as absurd as ignoring the end. Perhaps we should have a conversation about just what technology is, since it is the primary difference between our lives and those of our ancestors.

NAT: What do you mean by that?

SOCRATES: Simply that in the past nature dominated most of their lives, with technology confined to a small segment. Today, first because of the Industrial Revolution and now because of the computer revolution, most of our life is technologized, and the percentage of our lives in which we face nature face-to-face and not just on screens is far less.

NAT: I look forward to that dialogue.

Questions for Discussion or Personal Essays

1. Were you disappointed that this dialogue did not come up with an answer to its important question? If so, what does that psychological fact tell you about yourself or about the question?

2. Try giving your own answer to the question and criticizing it, by turning yourself into the two people in the dialogue. For we all of us have an inner Nat and an inner Socrates.

3. Were you disappointed when you discovered there were so few questions for essays or discussion about this dialogue? If so, what can you do about that? If not, why not?

4. Don't you think an author whose whole professional life consisted in educating students at a university should have given you a reasonable positive answer to the question of this dialogue? Why do you think he chose to be silent about this one, the one he has the most expertise in?

5. How many answers to the question were dealt with in this dialogue? How was each one refuted? Do you think any of them can be saved and their refutation refuted? If so, how?

6. Defend your alternative answer.

7. How are the answers to the two questions of this dialogue related, namely, What is the purpose of education? and What is the purpose of the university?

16

Philosophy of Technology: How Important Is Technology in Our Lives?

Since the rise, progress, and pervasiveness of technology has transformed our lives more than anything else in the last generation or two, except perhaps the decline of religion, it is fitting that we philosophize about it, that is, see what light the methods of philosophy can shed on its nature and value. As with the other dialogues, we confine ourselves to the questions a beginner is most likely to ask.

SOCRATES: You asked, last time, to explore technology and the technological revolution from the standpoint of philosophy. Here we are again on the log that is Socrates University. Where do you think we should begin?

NAT: If we are truly Socratic, by knowing what we are talking about, that is, by asking the "what" question that you and Plato always centered on. We need a definition—not just a nominal definition of the word, such as a dictionary would give, but a real definition of the real thing. And knowing that this must be our first question, and thinking about it, I came to the conclusion that the most basic definition of technology would be the practical application of science and scientific knowledge of the material universe outside us and around us, that is, to the production of artificial devices, such as machines and computers, that make some things in our lives easier to do or attain, or less painless, or quicker, or more efficient, or less costly to us. Francis Bacon, who perhaps more than anyone else discovered the principles of the modern scientific method, defined the purpose of technology as "man's conquest of nature", or acquiring the knowledge of nature for the sake of power over it. And all these things that constitute technology are things made of matter, things in the material universe. I do not think technology extends to thinking or moral living or religious holiness, although medical technology may well improve our thinking, especially when it is impaired by disease, diet, and depression; and it certainly improves our longevity and our happiness, or at least our freedom from pain.

SOCRATES: Well, now, that is quite a long and rather complete answer to the question—in fact, to more than one question. Before analyzing it and distinguishing different questions about it, I ask how you came up with it, what facts or data you used and what process of thinking.

NAT: That's easy and obvious. The data is the existence of the many examples of it, especially means of transportation; aids to health like medicines, pills, and surgical devices; means of communication; and machines for the mass production of goods, like clothing and weapons. And of course all the devices of the digital revolution of late, such as advanced computers, smartphones, and the Internet. As to the process of thinking I used, it was what Bacon would call the observation of data and then inductive reasoning, especially generalization.

SOCRATES: I see nothing inaccurate or even obviously controversial in your answer, so I will accept your definition, which contains, as I noticed, four things, corresponding to what Aristotle called the Four Causes, or four explanations, of a thing: its material cause or contents, its formal cause or essence, its efficient cause or origin, and its final cause or end. Its contents, or material cause, are all the artefacts you mentioned. Its essence is the control of things in nature by these artefacts. Its origin, or efficient cause, is science, that is, the knowledge of the things and powers in nature and how to harness them. Its end is, immediately, the conquest of nature and, ultimately, the increase of human happiness, that is, the satisfaction of human desires and the minimization of unhappiness or frustration or pain, by means of this control or conquest. Would you say that is a good summary of what you have said?

NAT: It is indeed. I am pleased that you think I have given the kind
of complete definition, of all four dimensions of it, that Aristotle
would give.

SOCRATES: So what do you think our next question about it should
be, now that we have defined what it is?

NAT: Pretty obviously, the question of the final cause, its end, especially whether it has succeeded in attaining that end. It has obviously attained its proximate end, the conquest of nature, or power
over nature, with remarkable success and rapidity. But whether
this has succeeded in its ultimate end, namely, the increase of
human happiness and the decrease of unhappiness, is the controversial question, I think. Our science has succeeded in its end of
knowing the universe ever better; and that knowledge has given
us what Bacon called "the conquest of nature"; and that conquest
has given us great *power*. But has that power given us increased *happiness*? I think the data are ambivalent here, for, on the one hand,
we like these things, but on the other hand, we seem to fear them
or be suspicious of them, and they do not seem to have made us
noticeably happier or wiser or more moral.

SOCRATES: Let's explore the first link in this chain: the knowledge
that underlies technology.

NAT: It's scientific knowledge, of course. What philosophical questions do you think we should ask about science? Should we enter
the rather technical discussions of what is called "the philosophy of
science", especially about the scientific method and epistemology
and truth?

SOCRATES: I was thinking, rather, of the human and practical question
about the end or goal or purpose of this knowledge. Aristotle said
there are three purposes of knowledge, three motives for seeking
the truth, and thus three kinds of "sciences" in the old, broad
sense of the word, that is, organized knowledge through causes
and reasons. He called them the theoretical sciences, the practical
sciences, and the productive sciences.

The purpose or end of theoretical science is simply to know the
truth. The end of practical science is to apply the truth to action, to
life. The end of productive science is to apply the truth to making or
improving or repairing new things in the world. Philosophy, mathematics, and physics are theoretical sciences. Ethics and politics and

economics are practical sciences. Writing plays, building bridges or weapons, and repairing shoes or houses or diseased human body parts are productive sciences. The Greek word for that third kind of knowledge is *techne*, from which we get the word "technology". It means "know-how, knowing how to make something".

"Theoretical" doesn't mean "uncertain". It means "seeking the truth simply for the purpose of seeing it, understanding it". "Practical" doesn't mean "efficient". It means "for the purpose of doing something about the truth, living the truth in some way". And "productive" doesn't mean "working hard". It means "producing or making something, whether a work of art, like a poem, or a work of technology, like a bridge". So this "productive knowledge" can include what we classify as art as well as what we classify as technology, for art is a human invention, an artifice.

NAT: Thank you for your little lecture, Socrates. I know you resist lecturing, but that linguistic and historical background is very useful to me in thinking about the place and function and value of technology.

SOCRATES: How?

NAT: Well, for one thing, it helps me to define it by giving me its genus, which is knowledge, and its specific difference, which is what makes it different from other kinds of knowledge. And defining things is always a necessary beginning. And it also answers our main question about technology, namely, its value or goodness or end or purpose. Its purpose is to improve the world, that is, those parts of the world that we want to use for our human purposes, whatever they are and however many and different they may be. So it increases our power; and, like all power, it can be used for good or evil ends, so it is morally neutral. For instance, a weapon can be used to protect the innocent or to kill the innocent, and a means of transportation can be used to quicken our progress toward a place, where we may hold a festival or commit a theft.

SOCRATES: And how does this fact about technology cast light on its value?

NAT: It locates its value in the realm of means rather than ends, and by this it refutes two opposite errors: worshipping it, so to speak, as an end in itself, and demonizing it, as responsible for evil rather than good. We see both extremes in today's controversy about technology, especially computer technology, artificial intelligence, the Internet, and social media. And this also shows something positive: that we need wisdom, especially moral wisdom, to judge it and use it for right ends rather than wrong ones. We don't want to put powerful weapons into the hands of fools, who will misuse them and add to the sum of all the evils in the world, or to take them away from the wise, who will rightly use them and add to the sum of all the goods in the world. But I do not feel at all competent to answer the question of *how* to do that, the question of who should regulate this power politically and socially.

SOCRATES: But surely you have the answer to the most important aspect of that question.

NAT: What do you mean?

SOCRATES: You are one of those people who have this power, and you have to choose how you will use it and how much of it is good for you, even if you claim little or no authority or wisdom to answer that question for others or for public society at large.

NAT: Yes. And clearly, part of the answer is to avoid both extremes: on the one hand, hating and fearing technology because of its proneness to abuse and misuse, and on the other hand, loving it so much that I idolize it and become addicted to it by underestimating its power to addict me and overestimating my power to control that addiction—like Sauron's Ring in *The Lord of the Rings*.

SOCRATES: So far we have come up with fairly noncontroversial common sense. And that is not a bad thing. But I relish controversy, so I would like to introduce one here. It is a controversy between the typically premodern mind and the typically modern mind about technology. And it centers on the difference between Aristotle and Francis Bacon, not in science and scientific method (about which history has pretty clearly shown Bacon's superiority) but in ethics, where many still maintain Aristotle's superiority. The question in ethics that I refer to is the question of the "summum bonum", the greatest good or the end of ends. Bacon accuses the ancients of prioritizing the wrong kind of science, what Aristotle called theoretical science, whose end is simply to know and understand and contemplate the truth for its own sake. He says the primary value should be put on the productive sciences, on technology, on "the conquest of nature" to "improve man's estate on earth". He says that this priority is almost self-evident. If a man is in pain, would he value a philosopher to explain and preach about his pain over a doctor who could relieve it? If a man is in danger of drowning, would he value one who offered him philosophical wisdom about death over the invention of a life jacket?

NAT: No, but what the man *would* prefer need not be assumed to be identical with what he *should* prefer. And it could be argued that not knowing why he was dying, and not knowing why he was living, is a greater tragedy than death itself, which we must all endure eventually anyway.

SOCRATES: You are becoming very philosophical, Nat.

NAT: But I want a reason for that preference. What was Aristotle's reason for prioritizing the theoretical sciences over the practical and productive sciences, prioritizing the search for truth for its own sake over the application of truth to life and to the improvement of the material world? It sounds pretty elitist and impractical.

SOCRATES: Aristotle used the same argument for the priority of the theoretical sciences over the practical sciences as he used for the priority of the practical sciences over the productive sciences.

NAT: What argument was that?

SOCRATES: He said that the practical sciences, especially ethics, improve our own behavior, our own active lives, while the productive sciences improve only something in the material world outside us. The practical sciences' object is closer to home, so to speak.

NAT: That makes sense.

SOCRATES: But the theoretical sciences improve something even closer to us than our actions.

NAT: What is that?

SOCRATES: Our very self, in fact an aspect of the self that distinguishes us from the animals: our mind, our reason, our intellect, our understanding, our wisdom.

NAT: Oh. I guess that logically follows. So then Bacon simply turned Aristotle's hierarchy upside down.

SOCRATES: Exactly. Technology, for him, was the meaning of life, the new summum bonum. And that is a total change, a radical change. Before Bacon, the primary aim of human life on earth, for just about every culture and philosophy and religion in the world, was to conform the soul to objective reality—the objective reality that was above it: God, or the will of God, or Platonic Ideas, or "the good, the true, and the beautiful". And the way to do that was virtue: intellectual virtues like wisdom, and moral virtues like justice and charity and self-control and the rest. But for Bacon, the aim of human life on earth was the opposite: to conform objective reality—the objective reality of nature—to the desires of the human soul: "man's conquest of nature". And the way to do that is technology. So that is a very great change indeed, a change in the answer to the greatest question of all!

NAT: I see. So our deciding to set aside a whole session for philosophizing about technology was a wise one, because for our society, technology is not a minor issue at all, as it was for every premodern society, but the central issue of our "brave new world".

SOCRATES: Indeed. However, there is a principle that governs this new, Baconian worship of technology that makes it even more disturbing. Assuming that there is a value hierarchy, that one thing is of greater value than others, whenever a greater thing is subordinated to a lesser thing, whenever a lesser thing is idolized and the greater thing neglected, what happens is exactly the contrary of what is intended. Not only is the greater thing neglected (that was indeed intended, or at least tolerated), but the lesser thing is also spoiled. It is made to bear greater burdens of importance than it can carry. It is an idol, that is, something false, and all falsities eventually show themselves and crack. What follows from this principle is that if technology, which is in itself a good thing, is idolized, it will become a bane rather than a boon.

NAT: I see this happening with teenagers who are literally addicted to their smartphones. Their souls and their identities have disappeared into their selfies and Facebook images.

SOCRATES: Well, if, as all the religions of the world agree, egotism is the great enemy of happiness, then iPhones are too, for they are the agents of egotism. The very name reveals that: they are not you-Phones but iPhones. They invite us to withdraw from the "I-Thou" relationship into loneliness, which is a terrible thing. In fact, I suspect that if there is a Hell, it is not made of fire but of loneliness.

NAT: So Hell is one gigantic iPhone!

SOCRATES: If so, the artist who wants to paint Hell should paint the picture of an isolated individual sitting alone before a supercomputer that at his direction creates his own perfect virtual reality.

He seems to himself to have godlike powers, but he cannot create anything real, only things unreal. And he lives in this unreality. He is living in two unreal worlds, both within and without. Within, because he seems to be God, and without, because his virtual reality seems to be real. He has listened to the stupidest and most common lie ever told, which is repeated by almost all commencement speakers, that "you can be whatever you want to be."

NAT: So we need good philosophy to free us from this cave of shadows. Is that why you departed from your usual method of logical argument this time and indulged in something deeper: wisdom, understanding, seeing?

SOCRATES: Yes. When a false "big picture" captivates, what is needed is more than little critiques. We need an alternative "big picture", a true one.

NAT: And I suspect that this will be *increasingly* needed. For if and when our technology invents a total iPhone, a "happiness machine" that obeys every whim and desire and creates another world of virtual reality, a matrix, with total realism and the satisfaction of all our desires, there may not be many people left in this poor old thing called the "real world", for they will all rush into that "happiness machine". How do we deter them?

SOCRATES: By getting them to ask the question put forth by a very realistic philosopher long ago: "What does it profit a man if he gains the whole world and loses or forfeits himself?" (Lk 9:25). When he finds his whole identity in his iPhone, he is literally losing himself, disappearing into IT.

NAT: Perhaps that is what Hell is made of: not pain and fire but "the happiness machine", total technological "happiness" surrounded by total loneliness. Sartre famously said, "Hell is—other people!"[1] Perhaps that is the exact opposite of the truth.

SOCRATES: We have found much darkness in our inquiry so far. Let us see whether we can also see some light. Do you see people recognizing this problem and protesting against this technologization of life and worship of technology?

NAT: Yes, in many ways. For instance, the "back to nature" environmentalist movement. It seems to be an unconscious compensation or reparation for the harm done by the "conquest of nature".

---

[1] Jean-Paul Sartre, *No Exit*, trans. Stuart Gilbert (New York: Alfred A. Knopf, 1946), 61.

I see it also in our choice of vacation spots. When people spend big bucks trying to arrange for a week or two of happiness on their vacations, they seem to be trying to *escape* technology, for they are happier in spots that are almost always less full of technology: oceans, beaches, wildernesses for camping, mountains.

I think it is also happening concerning *time*. All technological devices are ways of saving time. But we have less time today, not more, than our ancestors did. Everyone complains about being harried and hassled by responsibilities so that leisure is becoming as rare as virginity. All the time we saved by these technological time-saving devices—where did it disappear to? Technology has not improved our relationship with time but made it more problematic. And that makes a difference to everything in life because time is a dimension of everything in our lives, mental and spiritual as well as physical.

I also see this problem about technology in university education today, in the fact that little colleges that specialize in the humanities and Great Books are springing up everywhere, in conscious or unconscious protest against the fact that in nearly all our major universities, the courses in all the humanities and the arts are declining very rapidly and being replaced by the STEM courses, which exist for the sake of their technological payoff. This is an issue for the philosophy of education, perhaps the major issue today.

SOCRATES: It is an issue for philosophical anthropology as well. For you are learning more about everything else in the universe but less about yourselves. After all, the subject of the humanities is *humanity*, human nature. And that is where values are studied, including the value of technology. You are learning how to conquer nature but not why. You are forgetting to "know thyself", except insofar as you can try to turn that into a science too, a kind of spiritual technology, by a supposedly scientific psychology and sociology. But there is a great difference between knowing many facts about people and knowing people. The first piece of advice I would give to a student of psychology or sociology is to read great novels, not simply scientific textbooks.

NAT: Why do you think this change happened so radically and so quickly?

SOCRATES: I don't know all the historical reasons for it, but I can think of one philosophical reason. At the end of the Middle Ages, the popular new philosophy was Ockham's nominalism, which reduced the notion of nature, or the nature of a thing, to a mere word or concept, not a reality. The essential nature of a thing is a universal, like human nature, or the nature of justice, or the nature of the soul. Such universals were declared unreal by Ockham. Nature was reduced to mere matter, stuff to be conquered.

NAT: I see the connection between this apparently very abstract issue in logic and this very concrete change in the meaning of human life itself. There was a movement in the sixties called "camp" where it became fashionable to deviate from nature as much as possible, just to be cool, or to show it could be done, or to create alternatives. And that is obviously the philosophy behind the idea that our sex, our gender, is also simply something we can conquer or change at will—a subjective project rather than an objective truth.

SOCRATES: That philosophical controversy, I think, is behind many of the controversies in medicine: Is nature a standard, so that technology finds its rightful place in restoring nature, and protecting nature, both in the environment and in the body? Or is nature simply something to be conquered?

NAT: I don't understand why the same very modern or progressive movement seems to take nature more seriously as a standard when it comes to the environment, the planet, but less seriously when it comes to our bodies and their sexuality and their relation to our souls, our minds, and our wills.

SOCRATES: Perhaps the former is compensation for the latter. We tend to focus on some virtues at the expense of others, or in one dimension of human life at the expense of others. One of your political parties takes human life very seriously and very morally, or moralistically when it comes to some issues, like poverty, immigration, racial justice, and peace, yet shies away from doing that when it comes to life's beginning and ending, advocating for abortion and euthanasia. And the other party is exactly the opposite: highly moralistic about one area and highly pragmatic about the other.

NAT: I have here another question for you, Socrates, that seems related to these. I wonder why, when our lifetimes were short and life contained far more pain (after all, anesthetics were invented only a little more than a century ago), people seemed happier, while today, when technology has abolished most pain and radically expanded life expectancy, people are far more unhappy, depressed, nervous, and prone to suicide.

SOCRATES: Another good question, to which I have no single clear and compelling answer. But I think this, too, has something to do with nominalism and the denial of the very existence of such a thing as human nature, or the essential nature of anything, or any real distinction between the essential and the accidental. We might call that "the technological mindset". It is reflected in the very logic now taught: not the commonsense, ordinary-language logic that I used but the digital logic of the computer, mathematical logic, quantitative rather than qualitative logic. That is our new instrument, and the user tends to become more and more like his instrument.

NAT: So you would suggest studying the old logic, at least as a modest beginning?

SOCRATES: Yes. Perhaps I should write a book called *Socratic Logic* someday.

Questions for Discussion or Personal Essays

1. Is the definition of "technology" correct? Or should it be narrower or broader?

2. Is technology morally neutral or good?

3. Is Sauron's Ring in *The Lord of the Rings* morally neutral? If not, why not and what makes it not neutral but evil? Is this mere fantasy, or are there equivalents to the Ring in our real world?

4. Why is it so rare to see a commonsensical Aristotelian philosophical evaluation and explanation of technology?

5. What do Francis Bacon and Aristotle have in common? Where do they contradict each other? In those cases, who is right and why?

6. Evaluate Aristotle's argument for the priority of theoretical sciences over practical and productive sciences.

7. How much has technology changed our lives? Give specific examples.

8. Can technology change human nature itself?

9. What has changed our lives today more than technology, if anything?

10. How has the technology of clocks changed our lives?

11. If all technology saves time, why do we seem to have less time the more technology we have?

12. Would you use a technological "happiness machine"? Why or why not?

13. In the past, most books about nature were directed to contemplative admiration and enjoyment; today most are about the technology of environmental protection. Why?

14. We seek "unspoiled", natural places for happiness. Why, then, do most of us live in "spoiled" places (large cities)?

15. Why do we take nature as a standard when it comes to ecology and the environment but not when it comes to our own bodies? Or do we?

16. What do you think is the best technological invention of all time? Why? What do you think is the worst? Why?

17. How strong is the connection between our new quantificational (mathematical) logic and our lives?

18. If it is true that the user of a logic, a method, or a technology tends to become like his instrument, what should we do about that, both in general and specifically?

RECOMMENDED READING

Ancient Philosophy (Primary)

Solomon, *Ecclesiastes*
Plato, *Meno* and *Apology*
Plato, *Republic*, excerpts. (If you use the Rouse translation, *Great Dialogues of Plato*, and mentally divide each book into three parts—A, B, and C—you could cover Book I, Book IIA, Books VB through VIIA, Book IXC, and Rouse's helpful summary of the rest.)
Aristotle, *Nicomachean Ethics*, excerpts. (Select your own excerpts but be sure to cover Books I and VIII.)
Plotinus, "Beauty"

Ancient Philosophy (Secondary)

Parmenides' poem
The rest of Plato's *Republic*
Plato, *Gorgias*
The rest of the *Nicomachean Ethics*
A secondary source summary of Aristotle, either Adler's *Aristotle for Everybody* (easy) or Ross' *Aristotle* (intermediate).

Medieval Philosophy (Primary)

Augustine, *Confessions* 1-10 (Word on Fire Classics edition, which uses the Sheed translation)
Boethius, *The Consolation of Philosophy*
Anselm, *Proslogion*
Aquinas, *Summa theologiae*, at least 1.2.3 ("On God's Existence") and 1-2.2 ("On Those Things in Which Happiness Consists"). These and more, with explanatory notes, are included in my *A Shorter Summa*.

Medieval Philosophy (Secondary)

Bonaventure, *Journey of the Mind to God*
Aquinas, more of the *Summa*. My *Summa of the Summa* anthology is
five hundred pages, with many footnotes.
Nicholas of Cusa, *Of Learned Ignorance*

Modern Philosophy (Primary)

Machiavelli, *The Prince*
Descartes, *Discourse on Method*
Hume, *An Enquiry Concerning Human Understanding*
Kant, *Foundations of the Metaphysics of Morals*

Modern Philosophy (Secondary)

Pascal, *Pensées* (or my *Christianity for Modern Pagans: Pascal's* Pensées—
Edited, Outlined and Explained)
Descartes, *Meditations*
Leibniz, *Monadology*
Kant, *Critique of Pure Reason*, excerpts

Contemporary Philosophy (Primary)

Sartre, *Existentialism and Human Emotions* (or *Existentialism Is a Humanism*)
James, "What Pragmatism Means" and "The Will to Believe" (short
lectures)
Marx, *The Communist Manifesto*
C. S. Lewis, *The Abolition of Man*
Buber, *I and Thou*

Contemporary Philosophy (Secondary)

Mill, *Utilitarianism*
Russell, *The Problems of Philosophy*
Ayer, *Language, Truth and Logic*
Wittgenstein, *Tractatus Logico-Philosophicus*
Chesterton, *Orthodoxy*
Clarke, *Person and Being*

INDEX